MAJOR & MR
Battlefield Guide to
GALLIPOLI

"These by the Dardanelles laid down their shining youth
In battle and won fair renown for their native land."

*Inscription on marble monument in Athens to the Athenians
who lost their lives in the Dardanelles in 440BC.*

*Title page: View from Walker's Ridge: the sweep of North Beach towards Nibrunesi
Point, the Salt Lake and the Kirectepe Ridge with, in the foreground, the CWGC Base*

MAJOR & MRS HOLT'S
Battlefield Guide to

GALLIPOLI

Tonie and Valmai Holt

Leo Cooper

By the same authors:

Picture Postcards of the Golden Age: A Collector's Guide
Till the Boys Come Home: the Picture Postcards of the First World War
The Best of Fragments from France by Capt Bruce Bairnsfather
In Search of the Better 'Ole: The Life, Works and Collectables of
Bruce Bairnsfather
Picture Postcard Artists: Landscapes, Animals and Characters
Stanley Gibbons Postcard Catalogue: 1980, 1981, 1982, 1984, 1985, 1987
Germany Awake! The Rise of National Socialism illustrated by
Contemporary Postcards
I'll Be Seeing You: the Picture Postcards of World War II
Holts' Battlefield Guidebooks: Normandy-Overlord/Market-Garden/Somme/Ypres
Battlefields of the First World War: A Traveller's Guide
Visitor's Guide: the Normandy Landing Beaches
Major & Mrs Holt's Concise Battlefield Guide to the Ypres Salient
Major & Mrs Holt's Battle Maps: The Somme/The Ypres Salient/Normandy + Battle Map
Major & Mrs Holt's Battlefield Guide to the Somme + Battle Map
Major & Mrs Holt's Battlefield Guide to the Ypres Salient + Battle Map
Major & Mrs Holt's Battlefield Guide to the Normandy Landing Beaches + Battle Map
Violets From Oversea: 25 Poets of the First World War
Reprinted as 'Poets of the Great War'
My Boy Jack: The Search for Kipling's Only Son

First published in 2000 by LEO COOPER an imprint of Pen & Sword Books Ltd
47 Church Street, Barnsley, South Yorkshire S70 2AS

A CIP catalogue record for this book is available from the British Library

ISBN 0 85052 662-0

CONTENTS

ABBREVIATIONS/VOCABULARY

Abbreviations and acronyms used for military units are listed below. They are also printed in full at intervals throughout the text to aid clarity. Others are explained where they occur.

Abbreviations

AIF	Australian Imperial Force
ANZAC	Australian and New Zealand Army Corps
BWI	British West Indies
CCS	Casualty Clearing Station
CGS	Chief of the General Staff (Turkish)
CO	Commanding Officer
GRU	Graves Registration and Enquiries Unit
KOSB	King's Own Scottish Borderers
MO	Medical Officer
NSW	New South Wales
NZ	New Zealand
NZEF	New Zealand Expeditionary Force
OP	Observation Point
RDF	Royal Dublin Fusiliers
RIR	Royal Irish Rifles
RMLI	Royal Marine Light Infantry
RNAS	Royal Naval Air Service
RND	Royal Naval Division
RP	Reference Point
RSL	Returned Services League
RWF	Royal Welch Fusiliers
Sp Mem	Special Memorial
SWB	South Wales Borderers
VD	Volunteer Decoration (for Officers)

Turkish Vocabulary

Turkish is more or less phonetic...

Alai	regiment
Anit	memorial
Asma	vine
Bay	gentlemen (as in WC)
Bayan	ladies (as in WC)
Bimbasi	Major (bim = 1,000; basi = head of)
Cavus	Sergeant
Cesme	fountain
Cimen	grass
Ciftlik	farm
Coca	big
Dag	mountain
Dere [derray]	stream
Dikkat!	attention! (forbidden or 'Restricted area')
Er	Private soldier
Eski	Ancient/historical
Evet	yes
Gule gule	goodbye
Hayir	no
Kaba (gaba)	large
Kale [karlay]	fort
Koca	big
Kucuk	little
Lutfen	please
Merhaba	hello
Mezar	tomb/grave
Miralai	Colonel (Mir = Commander; alai = regiment)
Mirileua	Brigadier (Mir = Commander; leua = brigade)
Mishir	Field-Marshal (Liman von Sanders' final rank)
Mulazim and/or Tegmen	Lieutenant
Nerede	where
Nufus	population
Onbasi	Corporal
Sehit	martyr
Sehitligi/sehitlik	military cemetery
Tepe [teppay]	hill
Tesekkur ederim	thankyou
Ustegmen	First Lieutenant
Yarbay	Lieutenant-Colonel
Yuzbasi	Captain (Yuz = 100)

INTRODUCTION

'In January, 1915, the terrific affair was still not unmanageable. It could have been grasped in human hands and brought to rest in righteous and fruitful victory... It was not to be... Pride was everywhere to be humbled, and nowhere to receive its satisfaction... No prize was to reward the sacrifices of the combatants.'
Winston Churchill.

'After the first ten days fighting there was never any question of military "defeat". The field on which the British Navy and Army suffered their defeat was - not on Gallipoli - in Whitehall.'
Sir Ian Hamilton.

Gallipoli is probably the campaign which, above all others of the Great War, lends itself to the greatest number of 'If onlys' and 'What ifs' so beloved of the armchair military historian. So many good ideas ineptly executed, so many opportunities lost, and in what is now a strangely beautiful setting, where wild flowers and fragrant herbs mask the horror that was the Peninsula in 1915.

It is thrilling to be in Gallipoli on and around 25 April in any year. Dozens of young Australians travelling alone and in groups come to pay their respects to the men of ANZAC, and almost without exception they are strong, confident and sure of their place in history. Their vigour and enthusiasm match that of those who came in 1915, and to those of us who are part of an older nation there is a tinge of envy in our admiration of their dedicated pilgrimage.

It is also saddening to be in Gallipoli at that time. Not only because the currency of any war is that of young lives but because so many who fought and died here for their country are not acknowledged as the Australians are acknowledged. We heard one Turkish teacher pronounce that '1 million men died' in the 'Australian landings'. Much as the British often ignore the fact that the French actually fought on the Western Front, and treat that theatre as a purely British versus German affair, so the world seems to think that only Australians fought the Turks in Gallipoli.

Certainly the Gallipoli campaign gave the fledgling Australian nation a framework upon which to build an identity of national valour, independence, physical and martial prowess, and the superb accounts of C. E. W. Bean, their official historian, in which he painted with pride the achievements of the ANZAC Corps, became text books for an Australian character to which all could aspire.

This is splendid: there seems little to complain about there except that 'Gallipoli the battle' and 'Gallipoli the battlefield' have become synonymous with 'Australian' to the exclusion of everyone else - including New Zealanders. This impression is so strong that it reaches into the higher echelons of power. On the 75th Anniversary of the campaign, while the Ambassadors of Turkey, Australia, New Zealand and France attended the international ceremony at Gaba Tepe in an official capacity, the British Ambassador did not. Neither was the Union Flag flown nor the National Anthem played. Present were over seventy Australian Gallipoli veterans, flown to the Peninsula at Australian Government expense. Despite our many pleas to the then-Thatcher Government to host British veterans, only one British veteran, Captain Clarence Bennett, was present and he was our personal guest. Nowadays the Australian and New Zealand Governments alternate in organising the annual official ceremonies. The British only organise the low-key ceremony at Helles.

If one points out to a visiting Australian, or a local Turk, that the French had almost twice as many casualties as the Australians, or that the British had almost double the losses of the other Allies put together, they are usually totally surprised and in some cases disbelieving. They are not arrogant in their belief but merely victims of a myth that has helped to forge a nation. But that nation is changing and with that change it is now time for the story of Gallipoli to be told with balance so that the sacrifice of all the soldiers involved, of whatever nationality, is properly acknowledged. The portrayal in the 1981 film *Gallipoli*, starring Mel Gibson, of the brave Australians being sent to their deaths by inept senior British officers tells a slanted and inadequate story. Incompetence and ignorance are not exclusively British qualities. In comparison to the thousands who visit the landing beaches at Anzac and the cemeteries on the rugged ridges above them, the solitary and beautiful beaches and cemeteries in the Helles sector are comparatively little visited; the stories of British sacrifice and individual heroism rarely studied.

Our aim in this book is to provide sufficient information for the visitor to make a competent tour of *all* these battlefields and to derive from that tour at least a glimpse of the dreadful conditions that the men who fought here had to endure. It endeavours to show the extraordinary heights of bravery and endurance scaled by each side that led Turk and Ally to respect each other in a way that did not happen anywhere else.

Hopefully the new initiative by the Turkish Government to create a tranquil International Peace Park will preserve this site of extraordinary endeavour for generations to come and will present the events in an even-handed and balanced manner.

Tonie and Valmai Holt
Sandwich, 2000

HOW TO USE THIS GUIDE

HISTORY OF THE BATTLES/PERSONAL STORIES

This book is designed to guide the visitor around the main features, memorials, museums and cemeteries of the Gallipoli Peninsula, and to provide sufficient information about those places to allow an elemental understanding of what happened where. It makes extensive use of contemporary material (letters, diaries, regimental histories, literary accounts, newspaper reports etc.) where available, to bring the sites and past events alive and to help the modern reader to see them through the eyes of the 1915 protagonists.

Descriptions of the fighting are given at intervals. These are more detailed than those in our Guides to the Western Front, where the visitor may be equipped with more support material - such as Regimental Histories, personal accounts and the relevant cemetery registers - than may be available or easily transportable in Turkey. Also the Gallipoli visitor, having come so far, may well be prepared to do more walking over the battlefield to isolated sites where it is important to know what happened.

Some of the accounts may be difficult to follow in their spatial sequence, so tortuous is the ground over which the actions were fought. However, our purpose in decribing them is to illustrate the confusion experienced by the soldiers, the extraordinary intensity of the fighting in which they took part and the horrendous conditions under which they fought. Frequent reference to the Holts' Map, particularly in the Anzac area, will help the reader to grasp what was happening and where.

The historical notes given at each recommended stop and the personal anecdotes can in no way be continuous and sequential. It is therefore recommended that the visitor precedes his/her tour by reading the *Historical Summaries* below, which give condensed chronological accounts of the different phases of the fighting. It is also strongly recommended to make repeated use of the Index and the indication 'qv'. There are often multiple entries about, say, a regiment or an individual, each episode described on the spot where it occurred, which add up to a full picture.

PRIOR TO YOUR VISIT/TIMING IT
(see also Tourist Information below)

Before setting out, read this section thoroughly and study the accompanying map. Time your visit carefully, avoiding the extremes of cold in the winter (November to

February) and heat in the summer (July and August) The ideal time to tour the Peninsula is over the anniversary of the 25 April landings when the weather is pleasantly mild, the flora is spectacularly beautiful and there is the added bonus of the moving commemorative ceremonies - or in September/early October. It is important to consult your national Turkish Tourist Office for current regulations about visas. Make sure you are well insured for all medical, loss and theft eventualities and that you bring your driving licence if you wish to hire a car. You will need sturdy walking boots or shoes and thick socks, waterproofs, suntan lotion, sunglasses, a hat, insect repellant, a plentiful supply of all the medication you are on, plus a small medical kit with a general purpose antibiotic, treatment for headache/upset tummy/minor cuts etc. A thermos flask, torch and binoculars are strongly recommended and a compass would be of interest if you plan to walk any distance. A camera with plenty of film (although this is available in Canakkale, Eceabat or even Alcitepe) is a must and a mobile phone (with a local emergency number you can ring if in trouble, using the prefix 00 90 to get into the Turkish telephone system) would be desirable.

CHOOSING YOUR ROUTES

Touring the Gallipoli Battlefield is a different proposition to making a short trip to the Western Front, which can now be visited in a day from the UK. Reaching the Peninsula will involve a long and comparatively costly journey, so, once there, it is desirable to see as much of it as possible. If time is limited, in our experience, 'ANZAC' visitors want to see *their* beaches, cemeteries and memorials first, followed by the British, French and Turkish if time permits, while visitors from Europe first wish to see where their forces landed, fought and died. The five timed and measured Itineraries are designed to take this into account. Each one is described as starting and finishing in Eceabat and their number of hours of touring and visiting, without including time for refreshments, varies. Itinerary One (Helles) for instance, is the longest as, once embarked on the southern route, the journey to the British Landing Beaches is considerable and it seems logical to continue round them rather than make the long journey back to, and out again from, Eceabat. Numbers Two and Three (Anzac and the Sari Bair Ridge) are shorter and one can easily be followed by the other or followed by Itinerary Four (Suvla). Itinerary Five (on the Asian side) is also logically completed in one long journey.

GETTING AROUND THE PENINSULA

The distances between points of interest on the Peninsula are considerable and, for all but the very young and fit, motorised transport is recommended. See the **Tourist Information** section for details of taxi, car, motorbike and bike hire.

IF YOU WISH TO VISIT A PARTICULAR PLACE

If you are seeking a particular grave or name on a memorial, it is vital to contact your national Commonwealth War Graves Commission office before setting out as registers are only available in the cemeteries on 25 April and other days of ceremonies. Otherwise they may be consulted at the CWGC's offices in Canakkale (see below). To find a particular site, consult the index. If you are on the Internet you can now look up details of Gallipoli burials either on the CWGC Website or the ANZAC Officers Died at Gallipoli Website - see below.

APPROACH ROUTE

The majority of visitors to the Peninsula fly in to Turkey via Istanbul (the alternative being to fly into Izmir) and drive down to Eceabat. Therefore the Approach Route, assuming that the traveller has the independence to stop where desired, describes some points of interest in, and en route from, Istanbul. The alternative is to fly from Istanbul to Canakkale by Dardanel Air (see **TOURIST INFORMATION** below).

EXTRA VISITS

In addition to the main Itineraries, Extra Visits to sites of particular interest which lie near the routes are described. They are boxed so that they stand out clearly from the main route. Estimates of the round trip mileage and duration are given. Extra Visits 1, 2 and 3 are to military-related sites in Istanbul.

KILOMETRES COVERED/DURATION/OP/RWC/TRAVEL DIRECTIONS

A start point is given for each Itinerary, from which a running total of kilometres is indicated (but which does not include Extra Visits). Each recommended stop is indicated by a clear heading with that running total and the probable time you will wish to stay there. You may wish to stay longer at some and leave others out. For instance, each cemetery on the route is described. It is highly unlikely that you will have the time, or the wish, to visit them all.

As yet, signs to memorials and points of interest are not standardised, and they are not all in English. It is, therefore, of particular importance to notice the distances between points in order to locate them, and we recommend the zeroing of your vehicle's mileometer/kilometer at the beginning of each itinerary.

The letters **OP** in the heading indicate an observation point from which the salient points of the battlefield that may be seen are described. **RWC** indicates refreshment and toilet facilities. **RP** marks a reference point which can aid orientation as it is visible from more than one location.

Travel directions are written in italics and indented to make them stand out clearly. An end point is suggested, with a total distance and timing - without

Slow-moving obstacle in the road   *Sheep dog in protective mode*

deviations or refreshment stops. As refreshment opportunities are few and far between, packed lunches with plenty of liquid are recommended.

MAPS/ROAD SIGNS/PLACE NAMES

This guide book has been designed to be used with the accompanying *Major & Mrs Holt's Battle Map of Gallipoli* and the words 'Map ___' in the heading indicate the map reference for the location. Frequent use of this map will also assist you in orientating, give a clear indication of the distances involved in possible walks and show points of interest which are not included in the Itineraries or Extra Visits.

Commercially available modern detailed maps of the Peninsula are virtually non-existent and to the best of our knowledge our map is the only one available that gives comprehensive details of roads, memorials, cemeteries and battle lines. It was drawn by studying the ground and using original trench maps, the *Official History* maps and satellite mapping supplied by Professor Bademli (qv).

The CWGC Cemeteries are all clearly signed with their usual green signs, or Milli Park (National Park) brown signs with yellow lettering, and use the wartime names. Turkish memorials are often indicated on yellow signs.

Modern place names in the area often differ from those used in 1915 and there are many variations in the Turkish spelling, especially for the forts and villages. We have chosen the simplest version where possible. For instance, Abydos is now called Nara Burnu, Chanak (sometimes seen as Tchanak) is Canakkale (pronounced 'Chanakalay'), Ari Burnu is Ariburnu, Chunuk Bair is Conkbayiri, Gaba Tepe is Kabatepe, Kilid Bahr is Kilitbahir, Kiretch Tepe is Kirectepe, Krithia is Alcitepe (pronounced 'Alchitaypay'), Maidos is Eceabat (pronounced 'Echeabat'), Nibrunesi Point is Kucukkemikli Br, Sedd-el-Bahr is Seddulbahir, and the ancient Sestos is Kilye Koyu.

SOME WARNINGS

It is most unwise to pick up any 'souvenirs' in the form of bullets, shells, barbed wire etc. that may be found. These remnants of war are extremely dangerous to handle: explosions can occur with this volatile material, resulting in death or maiming. Cuts could cause tetanus or blood poisoning. It should also be noted that it is forbidden by the Gallipoli National Park and Turkish Government authorities to remove such objects and visitors in the past attempting to do so have been charged with a criminal offence. In addition, removing the historical remnants of the battles diminishes the experience for future visitors.

It is advisable to take a companion when walking off the beaten path. The ground can be very rough and ankles easily twisted. A stick - or a packet of biscuits - may be an asset, especially to discourage the packs of dogs that are sometimes seen near the remoter cemeteries. A bottle of water is essential and a mobile phone could be useful. Snakes are present, although few are venomous. Packs of jackals have returned to the valleys behind the CWGC complex at Anzac but present no danger: nor do the wild boars that are beginning to return after the disastrous fire of 1994. The large tortoises that abound present no threat!

HISTORICAL SUMMARY

A BRIEF HISTORY OF THE DARDANELLES AND TURKEY UP TO 1914

Due to its strategic importance as the link between the south (the Mediterranean and the Aegean) and the north (the Black Sea and Russia, via Constantinople), possession of the Dardanelles has been fought for throughout the Greek, Roman, Byzantine and Ottoman periods. The area covered by the Gallipoli Peninsula, named the 'Chersonese' by the Thracians, and the Asian coast of the Dardanelles is a traditional bridge between Europe and Asia, between Thrace and Anatolia, a migration, trading and invasion route redolent with ancient history. Jason and the Argonauts, Xerxes, Lysander and Alexander the Great, St. Paul, the Emperor Constantine, Attila the Hun, the Crusaders and the Venetians all passed this way.

In 1452 Sultan Mehmet the Conqueror established the Ottoman shipbuilding yards in Gelibolu and built the forts at Kilitbahir and Cimenlik (Canakkale). Between 1656 and 1659 Koprulu Mehmet Pasha built the forts at Kumkale and Seddulbahir and the importance of the Dardanelles as a path to Istanbul and Russia increased. More than half the commerce of the known world passed through the Straits. In the late 1790s Sultan Selim III upgraded the defensive system, though in 1807 Admiral Sir J. T. Duckworth passed virtually unscathed through the Straits with a squadron of line-of-battle ships to support British diplomacy in Constantinople. Only on their return was some damage sustained from shore batteries and twenty nine men were killed and 139 wounded. On 2 April 1915 Lord Fisher was to express the hope that de Robeck would not be 'Duckworthed'. However, new ramparts were added in the 1810s by Sultan Mahmut II, by Sultan Abdulmecit in the 1860s and Sultan Abdulhamit II in the 1890s.

The Ottoman Empire, described by Nicholas 1 of Russia as 'The Sick Man of Europe', gradually declined and during the Crimean War of 1854, Gelibolu (see **APPROACH ROUTE** below) was occupied by the British and the French. The war was ended by the Treaty of Paris, which settled the right of passage through the Dardanelles. The Russians later repudiated the Treaty and in 1878 another British Fleet under Admiral Hornby passed virtually unopposed through the Dardanelles to secure Constantinople against the Russians in the Russo-Turkish War. The phrase 'jingoism' was coined to describe the war fever then aroused as expressed in the popular music hall song written by G. W. Hunt, 'We don't want to fight, yet by jingo, if we do, we've got the ships, we've got the men, we've got the money, too!' After this episode German experts took the defence of the Dardanelles in hand and installed many guns. As the Ottoman star waned, so German influence in Turkey increased.

In 1908 came the revolt of 'The Young Turks' in Macedonia led by Enver Pasha and supported by the Germans. One of the Young Turks was Mustafa Kemal (most Turks did not have surnames until 1934 - 'Kemal' means 'Perfection') who was

born in Salonika in 1881. Striking- looking, with blond hair, he impressed all who met him. In 1904 he had passed out of the War College at Pangalti proficient in French (which he had learned from an interesting lady tutor), the waltz, the ability to hold strong liquor and with a burning desire to serve his country. He joined the Union and Progress Party (known as the C.U.P.), a political movement largely led by the military, but was often at odds with the party hierarchy. Kemal was convinced that a revolutionary government should throw off the stranglehold influence of the Islamic religion, discard the redundant parts of the Empire and build a new modern secular State with Turkish Anatolia at its heart. In spring 1909 NCOs loyal to the C.U.P. staged a revolt in Istanbul and the Sultan, Abdulhamid, was deposed. Kemal, however, strongly believed that the Army must distance itself from politics and the C.U.P. This unpopular view led to assassination attempts on his life and, when that failed, a slander campaign based on his alleged excessive drinking and womanising. Kemal survived, concentrating on his speciality - training - and learning from his new German military mentors, his 38th Infantry Regiment in Salonika became a model formation. In the Balkan War of 1912 Turkey lost all her European possessions to Bulgaria by the Treaty of London of 30 May 1913, save the Chatalja and the Gallipoli Peninsula.

Mustafa Kemal in his familiar Gallipoli uniform

In November 1912 Kemal had been posted to the Peninsula where, from his base at Maidos (present-day Eceabat), he headed the operations section of the force being assembled at Bulair to defend the Peninsula and the Dardanelles, an experience he was to put to good use in 1915. Like von Rundstedt in 1944, Kemal was convinced that no determined enemy could be prevented from landing and that once the main landings had been identified the invader must be pushed back into the sea.

Meanwhile the C.U.P. was now in power, and Enver led a force which recaptured Edirne, thus enhancing his standing. Kemal was banished to Sofia as the military attaché. Enver, appointed Minister for War despite his inexperience, was dazzled by his German colleagues, now in charge of military training under Liman von Sanders, leader of the German Military Mission established in December 1913. A one-time military attaché in Berlin, Enver believed that, with German strength behind Turkey, they could easily win a war against the Allies. Kemal subscribed to the Allies' theory that Turkey would be best to remain neutral. As well as the German Military Mission, there was a British Naval Mission, established the previous year in an attempt to influence the Turks into remaining pro-British, led by Rear-Admiral Arthur Limpus.

Thus Turkey was balanced between the British and the Germans - which way would she fall?

MILITARY BACKGROUND TO THE GALLIPOLI CAMPAIGN

In a Nutshell

By the end of the first year of the war a stalemate had been reached on the Western Front, with the adversaries facing each other across a virtually continuous line of 350 miles of trenches, and so the British and French searched for another theatre where they might win a victory. They looked towards Turkey and the opportunity of opening the sea route through the Dardanelles to their beleagured ally Russia.

Their chosen plan was that a purely naval force should sail up the Dardanelles to Constantinople in the hope that the city would fall in sheer fright, and that Turkey, who had entered the war on the German side, would capitulate, thus opening the sea route from the Aegean to the Black Sea. But was it possible to force the Straits? The coastline on each side was lined with guns and the waters sown with mines.

With a view to silencing the on-shore weapons, naval bombardments of the Turkish forts protecting the entrance to the Dardanelles began on 19 February 1915, but the attempt on 18 March 1915, to sail past them and up the Straits failed with the loss of several ships due to mines.

As a result, on 25 April 1915, British and ANZAC landings were made on the Gallipoli Peninsula. Their task was to clear a passage for the Navy by neutralising the Turkish defences on the banks of the Dardanelles. This attack also failed. Later on 6 August further landings were made at Suvla Bay in an attempt to take the Peninsula and, essentially through incompetence on the part of the Generals, this too failed. The Army did not try again.

The Navy, also, made no further attempt to force a passage to Constantinople and 8 months later the Allies withdrew, having sustained a quarter of a million casualties. Turkish losses were of the same order.

Where is Gallipoli?

Gallipoli, or Gelibolu as it is marked on Turkish maps, is a small town and port on the European side of the Dardanelles Channel and it gives its name to the finger of land that points southward into the Aegean. The town itself was not directly involved in the fighting. See Holts' Map 1.

Why Attack Gallipoli?

In searching for a solution to the Western Front stalemate the British hierarchy divided into two main camps - those who believed that the only way forward was to beat the main German armies on the Western Front, known as the 'Westerners', and those who felt that a major result could only be obtained by turning the enemy's flank in the Baltic or in the Mediterranean, and hence known as the 'Easterners'.

Sir John French, the British Commander-in-Chief on the Western Front, a staunch Westerner, advocated an attack along the Belgian coast supported by the Navy, while the First Sea Lord, Fisher, proposed a blockade of the Baltic. Both of these ideas were put aside following an appeal on 3 January 1915, by Grand Duke Nicholas of Russia for help in the Caucasus, thus prompting a renewal of interest in an expedition to the Dardanelles. Although not exactly of one mind as to the nature of the operation, both Winston Churchill, First Lord of the Admiralty, and Fisher, supported the idea of an expedition to Gallipoli, a venture that Churchill and Lord Kitchener, Secretary of State for War, had discussed as early as August 1914 and which had at that time included the participation of Greek forces.

Perhaps the most concise summary of the reasons for taking on Turkey, other than responding to the appeal by the Tsar, was made later by Sir William Robertson, who had actually opposed the idea of involvement in Gallipoli, as, 'To secure Egypt, to induce Italy and the Balkan States to come in on our side, and, if followed by the forcing of the Bosphorus, [to] enable Russia to draw munitions from America and Western Europe, and to export her accumulated supplies of wheat.'

How to Attack Gallipoli?

The British had formally studied the idea of forcing a passage northwards through the Dardanelles as early as 1904, but, as described above, that challenge had faced antagonists for centuries, usually in purely naval actions.

Two differing views existed as to how to effect that passage to Constantinople. One was that it could be done purely by naval forces as in 1657 and 1807. The other was that land forces were needed, either to silence the guns along the coast before the navy could make its attempt, or at least to occupy the Gallipoli Peninsula after the ships had passed in order to secure their line of passage. The August 1914 deliberations of Churchill and Kitchener - though they came to nothing - had included joint naval and military plans for 60,000 Greek troops to occupy the Peninsula in concert with a naval assault.

On 25 November, 1914 the War Council had its first meeting and Churchill raised the idea of a joint military and naval attack on the Dardanelles as a measure to protect Egypt. Kitchener objected on the grounds that all available troops were needed on the Western Front and the idea was rejected. However, following the Grand Duke's appeal for help, Fisher enthusiastically supported the idea of a joint naval and military attack, provided that it took place immediately.

One person who had recent first-hand knowledge of the strength of Turkish naval defences was Rear-Admiral Limpus, yet he was not officially consulted because London felt that to do so would push the as-yet-uncommitted Turks into the German camp. When the British Naval Mission was withdrawn on 9 September 1914, Limpus was sent to Malta to administer the Dockyard.

The Westerners felt that no land forces should be involved in the venture and much discussion and argument took place around the two basic options of 'without troops' and 'with troops', and some personalities, such as Fisher and Kitchener, suffered violent reversals of opinion that were, in the latter's case, to strike a major blow at the operation's chances of success. Churchill sought the views of Admiral Carden, commanding the British squadron in the Aegean, and

Carden produced a plan that envisaged four stages in a purely 'without troops' naval offensive:-

1. Destruction of the forts guarding the entrance to the Dardanelles
2. Silencing the guns along the inner shore line of the Straits
3. Clearing the mines
4. Neutralising the defences at the Narrows and those beyond to Constantinople

At the War Council meeting of 13 January Churchill enthusiastically presented this plan which was accepted with little discussion. He recorded that the Council had resolved '... that the Admiralty should prepare for a naval expedition in February to bombard and take the Gallipoli Peninsula with Constantinople as its objective.' There was no mention of land forces.

Thus, although the Easterners had prevailed, the advocates of 'without troops', the Westerners, had their way. Gallipoli was 'on'. It was to be a purely naval action.

What Happened

The development of the Gallipoli campaign may be divided into the following phases, each of which will be described separately below in summary form, further details being given in the commentaries accompanying the battlefield tour routes:-

Preliminary 1914

The Bombardments of 19 February - 16 March 1915

The Naval Action of 18 March 1915

The Landings and Actions of 25 April 1915

    The Bulair Diversion

    The Kumkale Diversion

    The Five Landings at Helles:

        Y Beach; X Beach; W Beach; V Beach; S Beach

    The ANZAC Landing and After

The First Battle of Krithia 28 April 1915

The Turkish night attack of 2 May 1915

The Second Battle of Krithia 6 May 1915

The Third Battle of Krithia 4 June 1915

The Battle of Gully Ravine 28 June 1915

The Landings and Actions of 6 August 1915

    The Helles Diversion

    The Anzac Diversion and the struggle for Sari Bair

    The Suvla Landings

The Battle of Scimitar Hill 21 August 1915

The Final Phase: Plans and Counter-Plots

The Evacuations of December - 9 January 1916

Preliminary 1914

The French and the Russians had formed an alliance to come to each other's aid if either were attacked by Germany, but Russia's ability to sustain a major war depended greatly on being able to use the Dardanelles for supplies. Russia and

Greece were traditional enemies of Turkey and Turkish inclinations towards an alignment with Germany were reinforced when in June 1914 the Greeks bought two battleships, the *Mississippi* and the *Idaho*, from the Americans - probably in anticipated defence against two other battleships, the *Reshadieh* and the *Sultan Osman*, that were being built for the Turks in Britain at Armstrong Vickers. On 28 July, a month before the *Reshadieh* was to be handed over, Winston Churchill requisitioned the two Turkish ships for the Royal Navy. Inevitably, feelings ran strongly against Britain and when, on 10 August, the German ships *Goeben* and *Breslau* sailed up the Dardanelles and were offered to the Turkish Navy, the slide towards declaring for Germany began. On 15 August control of the Turkish Navy by the British Naval Mission was removed and given to Rear-Admiral Wilhelm Souchon, on board the *Goeben*. Nevertheless, the Turkish politicians contrived to make the best of both worlds by remaining technically neutral for as long as possible, but, when, on 27 September, the Royal Navy forced a Turkish boat to turn round at the entrance to the Dardanelles, the Germans persuaded the Turkish Navy to close the Straits. Mines began to be laid and lighthouses were dimmed. One month later the Turkish fleet bombarded the Russian ports of Sebastopol and Odessa.

Hostilities between Turkey and Britain formally began on 31 October and on 3 November, on Churchill's orders, and despite Limpus's urgings not to undertake the attack, the Royal Navy shelled the forts at Seddulbahir and Kumkale, hitting a powder magazine at the former and killing five officers and eighty-one men.

The shelling was to prove a fatal move for the expedition that was to offer such high hopes in 1915. It prompted the Turks, under German guidance, to begin to strengthen their coastal defences. Under Liman von Sanders' energetic leadership, in a mode similar to that displayed by Erwin Rommel thirty years later in Normandy, gun positions were laid out, forts strengthened, roads built, beach defences of barbed wire and improvised land mines were prepared, submarine nets placed and sea mines laid. Even greater emphasis was given to the defensive preparations when, on 13 December, the 1874 battleship *Mesudiye*, anchored just below Canakkale, was sunk by the British submarine *B11*, winning for her commander, Lieutenant Holbrook (qv), the first submarine VC.

By February 1915 the defences had developed on both sides of the Straits, around three areas. Firstly there were the **Outer Defences** of the forts at Seddulbahir and Kumkale with some twenty medium-range weapons and 4 long-range, secondly the **Intermediate Defences** between Seddulbahir and Kephes Point with a small number of fixed weapons but with a couple of dozen of mobile howitzers pulled by buffalo teams, and thirdly the **Inner Defences** at the Narrows around Kilitbahir and Canakkale with some 80 guns, plus three land-based torpedo tubes at Kilitbahir. Between the shores were the minefields (see Holts' Map 2) comprising almost 350 mines. The Turkish defensive strategy was to face incoming warships firstly with artillery and then, as the waters narrowed, with mines. The sea defences were now formidable but on land only one Turkish infantry division was in the Peninsula.

After a lapse of three months the Allied fleet began its attempt to sail up to Constantinople. Their plan was first to silence the **Outer Defences** and then to send in the minesweepers to clear the minefields.

The Bombardments of 19 February - 16 March 1915

Twelve capital ships in three divisions, two British and one French, all under Admiral Carden, began the attempt to force the Dardanelles by naval power alone by bombarding the outer forts on 19 February. The shelling was inaccurate because the warships kept on the move while firing, an inept opening that might be said to characterise the entire campaign.

By 24 February doubts surfaced in London about the validity of the 'without troops', 'navy only', plan because the War Council decided that if the Navy failed 'the Army must see the business through' and Kitchener ordered Lieutenant-General W. R. Birdwood, commander of the Australian and New Zealand Army Corps (ANZAC) in Egypt, to go to the Dardanelles and report back. However 'K' was not prepared to release the only available trained division, the 29th, for duty in the operation.

The following day Carden resumed hostilities, in increasingly bad weather, and the long-range guns of the **Outer Defences** were silenced. Twenty-four hours later from inside the Straits the **Intermediate Defences**, including the Dardanos Battery, were shelled by HMS *Albion* and HMS *Majestic*. In conjunction with the naval actions, Allied landing parties were put ashore at Kumkale and Seddulbahir in order to complete the destruction of the Turkish guns. On 26 February Lieutenant-Commander Eric Gascoigne Robinson led a demolition party from HMS *Vengeance* and, advancing alone (he refused to allow members of his party to accompany him as their white uniforms made them too conspicuous) under heavy fire, infiltrated an enemy gun position, destroying two guns. He also took part in four attacks on the minefields, always under fire. For his bravery he was awarded the VC. [Robinson served on convoys in WW2, during which both his sons were killed, and retired as a Rear-Admiral. His grave in Langrish, Hampshire, was lost until, on 20 August 1965, a new headstone was erected in the presence of his two grandchildren, members of the VC Memorial Fund of the Greenwich RN Association, the local RNA and members of the Gallipoli Association.]

By 3 March some fifty guns had been put out of action with only a handful of casualties. Carden, encouraged by his success, sent a message to the Admiralty to say that, given fine weather, he hoped to get through to Constantinople in fourteen days. Fisher, meanwhile, was having severe doubts about the viability of the Gallipoli campaign. 'The more I consider the Dardanelles the less I like it,' he wrote to Churchill on 4 March.

On that day in the Dardanelles itself the pattern of events changed dramatically when landings were made at Seddulbahir by a company of the Plymouth Battalion. They met such fierce opposition that they had to be evacuated by the Navy under covering fire from the battleship *Majestic*. At the same time, a landing at Kumkale (meaning Sand Fortress) on the Asian side of the Dardanelles, by another company of the same battalion, also had to be withdrawn following an opposed landing, and suffered twenty-two men killed and a further twenty-two wounded.

This, then, was no longer an operation against a totally unprepared enemy as it had been in 1914. The Turks, supported and encouraged by their German advisers, used their mobile howitzers to harass the warships, keeping them on the move, and, as the task force moved further up the narrowing Straits, so the effect of these mobile weapons became more pronounced, particularly on the civilian crews of the minesweepers. Abortive efforts on 1 and 2 March to clear the Kephes minefield failed and on 3 March the mine-sweeping trawlers turned back down the Straits under a hail of fire from some seventy guns. Even the arrival of HMS *Queen Elizabeth* on 5/6 March, when she fired from off Gaba Tepe and hurled 29 of her huge 15-inch shells 20 kms across the Peninsula onto the forts at Kilitbahir, caused only temporary disruption of growing Turkish confidence. [Twin guns of the Elizabeth type can be seen outside the Imperial War Museum.]

On 7 and 8 March several battleships, including *Agamemnon, Lord Nelson* and *Queen Elizabeth*, continued the shelling from within the Straits. The weather was bad and Turkish batteries, including Kilitbahir, returned fire. The mobile batteries were proving particularly troublesome and it was difficult to locate them, despite the use of aircraft. It was beginning to look as if naval gunfire alone could not neutralise the shore defences and, as yet, the minefields up to Kephes Point had not been cleared.

On 10 March the trawlers tried again and failed. The draught of the vessels was such that in order to trawl the mines with a wire hung between two boats, they had to sail over the minefield, but if they did that and passed directly over a mine, they would probably be blown up. It was not surprising, therefore, that on the following day the trawlers turned back at the first sign of Turkish fire. It was now clear that the inner Turkish defences, although damaged, were still effectively protecting the minefields, the minefields had not been swept and the mobile howitzers had not been neutralised. It was close to a stalemate but Commodore Roger Keyes, Carden's Chief-of-Staff, assumed command of the mine-sweeping force, offered large financial rewards to induce the civilian crews to try again, strengthened their numbers with naval volunteers and on the night of 13 March set off with 6 trawlers and the cruiser *Amethyst* to tackle the Kephes minefield. It was a near disaster. Four of the trawlers were badly damaged by fire from the shore and *Amethyst* had her steering gear put out of action for 20 minutes, a sitting target for the Turks and twenty-seven men were killed with forty-three wounded. Despite strenuous efforts the minefield had not been cleared.

Constantly pressurised by telegrams from Churchill, Carden now decided to change his plan. Instead of first clearing the Straits of mines and then taking on the Turkish batteries, he proposed to sail a force directly up the channel to silence the guns. Meanwhile, in London, Kitchener clearly now felt that, despite Carden's new plan, the navy could not succeed alone and ordered the 29th Division to sail to the Aegean. To command the military force Kitchener chose Sir Ian Hamilton, who described in his diaries how Kitchener sent for him on 12 March and said in a matter-of-fact-voice,

"We are sending a military force to support the Fleet now at the Dardanelles and you are to have Command." At that moment K wished me to bow, leave the room and make a start ...but my knowledge of the Dardanelles was nil; of the Turk nil; of the strength of our own forces next to nil ...although I have met K almost every day during the past six months, and although he has twice hinted I might be sent to Salonika; never once, to the best of my recollection, had he mentioned the word Dardanelles.

Thus was the stage set for the inadequate military operation to come. Meanwhile, out in the Aegean, Carden found the pressures of the affair too much for him and resigned on 16 March to be succeeded by Admiral de Robeck, his Second-in-Command. De Robeck, calm and authoritative, supported by the energetic and resourceful Roger Keyes, determined that a more robust naval approach was needed and, following Carden's new concept, resolved upon a fleet assault through the Dardanelles. It began on 18 March.

The Naval Action of 18 March 1915

Just before noon on a warm sunny day *Queen Elizabeth*, *Agamemnon*, *Lord Nelson* and *Inflexible*, the four most powerful battleships of the British fleet, flanked by the battleships *Prince George* and *Triumph*, led the first wave of the armada into the Narrows and from the area of Eren Keui Bay engaged the shore batteries at Canakkale and Kilitbahir. Once this action was underway, the second wave, four French ships - the *Bouvet*, the *Gaulois*, the *Charlemagne* and the *Suffren*, commanded by Admiral Guépratte - accompanied by battleships *Majestic* and *Swiftsure*, sailed through the British vessels to within two miles of Kephes Point and opened an even fiercer bombardment on the defences of the Narrows which returned fire, slightly damaging all four French vessels.

This was an extraordinary confrontation, a naval 'army' of eighteen battleships and attendant destroyers and cruisers taking on a land army rather than an opposing navy. The forts and the shore lines were blotted by great clouds of dust rising from the impact of the huge shells hammering at their defences and overlaid with the sound of explosions, while the waters of the Narrows were speckled by tall spouts as the shells of the defenders dropped like grains from a giant's pepper pot amongst the fleet.

When, one hour later at around 1400 hours, the shore batteries fell silent, the third wave of British ships - the *Vengeance*, *Irresistible*, *Albion* and *Ocean* (*Canopus* and *Cornwallis* were held in reserve) - steamed in to relieve the French who turned to the right, arcing into Eren Keui Bay. As they did so, the *Bouvet* was rent by a violent explosion and sank in less than three minutes, losing over 600 of her crew. The forts re-opened fire and the ships countered, but at just after 1600 hours the *Irresistible* struck a mine and sank at 1750 hours, though the majority of her crew escaped. Shortly after, HMS *Ocean* hit a mine and sank, the larger part of her crew surviving, while the *Inflexible* had her forward control turret put out of action and struggled back to Tenedos. Nevertheless, the remaining ships continued their attack under continuous fire from both shores until fading light forced them to withdraw. The Turks had spent almost all of their heavy ammunition and were convinced that the attack would begin again the following day. It did not.

Admiral de Robeck, encouraged by Keyes and bolstered by his familiarity with Kipling's *If*, had every intention of continuing the assault as early as possible, but Sir Ian Hamilton, who had arrived the day before and had seen part of the engagement from the deck of the *Phaeton*, wired Kitchener on 19 March that in his opinion the Straits could not be forced by ships alone. That settled the matter, despite the fact that this was an opinion on a naval matter expressed by an army commander. London decided that it was now to be a combined operation with the landings coming next.

Meanwhile, in Turkey the following week, Liman von Sanders was appointed by the Turkish Government to command the defence of the Peninsula, and while at Eren Keui Bay on a tour of inspection, he turned to his aide, Colonel Kannengiesser, and said, 'If the English will only leave me alone for eight days'. In fact it would be twenty-nine days before the English returned, by which time the Turks would be as ready as they could ever be with six divisions assembled for the defence of the Peninsula, six times the force that had been present when the bombardments had begun.

The Naval Action of 18 March 1915 from the Turkish point of view

Turkish artist's impression of the sinking of the Bouvet

The Landings and Actions of 25 April 1915

Despite the Commander's pessimism, stemming from the fact that he had left England on Friday the 13th and that April 25th was a Sunday and not in his view a propitious date on which to begin an attack (a view to be held by some Commanders in September 1944 when the drop at Arnhem was made on Sunday 17th) Hamilton's plan for the assault seemed to be a good one. It involved a dummy landing by the Royal Naval Division well to the north at **Bulair** in an attempt to persuade the Turks to keep their main forces on the Peninsula away from the areas of the actual landings in the south, a minor landing by the French on the Asiatic coast at **Kumkale**, with a similar objective of misleading the defenders, and two major seaborne assaults. One of these, by the ANZACs north of the promontory **Gaba Tepe**, was to drive inland past the Sari Bair Ridge which culminated in the hill, **Chunuk Bair**, while the other, by the 29th Division, was to use five small, unconnected beaches at **Helles** from which to launch an attack on the commanding hill, **Achi Baba**. Control of these two heights would give the Allies effective occupation of the Peninsula. In all, Hamilton had under command some 77,000 fighting men, including 17,000 French, and an armada of 200 ships to transport and support them.

    The Bulair Diversion. On the evening of 24 April part of the RND in seven of their own transports, escorted by the battleship HMS *Canopus*, sailed into the Gulf of Saros. During the night Lieutenant-Commander Freyberg (qv) swam ashore at Bulair and lit a number of flares as a ruse to persuade the Turks that a landing was imminent. The courageous effort by Freyberg added to Liman von Sanders' conviction that a landing from the Gulf of Saros was likely, and he delayed sending troops south, even after he heard of the Helles and Anzac landings. Sanders had positioned two of his divisions - the 5th and the 7th - to cover his imagined threat, but on the 26th, now certain that the southern landings were the main threat, he took personal command of his forces and moved them down the Peninsula.

    The Kumkale Diversion. On 25 April five French battleships, plus HMS *Prince George* and the Russian *Askold*, began a bombardment of the fort and village of Kumkale shortly after dawn. The French 6th Colonial Regiment, despite starting late and experiencing difficulties with the strong current, landed around 0930 just south of the fort and carried both it and the village with the bayonet. When the French withdrew during the night of 27 April they had lost 7 officers and 183 men killed and 13 officers and 575 men wounded. Von Sanders had considered the Asiatic coast a likely target both here and in Besika Bay, where the presence of Allied warships on the day added to the effectiveness of the feint and it seems probable that the diversion here at least delayed the sending of troops from Asia to the Peninsula.

    Helles. The landing force was the 29th Division which went ashore on three main beaches, V, W and X, and two minor beaches, S and Y. The naval operations were commanded by Rear-Admiral Wemyss and the Division by Lieutenant-General Sir Aylmer Hunter-Weston. A preparatory naval bombardment began at 0500 hours. The actions, anti-clockwise around the beaches, are summarised below.

    Y Beach (hardly a beach at all, but the base of a 200-foot-high cliff) was the northernmost beach on the western coast, below the sharp face of what came to be known as Gurkha Bluff. Here the 1st King's Own Scottish Borderers landed unopposed and, supported by a company of the South Wales Borderers and the Plymouth Battalion, Royal Marines, sat around most of the day trying to decide which officer was in command and awaiting orders from Hunter-Weston. The landing had been seen by Hamilton as a way to get behind the Turks holding the Cape. Forays were made, in particular to the south by a KOSB company, but progress proved to be impossible as the Turks rapidly brought up reserves of the 9th Division to hold the ground about Gully Ravine, thus effectively reducing any hope of a link-up with X Beach [see Holts' Map 5] and subjecting the small British force to withering artillery fire. The shape of the terrain prevented the accompanying naval force of HMS *Amethyst, Sapphire* and *Goliath* from giving effective fire support and by the following morning the troops were exhausted and likely to be overwhelmed. The KOSB and the SWB had lost about half their officers and men. Later that morning they were evacuated, virtually unmolested, in an operation that was a portent for another withdrawal nine months later.

X Beach, a small strip of sand some 180 metres long, lay beneath a low escarpment which presented little obstacle to the assault force. HMS *Implacable* gave close fire support to the leading troops, the 2nd Royal Fusiliers, as they went ashore at 0600 hours and, although there were well-prepared defensive positions above the beach, there were but a dozen defenders manning them. The Fusiliers gained the top of the escarpment and by 1100 hours had taken Hill 114. They then continued south in an attempt to join up with forces on W Beach. Strong Turkish counter-attacks were held off as reinforcements in the shape of the 1st Inniskilling Fusiliers and the 1st Border Regiment landed and, with the help once again of HMS *Implacable* which silenced a particularly troublesome Turkish artillery battery near Krithia, a junction with W Beach was made at Tekke Burnu (meaning Cape Shrimp). Because of the particularly effective fire support given by the Navy (*Implacable's* captain, Hughes Lockyer, had brought his vessel close to the shore) the beach became known as "Implacable Landing".

W Beach was probably the most physically suitable for a landing of all of the beaches. It was sandy, about 350 metres long, bordered at each end by high ground, but in the middle there were gentle sand dunes and a gully that led inland to the ridge overlooking the sea. The Turks had prepared their defences well, using land and sea mines and running a thick barbed wire fence along the entire length of the shore. Machine guns had been placed in the cliffs to cover not only the beach but also the exit via the gully. The naval bombardment began at 0500 hours and at 0600 hours a small flotilla of boats carrying the complete battalion of the 1st Lancashire Fusiliers set off for the shore, some craft heading for the heights at each end of the beach. Initially there had been no response from the Turks, but, as the boats hit the beach, a torrent of rifle and machine-gun fire fell upon them from the 26th Turkish Infantry Regiment. Many men were killed before they could leave the boats, others wounded in the water, drowned, and yet more, struggling to force a way through the thick belt of barbed wire, got no further. Nevertheless, thanks to the troops that had landed against less opposition below Tekke Burnu at the northern end of the beach, who climbed the cliffs and after a short but furious tussle silenced the machine guns that were doing so much damage, the main body struggled ashore. At 0900 hours the 4th Worcesters arrived as reinforcements and, having seen what had happened to the Lancashire Fusiliers on the main beach, made their landing below Tekke Burnu. Together the battalions cleared the remaining Turks from around that position and established contact with the Royal Fusiliers moving down from X Beach. By the end of the day the British hold on W Beach was firm, although no progress had been made south towards Cape Helles. The cost had been high and in recognition of the extraordinary bravery of the Lancashire Fusiliers in making their landing, six VCs were awarded 'before breakfast' and the beach was named by Ian Hamilton to honour the regiment's bravery, and still is named, "Lancashire Landing".

V Beach. This beach, which was to receive the main landing force, was about 300 metres long and sealed at the western end by high cliffs surmounted by Ertugrul Fort, and at the eastern end by the fort and village of Seddulbahir. In the centre, behind the small beach of less than 10 metres width, the ground rose steadily to a height of some 40 metres as from the bottom of a giant saucer. The ground was chequered with lines of trenches and barbed wire. At around 0500 hours HMS *Albion* opened fire on the beach area and some 90 minutes later three companies of the 1st Dublin Fusiliers in towed boats approached the shore together with an old collier, the *River Clyde*. On board the *Clyde* were another 2,000 men - the rest of the Dubliners, the 1st Royal Munster Fusiliers, two companies of the 2nd Hampshires, a field company of the West Riding Royal Engineers (Territorials) and a platoon from the Anson Battalion RND. The *Clyde* drove straight at the shore towards the Seddulbahir end and grounded about 100 metres out. On each side of the ship were four large sally ports through which it was planned that the men would storm onto lighters and pontoons and thence to the shore. The Turks held their fire until the invaders reached the shore line and then poured down upon them a murderous fire from small arms, machine guns and pom poms. Only about 300 of the 700 Dubliners in the boats reached the shore where they were pinned down behind a small sandbank and the men trying to leave the *Clyde* were decimated, their bodies filling the sally ports. Fifty metres out to sea the water ran red with blood. To add to the chaos, the intensity of the gunfire, and the strength of the current prevented the construction of the walkways to the beach, despite the efforts of Commander Unwin RN (qv), for which he would win the VC. The men trapped in the ship, although safe from small arms fire, were a sitting artillery target, and four times she was hit by fire from the Asian shore, but each time the fuses failed and the shells did not explode - a parallel to the failure of the fusing of Argentinian bombs that hit British ships during the Falklands conflict. One tow of two platoons of the Dubliners had veered to the east and made a good landing at the Camber, a small harbour below Seddulbahir fort, but they were soon overwhelmed. For those on the *Clyde* there was little to do but to wait for darkness when the survivors were able to file off without a single casualty and to prepare for the struggle to come on the morrow.

S Beach. This was the largest beach - a sweep of about 3 kilometres from Seddulbahir Fort to de Tott's Battery at Eski Hisarlik Point (qv) - onto which landed

Suvla Bay: view from 'A' Beach, with Suvla Point on the extreme left and Ghazi Baba on the right

W Beach from the sea, with Helles Memorial on the heights to the right

Ari Burnu CWGC Cemetery with North Beach to its left and to its right the Turkish Monolith and Anzac Cove. Above is the Sphinx with the flat top of Plugge's Plateau to its right

the smallest force, three companies of the 2nd SWB with support detachments. HMS *Cornwallis* gave fire support and, landing later than the others (at 0730 hours), the Welsh secured the area by 1000 hours. The landing was a complete success.

The ANZAC Landing and After

The ANZAC force was planned to land at the wide Z Beach, adjacent to the Gaba Tepe headland, and to strike inland to Gun Ridge, but a strong current swept them some 1.5kms north into a small cove beside Ari Burnu with a narrow beach overlooked by steep cliffs. It was little defended, unlike the area where they had been scheduled to land, and the 3rd Australian Brigade met only minimal resistance as they went ashore early in the morning of the 25th. Within half an hour some 4,000 men had been landed. As daylight broke it was realised that the landing had been made in the wrong place and, although small parties of determined ANZACs scaled the cliffs and even made their way far enough inland to see across the Peninsula to the Narrows, the enthusiasm of the troops at being safely ashore, their inexperience, the cramped conditions and the savagery of the terrain, made the organising of concerted efforts very difficult. Mustafa Kemal at his HQ at Bigali (qv) had quickly appreciated that the Chunuk Bair and Sari Bair heights were the key to the struggle, rather than the beaches and, without higher authority, led his 55th and 77th Regiments to meet the enemy. The struggles on the cliffs and in the ravines were bitter and bloody; on each side every second man engaged in fighting becoming a casualty. By midnight the situation for the ANZACs seemed so critical that General Birdwood, commanding the Corps, advised immediate evacuation (an oddly parallel situation to that on 6 June 1944, at OMAHA Beach, also overlooked by high cliffs, where the American assault forces were under so much pressure that the Army Commander, General Bradley, considered evacuation). Ian Hamilton decided against it and that, until he had taken Achi Baba, the ANZACs should act as a detaining force in the north. He issued an order to General Birdwood that included the words, 'Until you receive further instructions no general advance is to be initiated by you.' Fighting at Anzac therefore consisted of local hand-to-hand battles, sniping, the exchanging of grenades, mining, patrol excursions and the strengthening and developing of trench works supplemented by artillery exchanges including the participation of the Royal Navy. On 19 May the Turks made a major attack which was repulsed with heavy casualties, but during June and July neither side attempted any major action at Anzac. At Helles, however, in the heaviest fighting of the campaign, Hamilton set out to take Achi Baba several times and brief accounts of those battles follow.

The First Battle of Krithia 28 April 1915

The Turks had planned to defend the Peninsula by first of all meeting the invasion on the beaches and then, if that failed, to fall back to a line some 6kms north of Helles below Krithia (Alcitepe). Thus, following their successful landings, the British, on 27 April, were able to advance almost 4kms up the Peninsula virtually unopposed. However, the lower half of the Peninsula, the Helles area, is commanded by the heights of Achi Baba about 2kms to the east of Krithia, from which the Turks could observe most of what was going on to their south. The Turks, guided by their German officers, had made much use of camouflage and the gullies running down from the hill to the sea (Kereves Dere on the French front, Krithia Nullah, Kanli Dere and Gully Ravine on the British front) to conceal their artillery and machine-gun positions and to ease movement around the battlefield. Ian Hamilton, realising the importance of Achi Baba, ordered Hunter-Weston to take the hill. On 28 April, the day that Hunter-Weston moved his HQ on shore to the seaward slopes of Hill 138 (thence known as 'Hunter-Weston Hill'), 29th Division, with the French 1st Division on their right and beyond them the 2nd SWB, attacked at 0800 hours and were on the lower slopes of Achi Baba before noon. However, despite fire support from the *Queen Elizabeth*, the Turkish counter-attacks drove the Allies back, causing them some 3,000 casualties, about 20% of the forces engaged. The French had made gains of about 900 metres and the British, exhausted from the efforts of the landings, far less, but the ground that they gained by the end of the day (just short of what would become the Eski Line - see Holts' Map 5) was held until the Evacuation.

The Turkish Night Attack of 2 May

At 2200 hours the Turks began a heavy bombardment and followed it by an attack in the centre of the line about the Krithia Nullah, which fell upon an under-strength composite battalion formed from the Dublin and Munster Fusiliers, known as the 'Dubsters'. A prompt counter-attack by the 5th Royal Scots and the 1st Essex helped to hold the line, though Lieutenant-Colonel Godfrey-Fausset, the latter's CO, was killed (he is buried in Redoubt Cemetery). By attacking in the dark Liman von Sanders hoped to negate the power of the Allied naval force and the Turkish soldiers were primed to fight a hand-to-hand battle with a spirit of religious fervour, shouting 'Allah! Allah!' as they charged. The fighting developed along the line, with the French on the right taking the major brunt, one of their Senegalese battalions breaking. The Anson Battalion was sent to help the French and the Hood and Howe battalions to strengthen the 29th Division, and the fighting went on until dawn. British casualties were under 700 and the French were over 2,000, but the Turks had gained nothing.

The Second Battle of Krithia 6 May 1915

By 5 May, in answer to Hamilton's pleas for reinforcements, the leading elements of 42nd Division had arrived from Egypt and that evening Hamilton moved the New Zealand Infantry Brigade and the 2nd Australian Brigade from Anzac to Helles. He was determined to take Achi Baba. The Allies now mustered around 50,000 troops and seventy guns against the Turks' probable 30,000 troops and 56 guns and on 6 May a heavy artillery and naval barrage was followed at 1100 hours by a general advance which faltered and stopped. The next day the attack resumed at 1000 hours without result and on the 8th, although Gurkha Bluff was taken, it was lost again and stalemate followed, only a few hundred yards being gained along the whole front. Hamilton had by now had a total of some 15,000 casualties at Helles (the French around 4,000), yet he himself and his HQ were still at sea on the *Arcadian*, detached from what was happening on the ground, and Achi Baba, its top ringed with poppies, still stood sentinel in Turkish hands. On 9 May Hamilton told London that he could not break through the Turkish lines without at least a fresh Army Corps at his disposal.

The Third Battle of Krithia 4 June 1915

The next major attempt to take Achi Baba was a joint British and French offensive, but this time, instead of attempting to take the heights in a single day, Hamilton set a series of objectives starting with the Turkish front line trenches, each one never more than 500 metres ahead. This was now trench warfare in earnest. The French, on the right, were set to take the high ground overlooking Kereves Dere (1st and 2nd Divisions) while the British Corps (the 29th, 42nd and RND were now amalgamated into VIII Corps), guided for the first time by a trench map showing the Turkish trenches, (based on aerial photographs taken by the RNAS) were to head for the Turkish support lines. No new formations had arrived from England although there had been unit re-inforcements, but Hamilton had yielded to pressure from London to mount the attack and, because of the amount of planning that had taken place, there was an air of confidence at Allied HQ. The British mustered an attacking force of 20,000, the French 10,000, and offshore there were destroyers and battleships (*Swiftsure* and *Exmouth*) to provide fire support. The preliminary bombardment began at 0800 hours and the infantry assault at 1200 hours. On the French front, where the opposing lines were but 100 metres apart, the preliminary bombardment had been made beyond the Turkish front line and the front trenches were virtually untouched. Thus the French attackers were met with a hail of machine-gun fire and the attack was a failure. The RND advanced in a long straight line as if on parade (shadow of the things to come on 1 July 1916) and were so heavily punished that the newly-arrived Collingwood Battalion ceased to exist and its survivors were later amalgamated with the other battalions. The 88th Brigade, reinforced with the KOSB and the RIF from 87th Brigade, in the sector from Gully Ravine to Krithia Nullah, made the best advance of the day, reaching as far as The Vineyard (qv), but the early failures on the flanks meant that in the evening the 29th and 42nd Divisions had to retire, leaving only gains of 200-450 metres along the 1.6kms front line. Allied casualties were of the order of 6,500 and Turkish estimated at 9,000. The German General Kannengiesser (qv) later wrote, 'Had the British continued the attack the next day with the same violence all would have been lost'. Neither the French nor the British had the means - or, perhaps - the will - to continue. During the battle a German naval officer and machine-gun crew from the *Goeben* were captured by the 4th Worcesters and as they were being brought in to Battalion HQ the officer shot himself in the chest, presumably in an attempt to commit suicide. Lieutenant-Colonel Cayley, commanding the Worcesters (and later to command the 29th Division), saw the incident, saying, 'He was last seen by me being carried down the trench smoking away placidly'. On the following day the Turks made a spirited counter-attack at the junction of two battalions, each commanded by a 2nd Lieutenant. 2nd Lieutenant G.R.D. Moor, commanding the 2nd Hants, rallied panicking soldiers, reportedly by shooting one or two, and held the line, winning the 29th's ninth VC. An example of the international composition of the Allied forces, he had been born in Australia. Sadly he died from influenza a week before the war ended. Another unsuccessful Turkish attack on the 6th brought the battle to an end, but Achi Baba was still in Turkish hands.

The Battle of Gully Ravine 28 June 1915

At 0900 the British guns opened fire and one hour later the attack began opposite Y Beach and Gurkha Bluff. The area between the Gully and the sea was the responsibility of 87th Brigade and that east of the Gully to just below Krithia of 156th Brigade (part of the newly-arrived 52nd Lowland Division). The action had limited objectives and unlike previous affairs did not stretch across the entire line but less than 2kms inland from the sea. The fighting went on until 5 July, by which time an advance had been made beside the shore as far as Fusilier Bluff and some 500 metres of the Ravine itself had been taken. Further east, however, little had changed. The fighting had been intense and the Turkish official version of the struggle called it 'the most costly action yet fought on the Peninsula'. Their losses were estimated at 14,000 men and the effect on their morale was such that some soldiers refused to continue the counter-attacks and the Turks made no further effort to re-take the lost ground.

The Landings and Actions of 6 August 1915

As the fighting in Gallipoli slowed to a bloody stalemate, back in London the prime movers were at odds with each other. Fisher, who had removed the *Queen Elizabeth* from the Dardanelles because of the U-boat danger, declared, 'I was against the Dardanelles from the beginning' and resigned. Kitchener asked Hamilton what force he would need to ensure success and got the answer, 'two Army Corps in all'. That meant four more divisions and Kitchener was not pleased. Meanwhile a storm blew up over Fisher's departure and Conservative Bonar Law forced Asquith, the Liberal Prime Minister, to form a Coalition Government. Churchill was replaced as First Lord of the Admiralty by Balfour, denting the morale of the troops in Gallipoli. To oversee the future conduct of the Gallipoli campaign a Dardanelles Committee was formed and on 9 June it confirmed that three divisions of Kitchener's New Army would be sent to Hamilton for a new attack. On the Peninsula, however, ten new Turkish divisions had arrived. Frustrated at Helles, Hamilton wanted to extend the bridgehead at Anzac, but there was little room in which to manoeuvre and so he planned to land at **Suvla Bay**, 8kms north of Anzac, an area known to be lightly-defended and from which a flat plain gave easy access to the high ground. Thus he could turn the Turks' right flank. In order to mislead the enemy as to the intent of the landing he ordered two simultaneous diversionary attacks - one at **Anzac** and the other at **Helles**. Hamilton's strategic plan looked good - the 10th (Irish) Division under Lieutenant-General Sir Bryan Mahon would take the left flank, landing at the top end of Suvla Bay, the 11th (Northern) Division under Major-General Hammersley would form the right flank just below Nibrunesi Point at the southern end of Suvla and Lieutenant-General Sir William Birdwood would deliver the main assault on Sari Bair from Anzac. During the time of one of the authors at the Army Staff College a favourite phrase amongst the directing staff was, 'No plan survives contact with the enemy'. It certainly didn't here as it had not done at V Beach, nor would it at Arnhem in 1944, as General Sosabowski predicted.

As a result of the difficult terrain and the muddled execution of the enterprise, the account that follows, though greatly condensed, is inevitably complicated. It will help the reader to follow the actions described if the Holts' Map is kept to hand and referred to as appropriate.

The Helles Diversion. Around midday on 6 August a heavy bombardment of the Turkish trenches began and just before 1600 hours the 29th and 42nd Divisions attacked towards Krithia. The 88th Brigade, the only one supposed to advance rather than demonstrate, took heavy casualties - over 60% in the three battalions involved, 1st Essex, 2nd Hants and 4th Worcesters - and, far from being just a diversion, the stuggle became yet another attempt on Krithia. The 29th Divisional Commander described it as, 'Besides being a failure this was far and away the heaviest day of casualties the brigade had in the whole war.' Fighting continued for about a week with particular intensity around The Vineyard (qv), a small patch of land hardly 300 metres long and 150 metres wide, to the west of the Krithia road. It is difficult to know whether the attack succeeded in persuading the Turks to keep up the strength of their forces at Helles since they did transfer their 4th Division from there northwards towards Anzac.

The Anzac Diversion and the struggle for Sari Bair (Turkish Yellow Ridge). This diversion from the Suvla Landing had another diversion within itself. Secretly, the force at Anzac was reinforced at night by the 13th Division which brought the strength there up to around 40,000 men. A tunnel had been built which would allow part of the attacking force to emerge directly into some of the Turkish trenches around Lone Pine and it was intended that the Turks should see this attack as the main effort. Then, after dark, the real major effort would be made towards Sari Bair further north. Several days before the attack Lone Pine had been bombarded by warships and on 6 August at 1730 hours the guns stopped abruptly. Immediately men of the 1st Australian Brigade leapt out of their trenches and, on a front of less than 200 metres, headed for the enemy a stone's throw away in their covered positions at Lone Pine. Bitter hand-to-hand fighting with bomb and bayonet, attack and counter-attack left the position in Australian hands. At Quinn's, Pope's, Russell's Top and the Nek, the Australian Light Horse dashed across open ground to certain death: of 450 men who charged at the Nek, 435 were casualties. When, at midnight, more Australians ventured into the tunnel that led into German Officers' Trench they were mown down, but these actions on the right and centre of the Anzac line had captured the Turks' attention and on the left there was now an opportunity to assault and to take the commanding height of Chunuk Bair and from there to threaten the Narrows. The fighting that ensued on the left is often known as 'The Battle of Sari Bair' and it followed one of the most complicated assault plans ever conceived. As the Lone Pine assault began, two columns of a composite force of Australians, New Zealanders, British and Gurkhas set off in the dark over mountainous terrain that would tax healthy men in daylight. Inevitably they fell out of synchronism, became tired and were unable to press on. Meanwhile Mustafa Kemal sent his 19th Division to occupy the Sari Bair Ridge and, as further re-inforcements were brought in from around the Peninsula, the fighting went on until 10 August. The Wellington Battalion of the NZ Infantry Brigade had reached the summit of Chunuk Bair but were virtually eliminated, being replaced by the 6th Loyal North Lancs and the 5th Wiltshires. Hill Q overlooking Chunuk Bair from the north was taken at bayonet point by the 1/6th Gurkhas who were then driven off their prize by 'friendly fire' from one of their supporting ships. Kemal, aware of the critical importance of the high ground of the ridge, drove his men forward by personal example and in an attack on 10 August retook the ridge at a cost of 5,000 casualties, though the Gurkhas hung on for another six hours. Allied casualties in the four days were about 12,000 which, had the Suvla landing been properly managed, might have been militarily acceptable, but here no substantial high ground had been gained and at Suvla ineptitude was to reign supreme.

The Suvla Bay Landings. Lieutenant-General the Hon. Sir Frederick Stopford, age 61, was selected to command the operation on the grounds of seniority. He had never before commanded in battle and was eventually removed by Hamilton for his incompetence.

The bay, a sweep of flat sand some 5kms around, between Suvla Point in the north and Nibrunesi Point in the south, offered an ideal landing place for putting men ashore. A quarter of the way up the bay from Nibrunesi Point was a 'Cut' across the beach leading into a large Salt Lake which was dry at the time of the landings, and around and behind was the high ground starting with Karakol Dagh (the western end of the Kirectepe Ridge) at Suvla Point and continuing around Anafarta, eventually leading to the Sari Bair Ridge. The landing and what followed is a chapter of inadequacy and incompetence, of officers who did not know even the plan for the attack, of bungled landings, of total absence of leadership that allowed the troops to sit around for two vital days while the Turks assembled their defences. In a parallel situation twenty-nine years later on 22 January 1944 the Allied VI Corps under General Lucas landed 120kms behind enemy lines on the beach at Anzio. Instead of immediately heading inland for the clearly visible high ground the General delayed in order to build up his base and it took four months to break out. Lucas was relieved of his command. Hamilton would be too.

The force here was IX Corps comprising Mahon's 10th (Irish) and Hammersley's 11th (Northern) Division and the plan was to land on the night of 6/7 August on three beaches: 'A' in the centre of the bay above the Cut and 'B' and 'C' south of Nibrunesi Point. Hammersley's 11th Division was scheduled to land 34th Brigade on 'A' Beach north of The Cut with the task of swinging inland and to the left, taking Hill 10 and Karakol Dagh, and 32nd and 33rd Brigades to land on 'B' Beach with objectives Lala Baba and Chocolate Hill. Mahon's 10th were to land on 'A' early on 7 August to reinforce the 11th and to head for the Kirectepe Ridge with a view to both divisions driving on in a pincer movement to Tekke Tepe.

At 2130 hours on 6 August, as planned, 32nd and 33rd Brigades of 11th Division got ashore unopposed on 'B'. The 6th Yorkshire Regiment of 32nd Brigade took Lala Baba and Nibrunesi Point by midnight and suffered considerable casualties, although they were defended only by a few Turkish snipers. Indeed the Turkish defenders, the Anafarta Detachment commanded by Major Willmer, only numbered around 1,500 distributed around the various heights, while Stopford had a force of 25,000.

The landing of 34th Brigade (Brigadier-General Sitwell) on 'A' Beach just after 2230 hours was a shambles. The destroyers carrying the troops anchored in the wrong place, much as they had done at Ari Burnu for the ANZAC landing. Thus the 11th Manchesters were put ashore below The Cut instead of above it, several hours before the rest of the Brigade, whose lighters continually stuck on sand bars. Nevertheless, the Manchesters cleared the Turkish posts on Ghazi Baba and were more than 3kms along the Kirectepe Ridge by 0300 hours despite opposition from a battalion of Turkish gendarmes. Hill 10 proved more difficult. First it could not be found and then, as the bulk of the Brigade came ashore, it came under fire causing some of the force to be landed at 'B' instead of 'A'. Eventually Hammersley sent some of 32nd Brigade, who had been sitting around for five hours at Lala Baba doing nothing, to help, and the hill was taken by 1900. Sitwell determined to dig in and stay there. 'Sit'well was proving an appropriate name – as was 'Stop'ford.

The 10th Division, accompanied by Brigadier-General Hill (who on arriving in the bay had no idea where he was, had no map of the area and did not know what to do), were meant to land at 0500 hours on 'A' beach, but a number of 'Beetles' (a steel-plated bullet-proof motor lighter which could carry 500 men at a speed of 5 knots - designed by Lord Fisher) stuck in the shallows. The Navy baulked at continuing at 'A' and, after taking some hours to decide what to do, Stopford landed the first five battalions on 'C' Beach, i.e. completely on the wrong side of the bay and in broad daylight instead of darkness. He also put them under command of the 11th Division. There was confusion and chaos. Almost at the moment that Stopford decided to send the main body of 10th Division to 'C' Beach a more suitable beach was found below Ghazi Baba (later known as West Beach) close to the Karakol Dagh objective and Stopford told Mahon, the 10th Division commander, to land his remaining three battalions there and to take on the Kirectepe Ridge. Mahon, the senior Lieutenant-General at Suvla, was furious at only having three battalions of his division and thought of resigning on the spot. Nevertheless he began landing with the rump of his division at 1130 hours, but moved only as far as the Manchesters and then stopped. Meanwhile Hammersley (who was suffering from phlebitis) had established his HQ between Nibrunesi Point and Lala Baba. Brigadier-General Hill, now faced with the task of taking Chocolate and Green Hills, left his three battalions beside Lala Baba and tramped to Hill 10 to see if Sitwell would support him. He wouldn't. Having struggled back to Hammersley's HQ (making a round trip of some 8 kms while gripped by dysentry) he was told that the attack was to begin at once. Off went the tired Hill with three of his battalions and, forbidden to head directly for Chocolate Hill only some 3kms in a straight line away (it was thought that the Turks had formidable defences on the southern slopes of the hills - they had not), marched in the heat of the day over 8kms around the Salt Lake before making his assault. In spite of everything, they took both hills by evening. Thus, despite the ineptness of command, the innocence of the New Army troops, Turkish artillery and sniper fire, the confused landings and the chaotic inter-mixing of units, as dawn broke on 8 August the army was ashore and established at Lala Baba, on Chocolate and Green Hills and on the Kirectepe Ridge. It was time to move quickly.

The Suvla affair was essentially a race for the hills and Liman von Sanders was sprinting. He ordered the 7th and 12th Divisions at Bulair to march at once to Suvla and all of the troops on the Asiatic side to cross to Gallipoli - but it would take the whole day of 8 August for them to arrive. Their commander claimed that they would be too tired to attack when they got there and von Sanders sacked him on the spot, replacing him with Mustapha Kemal, an action that might be claimed to have doomed the Gallipoli affair for the Allies then and there. The British did virtually nothing that day, though the 6th East Yorks advanced and occupied Scimitar Hill (also known as Hill 70) apparently without the higher command being aware of it (Stopford was still at sea on the *Jonquil* nursing a sprained knee) because later in the day they were ordered back to Sulajik beside the Salt Lake to prepare for an attack on the morrow. The attack on the 9th, led by 11th Division, was stopped by Turkish reinforcements that the *Official History* claimed had been in position less than 30 minutes. The Turks had won the race. They had the high ground, and after 18,000 casualties the British had another stalemate. Further unsuccessful attempts were made to move inland, including that on 12 August when the 1/5th Norfolk Regiment disappeared, and another on 21 August (a week after Stopford was replaced by de Lisle) for which the 29th Division was transferred from Helles. There was no gain, just 5,300 casualties in the force of 14,300. Thus the Helles/Anzac/Suvla venture had achieved nothing except that the left at Anzac did manage to join up with the right at Suvla to form one continuous front line and eventually - but too late - there was a clear-out of incompetent generals.

The End Game

Keith Murdoch (father of the media magnate Rupert Murdoch) the Australian journalist who had been at Anzac and seen the conditions in which the troops operated, agreed to take a letter from the outspoken British journalist, Ashmead-Bartlett, which was highly critical of the conduct of the campaign, to London to give to the authorites. Although the letter was confiscated he personally saw to it that the Dardanelles Committee learned of his and Ashmead-Bartlett's views and met Asquith and Lloyd George.

On 11 October Hamilton was asked for his opinion on evacuation. 'Unthinkable', he said. It sealed his fate and he was replaced on 16 October by

General Sir Charles Monro. On his arrival in Gallipoli on 27 October Munro visited all three fronts and concluded that evacuation was inevitable. The French had considered reinforcing the Dardanelles but internal differences between Joffre and the powerful General Sarrail (known as *L'Affaire Sarrail*) prevented this, lending strength to the view that it was time to pull out. Early in November Kitchener visited Gallipoli and decided that Anzac and Suvla should be evacuated but that Helles should be held. The War Council demurred and ruled that evacuation should be total. It was now a matter of how it was to be done.

The Evacuations

The detailed plans were made by Cecil Aspinall-Oglander and Birdwood's Chief-of-Staff, Lieutenant-Colonel (later General Sir Brudenell) White. White devised the effective idea of 'Silent Stunts'. It occured to him that one of the biggest give-aways of a withdrawal would be the unnatural silence that would accompany it. He therefore instigated periods of complete silence and no-action, the first of which started at 1800 hours on 24 November. It was repeated on 25 and 26 November, during which time the perplexed enemy showed considerable curiosity, sending out patrols and even messages to the ANZACs at Quinn's. When hostilities resumed, the Turks mounted a fierce artillery bombardment on the ANZAC Front from Russell's Top to Lone Pine, shattering many of the already storm-battered trenches and causing many casualties.

The Great Storm. On November 27 a ferocious blizzard and thunderstorm hit the Peninsula. Great waves lashed the shore followed by enormous hailstones and torrential rain that coursed down the gulleys, flooding trenches and sweeping dead Turks, mules and all manner of supplies down to the sea. Fighting was forgotten as men, shivering with cold in their inadequate and tattered campaign clothes and without any food, battled for their very survival. Then the wind changed to the north and the Peninsula was covered in frost and snow - a sight that many of the ANZACs and Indians had never before experienced. Frostbite and exposure abounded - many thousands of cases were reported at Suvla, 3,000 at Anzac and 1,000 at Helles [Rhodes-James]. Men even froze to death: 204 men died of exposure at Suvla and 1 man at Anzac. Along the whole front 4,795 cases of trench foot were reported and 15,791 casualties were evacuated between 30 November and 8 December. Rhodes-James described how some of the starving and frozen men broke into a rum store with devastating and sometimes fatal effects. The appalling conditions lasted for nearly a fortnight. On 1 December Monro telegraphed to London, 'Experience of recent storms indicates that there is no time to lose. General Birdwood telegraphed yesterday that if evacuation is to be made possible it is essential to take advantage of every fine day from now.' The hyper-active Keyes argued for one last effort but on 8 December the unequivocal decision was made.

The Evacuation Plans: Anzac and Suvla. The daunting task of the planners was to take off 50,807 men, 3,000 animals and 91 guns from the 10,000 metre front at Suvla; 41,218 men, 2,368 animals and 105 guns from the 10,000-metre front at Anzac and

42,697 men, 9,219 animals and 197 guns from the 6,300-metre front at Helles. The operation was divided into three phases.

The Preliminary Stage was to reduce the garrison to a number sufficient to maintain a defensive winter campaign. This was started even before final and official approval had been granted. **The Intermediate Stage**, which was to start as soon as the word was given, was to reduce the force to the minimum required to hold final positions for about a week. **The Final Stage** was to withdraw with all possible speed, leaving any remaining material. Secrecy was vital. Messages were sent to Corps Commanders at Suvla and Anzac asking them to prepare to send ammunition to Salonika and troops to winter rest camps on Lemnos and Imbros. Tactics for the final withdrawal were left to individual Corps Commanders. At 0930 hours on 8 December Birdwood briefed Godley (newly-appointed as Commander of the ANZAC Corps) and White (the principal planner) and withdrawals began immediately.

The first to go were the non-combatant units - the Egyptians, Maltese and British Labour companies. Next were the sick and part of the hospitals. They were quietly moved to North Beach for embarkation on 11 December. Still keeping up the pretence that this was a planned winter garrison reduction, Divisional Commanders were then asked to prepare the removal of 2,000 troops of the 1st Australian Division on the 11th, 3,300 of the 2nd Australian Division on the 12th/13th, 2,750 of the NZ & A Division on the 13th/14th and 1,300 men of General Hodgson's Indian and Eastern Mounted Brigades from Suvla on the 14th. A considerable number of guns were to be taken away each night until the 17th. The movements were planned in meticulous detail and to a strict timetable. Birdwood paid daily visits to Suvla and to Anzac each day to confer with the Corps Commanders. Troop movements took place entirely after dark. Even the Indians' mules had been trained to move quietly and many of the men themselves did not realise that a real evacuation was under way during the Intermediate Stage. The rumour, like all Gallipoli rumours, soon spread quickly however, and to many it was 'a heart-breaking disappointment' [Bean]. Their main cause of grief was in leaving their dead comrades, many of whose graves they tidied up during the final hours. 'I hope they won't hear us marching down the deres,' remarked one departing man to Birdwood. The final stage took place on the nights of 18 and 19 December. During the early morning of 18 December a large supply dump on North Beach accidentally caught fire and thousands of cases of biscuits and tinned meat burned, fuelled by oil drums, but fortunately it was soon contained and seemed to cause no great curiosity on the part of the Turks. On the first night 9,900 men from both fronts were embarked and the final 10,040 on the second night, in three parties: 'A', 'B' and 'C'. When volunteers were called for to be in the last Australian parties, every man wanted the privilege. Men with boots covered by socks or sandbags filed down from the trenches which had been sprinkled with soft soil or carpeted with blankets along paths marked by flour, salt, and dim lights in biscuit tins to the sack-covered piers. Fuses were placed on the guns and ingenious devices were attached to rifles to cause them to fire automatically once the last man had left. Mines had been laid under the Nek and at 0330 hours they exploded, killing many Turks. A huge bonfire was made of remaining stores and equipment and lit at Suvla as General Maude and his staff left at 0400 after the final garrison had passed through the Salt Lake defences and the Lala Baba lines. The last picketboat to steam out of Suvla carried Captain Unwin VC (qv), the hero of the *River Clyde* (qv) during the Landing at V Beach on 25 April.

The successful operation had been carried out with a success that exceeded the wildest hopes of the planners - without the loss of one single life and to the apparent complete surprise of the Turks. It was a perfect exercise in the carrying out of well-laid plans with absolute discipline. Now the Helles Front had to be protected until a similar operation could be carried out at the foot of the Peninsula.

Helles. Government policy for the continuation of operations at Helles was vague to say the least. The French were threatening to withdraw their garrison and batteries. Their Senegalese infantry were evacuated between 12 and 22 December and this was only achieved by sending in yet again the remnants (then only 1,400 strong with only four regular officers) of the overworked 29th Division after a brief period of rest at Mudros following their evacuation from Suvla. By Christmas Eve they were reholding their old position in the line on the southern front. Monro and Birdwood were all for abandoning the position as soon as possible - certainly before the weather finally broke for the winter - and anxiously awaited orders from the Government.

Plans for the Evacuation were to follow the Anzac-Suvla formula of three stages, with the final exodus to be carried out in one single night. The deception plan - of maintaining normal activity - had to be meticulously adhered to.

On 23 December Sir William Robertson replaced General Murray as CIGS and at once pressed for immediate evacuation and opened a direct line of command to Monro, by-passing the Secretary of State. His first order, which had an instant psychological effect, was to make all preparations for evacuation. Birdwood, and the French Commander, General Brulard, decided to take the remaining French off as soon as possible, but to leave their artillery.

Piers on W Beach were repaired and animals and unwanted material were gradually withdrawn. After consultation with the Navy it was decided that two nights would be needed for the final evacuation and the men were to be gradually withdrawn from the Eski Line to a line from de Tott's through Zimmerman's Farm to Gully Beach into an 'embarkation zone'. There they were to come under Major-General H. A. Lawrence for movement to, and evacuation from, the beaches.

On 31 December, confident that all plans had been well laid, Monro left for Cairo. The following day the remaining French Colonials were relieved by the RND but bad weather hampered embarkations. The French battleship *Suffren* collided with and sank the British transport *St Oswald*, newly arrived to take off 1,000 mules and by 4 January Birdwood had to make the decision to sacrifice large numbers of animals and vast quantities of supplies in the hope of being able to get all his men safely off. In an attempt to alleviate the high seas on V Beach two old French 'men-of-war' were sunk to form breakwaters (a portent of things to come in Normandy in 1944).

On 7 January Liman von Sanders opened a major offensive at midday on Gully Spur, held by the 13th Division. The 7th North Staffordshires held on but with heavy losses, including their commanding officer, Lieutenant-Colonel H. F. Walker [commemorated on the Helles Memorial]. When the attack died down, 2,300 men, about 1,000 animals and 9 guns were taken off leaving a garrison of 17,000 men. It was the final stage.

At nightfall two long rows of ships set off from Mudros and Imbros to pick up three echelons of men from W and V Beaches. Heavy seas and high winds battered the flimsy floating bridges that the troops needed to reach the boats, only kept open by superhuman efforts by the Engineers. The last 400 men (of 13th Division) were to be taken off Gully Beach at 0200 hours but a lighter grounded and the resourceful General Maude, who had insisted on remaining with the rearguard party, marched 160 men three kilometers round the coast to W Beach, the bulk of the men arriving at 0315. Maude and his chief staff officer, having gone back to Gully Beach to retrieve the General's valise, arrived some twenty minutes later, in the nick of time before the rough seas stopped all further embarkation. This prompted the parody of Tennyson's famous poem,

'Come into the lighter, Maude,
For the fuses are all lit,
Come into the lighter, Maude,
And forget your ruddy kit.'

The fuses were set to light the fires under the huge piles of stores and equipment and the dazed men on the lighters looked back to see the enormous explosion of the main magazine reddening the sky. A frenzied but futile Turkish artillery bombardment then rained down on the empty trenches and beaches.

It was all over.

Did the Turks Know? The Allied propaganda was that the disastrous and costly failure of the Dardanelles Campaign was somewhat redeemed by the perfect exercise of the Evacuations: that the Turks and their German leaders had been totally hoodwinked by the skilfully executed deception plans and were taken by complete surprise. The lessons learned from the operation were undoubtedly put to use at Dunkirk in May 1940 and in Arnhem (where once again men with muffled shoes made their way in the dark to the water at Oosterbeek on the night of 25 September 1944).

Bean, who was one of the last to leave Anzac said, 'There had been no interference whatever by the Turks, and it was obvious that they had been completely deceived.' In February 1919 he asked Zeki Bey (qv), commander of the 57th Regiment at the time of the Evacuation (who went on to become Chief of Police under Kemal Ataturk when he became President of Turkey), what the Turks knew of it. He told Bean that the Turkish lines, like the ANZACs', were rife with rumours of evacuation and the men were instructed to keep a keen watch for any signs of withdrawal. The great fire on Suvla Beach confirmed the fact that the enemy had indeed left. Men helped themselves to the abandoned stores and equipment - 10,000 boxes of biscuits, jam, meat, tea and sugar were found near Hill 60 alone. Rhodes-James recounts that the supplies left on all three fronts were enough to feed and clothe four divisions for four months.

Bean also asked Kiazim Pasha, who in 1915 had been CGS of the Turkish 5th Army and who in 1919 was Chief of the Turkish General Staff, the question, 'What was the first news of the evacuation of Anzac?' Kiazim answered that at 0430 hours on 20 December the 19th Division reported the explosion of three mines to their command group. A Turkish patrol investigated and found the enemy trenches empty and an order was issued at 0640 by the Northern Group Command to all divisions to advance. Presumably it was then that the extent of the evacuation was realised. Kiazim also told Bean that he regarded the Evacuation as one of 'the best British operations'.

When, in 1998, the authors asked a serving Turkish military historian, Lieutenant Mehmet Gunes, who acted as official guide on the Gallipoli battlefield to Turkish Staff Officers, if he considered the fact that the Turks had not attacked the departing Allies proved that they had not known about the Evacuations, he answered that the Turks were probably aware of what was taking place. However, as the enemy was leaving the land they held so sacred, and for which they were prepared to fight to the death, they saw no further reason to take life or to risk their own.

Lieutenant Gunes, Turkish Military Historian at Lala Baba CWGC Cemetery

Aerial Activity in the Dardanelles

[For further details, consult *Royal Naval Air Service 1912-1918* by Brad King, pub. Hikoki 1997.]

In February 1915 Commander Charles Rumney Samson and his Eastchurch Squadron of the RNAS were called upon by Churchill to provide air support to the Dardanelles fleet. Samson with an Advance Party of 4 officers and 27 men crossed the Channel on 11 March and motored to Marseilles where their aircraft (including Samson's favourite B.E.2a 'Old Number 50') were loaded onto the *Abda*. Samson's second-in-command was Squadron Commander Richard Bell-Davies who travelled with the ground crews on the journey to the Dardanelles.

The main party arrived at Imbros on 21 March and moved on the next day to Tenedos where the crew of seaplanes from the *Ark Royal* were constructing an airfield. Their aircraft (two Maurice Farmans and eight Henry Farmans) were landed and transported to the airfield with great difficulty and from 28 March they began their work of mine and submarine spotting, engaging the occasional Turkish aircraft and dropping the occasional bomb. The rest of the squadron and their equipment then arrived, including two Sopwith Tabloids. The officers now numbered 18 (including Samson's brother, Bill) and Samson ordered more Maurice Farmans and was allocated some extra observers. From 11 April regular flights mapped and photographed the whole area and Lieutenant-Commander Brodie of Submarine *E15* was taken on an observational flight.

On the day of the Landings Samson was aloft, but unable to do anything other than to observe. He reported that the sea for 50 yards from V Beach was 'absolutely red with blood, a horrible sight to see'. Bell-Davies acted as an aerial spotter for HMS *Prince George* which was supporting the French Landings at Kumkale.

Once the tenuous hold on the Peninsula was assured, Samson recced a site for an airstrip. He had to make do with 'a scrubby, miserable, though relatively flat piece of ground' above Lancashire Landing. It was in full view of the Turks on Achi Baba and regularly shelled. After five aircraft had been lost there it was decided to use the airstrip for emergencies only.

The Eastchurch Squadron continued to make observation flights, spotting Turkish movements, but felt that the information they supplied was not valued or acted upon. On 17 May, however, Flight Lieutenant Reginald Marix spotted unusual Turkish activity at Akbas Bay and was able to prepare the ANZACs for the attack of 19 May. On that day Marix and Samson dropped several bombs behind the Turkish lines, causing considerable damage.

By June the small team was exhausted by its continuous efforts; Charles Samson had clocked up 180 hours in the air, Bill Samson was badly wounded and was sent home and Bell-Davies was down to nine stone in weight. A leave rota in Egypt was instituted and Colonel Frederick Sykes, commander of the RFC in France, was sent out to assess the situation. He moved the squadron's base from Tenedos to Imbros the better to support the impending landings at Suvla, but this airstrip was also regularly bombed by the enemy aircraft, notably by Taubes. Sykes exerted his organisational skills to improve conditions and performance, but relations between him and Samson, who felt under-valued, were difficult. Achievements continued, however, notably the torpedoing of a Turkish supply ship on 12 August by Flight Commander Charles Edmonds. It was the first ever successful torpedoing from the air. Edmonds then torpedoed three tugs at Akbas Bay on 17 August. On 31 August No 2 Wing arrived, with a mixture of Morane Parasols, B.E.2cs, Caudrons and Bristol Scouts, an additional sixteen pilots and 200 ground staff.

On 19 November the squadron set off 200 miles across the Gulf of Saros to bomb a railway station at Ferejik in Bulgaria. As they started the return after the successful raid, Flight Lieutenant Gilbert F. Smylie's Farman was hit and forced down. Bell-Davies landed nearby, whereupon Smylie shot an unexploded bomb under his aircraft which detonated and destroyed the plane. Bell-Davies, in true 'Boy's Own' style, scooped him up, stuffed him into his tiny cockpit and managed to get back safely to Imbros. Smylie was awarded the DSO and Bell-Davies the VC. Bell-Davies went on to become a Vice-Admiral in the navy, serving again in WW2. He died in 1966. His son, Sir Lancelot Richard Bell-Davies, also served in WW2 and became a Vice-Admiral.

In their nine months in the Dardanelles, 3 Squadron clocked up an amazing 2,600 hours of flying time, with many solid achievements, not the least being the morale effect their presence had on the exhausted ground troops.

The Royal Commission Enquiry

In October 1916 a Dardanelles Commission was set up to examine what went wrong at Gallipoli, and why. Practically every major player concerned in the planning and execution of the campaign was interviewed. Its damning Report, published by HMSO in 1917, with a Final Report in 1919, concluded that the operation had been ill-conceived and ineptly executed and that many thousands of lives had been lost in vain. Only Monro (qv) received any praise. Many justifications, notably by Churchill and Hamilton, were subsequently published and the debate, for and against, continues to this day.

SOME STATISTICS ABOUT THE GALLIPOLI CAMPAIGN

Turkish losses in the campaign have been recorded as 86,692 deaths, 164,617 wounded and sick. This is held to be a gross under-estimate and some sources put the total casualties as high as 470,000. The *Official History* quotes either 251,000 or 350,000. Such is the fog of war and the unreliability of record-keeping.

Figures for Allied losses also vary enormously. The *Official History* records that Sir Ian Hamilton's initial army strength was 75,000 and by the end of the campaign a total of 410,000 British and Commonwealth and 79,000 French had been sent to the Dardanelles. Of this, the French casualties totalled 47,000, total British and Commonwealth casualties were 205,000 (115,000 killed, missing or wounded, 90,000 evacuated sick). The 29th Division alone suffered 34,011 casualties: 9,042 killed or missing; 10,993 wounded in action; 13,977 incapacitated by sickness or disease. [These figures can be particularly confusing as they represent roughly twice the actual establishment strength of a division. The explanation is that, as casualties occur, so they are replaced by reinforcements who themselves become casualties and so on. It is, therefore, true to say that the entire strength of the 29th Division became casualties twice over.]

Australian sources quote the following breakdown:

Nationality	Total casualties	Killed
Australian	26,094	7,594
New Zealand	7,571	2,431
Rest of British Empire	171,335	119,696
French	47,000	27,000
Turkish	251,309	N/A

These interesting figures competely blow the myth of Gallipoli being a predominantly Anzac show and sacrifice. The proportion of dead to total casualties is also revealing, the rest of the British Empire suffering the highest ratio of killed to casualty and the Australians the lowest. The French - almost the forgotten combattants in Gallipoli - had more men killed than the Australians had total casualties.

TURKEY AND THE GALLIPOLI PENINSULA AFTER THE CAMPAIGN

In 1918 the British and the Turks fought over the oil wells of western Persia, the British force under Major-General L. C. Dunsterville (see Haidar Pasha entry below) eventually withdrawing from Baku in September. Meanwhile Lawrence of Arabia, leading the Arab rebellion against Turkish rule in Palestine, pinned down

25,000 Turkish troops along the Hejaz Railway. Liman von Sanders replaced Falkenhayn in command of the Turkish Fourth, Seventh (led by Mustafa Kemal) and Eighth Armies and on 19 September Allenby began his great offensive at Megiddo, routing the Turkish armies, von Sanders narrowly escaping capture. Lawrence cut the railway line at Deraa on the 27th and Allenby pressed on to Damascus and Beirut. On 30 October 1918, an Armistice was signed on Mudros between the Ottoman Empire and the Allies.

Turkey fell into anarchy as the Allies squabbled over the terms of the Peace Settlement and an Allied force was sent to Turkey to reinforce them. According to Bean, 'In carrying out the Armistice terms [Kemal Ataturk] proved, from the very first, a stubborn, determined opponent of the Allies' demands,' and the GHQ of the British Balkan Army, to which Allenby came in February 1919, was set up in Constantinople. He was followed by the ostentatious arrival of the Allied Commander-in-Chief, the French General Franchet d'Esperey, who had commanded the French in Salonika and whom the British deflatingly christened 'Desperate Frankey'. The British 28th Division was based in Canakkale where they created a comfortable officers' rest house known as 'The Red Lion'. A Greek Army was landed at Smyrna in May 1919 to protect Allied interests and several atrocities were perpetrated by them on their old enemies, the Turks. In October King Constantine came to the Greek throne. Pro-German during WW1, he was mistrusted by the Allies who withdrew their support from the Greeks. Then Mustafa Kemal, hailed as the hero of Gallipoli, inspired a new Turkish Nationalist Movement, set up a Government in Ankara in April 1920 and led his people in the Graeco-Turkish War of 1920-22, eventually routing the Greeks. There followed many massacres of Greeks by the Turks. Kemal then advanced on Constantinople in October 1922 and the Sultanate was abolished. Relations between Turkey and Britain deteriorated and the countries were once again on the brink of war - a period known as the 'Chanak Crisis' - but things were defused by the 1923 Treaty of Lausanne (qv) which restored Turkey's Thracian territory. The Allies evacuated Constantinople and Gallipoli was declared neutral ground, allowing the Allied war cemeteries to be completed and maintained by the War Graves Commission. Mustafa Kemal took the surname 'Ataturk' - 'Chief of the Turks' - the first President of the new Republic established on 29 October 1923. The streamlining of the old creaking empire and the 'westernisation' of this vast country began.

Meanwhile pilgrims began to visit the Peninsula as soon as the war ended. During his 1919 visit, Bean felt that Gallipoli would become 'the goal of pilgrimages from Britain and the Anzac countries'. On Anzac Day 1920 the first considerable party of British civilians held a service at Anzac Cove.

In 1924, the cemeteries completed, the pilgrimages began in earnest with a visit by the Australian Prime Minister, S.M. Bruce. In 1925 a series of important delegations unveiled the national memorials: in May there were four hundred pilgrims including the High Commissioner of New Zealand, and in August Sir Ian Hamilton, Aspinall-Oglander and Sir Roger Keyes arrived on the *Queen Elizabeth*. In 1927 the Prince of Wales, President of the Commission, visited, and in 1935 the *Lancastria* (the ill-fated ship that would sink off St Nazaire on 17 June 1940, with the loss of at least 5,000 B.E.F. lives) brought General and Lady Birdwood, Sir Roger Keyes and Captain Unwin, VC. Widows, parents and childen then began to visit, all greatly affected by the haunting nature of the Peninsula, its wild beauty and its enduring echoes of the terrors that were enacted upon it.

The League of Nations guaranteed the neutrality of the Straits until, later in 1935, Germany and Italy left the League. After Mussolini attacked Abyssinia, the Turks requested permission to re-establish their forts and garrisons on the Peninsula and the Dardanelles was remilitarised, although the land granted in perpetuity by the Treaty of Lausanne was assured, despite the building of Turkish concrete machine-gun posts along the Anzac area coast (qv). Ataturk died in 1938 and was succeeded by his former Chief-of-Staff, Ismet Pasha.

During the Second World War the Imperial War Graves Commission tended the cemeteries – the Turks had remained neutral – but afterwards the area became sensitive because of Russia's renewed desire to control the Straits, and armed

Wreath-laying ceremony at the Helles Memorial, 25 April

escorts and permits were required for pilgrimages. In August 1947 a British squadron visited Helles and was treated cordially by the Turkish military authorities but as relations between Greece and Turkey deteriorated certain areas were restricted, notably Lancashire Landing/W Beach, Akbas Harbour, Nara, Seddulbahir Fort and the Camber.

By 1999 only actual military garrisons, such as Fort Hamidiye, Degimar Burnu Garrison, the Gelibolu Military Complex, the naval Barracks at Canakkale, and Kumkale Fort, were still prohibited.

THE PENINSULA TODAY
(see also the entry on the International Peace Park project below)

As Turkey gradually became more open in its relations with the West and the country began to be a popular tourist destination, guided battlefield tours and pilgrimages to the Peninsula started to boom. Local tours, organised by Turkish historians and tour guides (see Tourist Information below) are also readily available.

The ANZAC and other Annual Commemorations

The 25 April Commemorations are alternately organised by the Australians and the New Zealanders. The day always starts with an 0530 Dawn Service at Anzac Cove, originally held in Ari Burnu CWGC Cemetery and nowadays held in an area cleared by the CWGC at Ari Burnu in 1998. This is normally followed by an 0930 ceremony at the Turkish Memorial at Helles, a 1030 service at the French Memorial, an 1100 service at the British Memorial, Helles, a 1200 Service at Lone Pine, a 1250 Service at the Turkish 57th Regimental Memorial and a 1330 Service at the New Zealand Memorial at Chunuk Bair. These ceremonies increasingly are attended by thousands of pilgrims, severely straining the narrow road system. Entry to the Upper Route is limited, but plans are in hand to make a one-way system to ease the congestion.

Major Turkish commemorations are also held to celebrate the Turkish victory at sea of 18 March 1915, and the repulse of the Allied attack following the Suvla landings on 6 August. In March the celebrations start in Canakkale with parades, speeches and a visit to the Military Museum and move on to the Turkish Memorial and other Turkish symbolic graves in the Milli Park. In August the commemorations start at the Gaba Tepe Information Centre and continue at the 57th Regiment Memorial area.

THE APPROACH ROUTE

This assumes that the visitor is flying into Istanbul and will probably spend one night in this fascinating city (see Tourist Information below). Whilst there, the following Extra Visits - which are not timed precisely because the start point is not specified - are recommended.

Extra Visit 1 to Haidar Pasha Cemetery

From Istanbul centre take the suspension bridge across the Bosphorus to the Asian side, follow the dual carriageway to Ankara for about 4 km, turning off for Haydar (local spelling, the cemetery is 'Haidar') Pasha to the right. Continue along the Izmit Ankara, crossing the Karacaahmet Ibrahimaga Yolu road, then take the exit road off to the right, linking with the Kadikoy Rihitim Cad road. Turn left (south) along it and then turn right at the traffic lights, onto the road leading to the cemetery. The familiar green CWGC sign points to the cemetery down a path which is just past the military hospital main gate. Alternatively take the ferry from Karakoy, near the Galata Bridge, to Haidar Pasha Pierhead. Go around to the right (south) side of the main station building and follow the road east approximately 400 metres. Close to the mosque with two minarets there are steps up to the Kadikoy Rihitim Cad Road. Turn left (northwards) along this road, crossing the railway, and continue approximately 700 metres. At the traffic lights turn left to the cemetery entrance - just past the military hospital main gate. Allow a good 30 minutes for the visit.

This unusual cemetery, a haven of peace in the bustle of Istanbul, is constructed on two separate plots of land donated by the Turkish Government in 1855. In 1867 further land was granted to link up these plots. The first burials were of some 6,000 British soldiers from the Crimean War who mostly died as the result of a cholera epidemic in the military hospital at nearby Scutari Barracks. There is a bronze plaque, unveiled on Empire Day 1954, to the memory of Florence Nightingale, on the large and imposing Crimean War Memorial obelisk. There is also a symbolic broken column to the memory of German Jäger officers who died in the Crimea and a British memorial transferred from the Therapia Crimean Cemetery with the bodies of 18 officers and men of the Royal Navy and Royal Marines.

The civilian plot contains more than 700 burials, including Sir Edward Barton, British Ambassador to Turkey during the reign of Elizabeth I and a chapel in memory of Sir Nicholas O'Connor, Ambassador at Constantinople at the turn of the century.

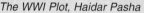

Crimean War Obelisk, Haidar Pasha CWGC Cemetery

The WWI Plot, Haidar Pasha

The WW1 plot contains 414 burials, many of POWs from the Gallipoli campaign, with a few from the post-Armistice occupation of Constantinople, mainly from No 82 General Hospital used by the Fleet and the Army. At the side of the plot is a WW1 memorial to 31 casualties who died in Turkey with no known graves and the 173 dead of the United Kingdom and India who lost their lives in Russia and on the Turkish borders. Most are members of 'Dunsterforce' led by Major-General Lionel Charles Dunsterville, the original of Rudyard Kipling's Stalky. The episode is fully described in Dunsterville's book, *The Adventures of Dunsterforce*, 1920, but Kipling summarised it, '...with an equipment of doubtful Ford cars and a collection of most-mixed troops, he put up a monumental bluff against the Bolsheviks somewhere in Armenia... and was as nearly as possible destroyed'. Also commemorated is Lieutenant Ewart Austen Wimbush Bourchier of C Sqn (Imbros Air Station), RAF, DFC, aged 21, killed whilst flying over the Peninsula on 23 May 1918. A third memorial is to soldiers of the Indian Army who died in 1919/20, whose remains were cremated and who were commemorated at Mashlak and Osmanieh Indian Cemeteries. In 1961, when those cemeteries could no longer be maintained, the earth with which the ashes of these men had mingled was scattered near this memorial, while the remains of the Muslim comrades were brought here and re-interred.

The WW2 plot contains 39 burials.

Nearby is the military hospital also used by the British during the Crimea and by the Turks during WW1, where Allied POWs were also treated.

Extra Visit 2. Florence Nightingale Room, Scutari (Selimiye) Barracks.

Prior permission to make this visit should be made to the Duty Officer on Tel: +90 216 343 7310

From the cemetery, continue north (approx 700m) to the large barracks with towers at each corner. Report to the guard room.

You will be escorted to visit the Florence Nightingale exhibition in the NE

Extra Visit continued

tower through the wide corridors which in 1853/4 were packed with hospital beds. The Scutari Barracks, then new and modern, became the base of the British when they moved up from Gallipoli (see below). Here on 24 May 1884, the Earl of Cardigan arrived at Scutari and called on his brother-in-law - Lord Lucan, whom he loathed, and who loathed him in return. The seeds of failure of the whole expedition were already sewn in the crucial relationship of these two aristocrats.

In the barracks, hospitals for the wounded from the Crimea were soon set up. Those who had the strength to survive the horror of the week-long crossing from Balaclava to Scutari across the treacherous Black Sea would finally be dumped on a filthy floor - up to November 1884 there were no beds, blankets, furniture or medical supplies. Sanitary arrangements were practically non-existent and revolting. Then on 5 November Florence Nightingale arrived with thirty-eight nurses. At first the male doctors spurned her assistance and gave her no support. But as the wounded flooded in from Balaclava and Inkerman they were forced to accept her efficient help. Under her organisational skills - and with the £30,000 she had to spend - beds, linen and clothing were provided, a hygienic regime instituted, and the death rate fell from 44% to 2.2% in six months. This improvement Nightingale achieved by sheer hard work and the force of her determined personality. She stayed in the barracks here (apart from the two visits she made to the Crimea) until the last patient left the hospital. Florence Nightingale's spartan quarters are kept much as she left them and contain several personal items, including the famous lamp.

Extra Visit 3 to the Military Museum

This splendid museum which contains impressive collections of uniforms, arms and armour has sections on Ataturk and the Gallipoli campaign and should ideally be visited between 1500 and 1600 hours when the impressive Mehter Janissary Band performs on replicas of early Ottoman military instruments. **Opposite the Sports and Exhibition Hall at Harbiye to the north of Taksim Square. Open: Wednesday-Sunday 0900-1700 hours.**

If time permits, the following Extra Visits are also recommended:

4. Pera Palas Hotel

Established in 1892 for travellers from the Orient Express, it is furnished in faded Belle Epoque style. The rooms where Ataturk (no. 101) often stayed in the Twenties and Agatha Christie (no. 411) is said to have stayed (although recent research questions this claim) may be visited. The spy Mata Hari was another famous visitor.

Mesrutiyet Caddesi 98-100, Tepebasi. Tel: +90 212 251 4560

5. Naval Museum

Established in 1897, the museum is now housed in the Treasury Building at Besiktas, below the Dolmabache Palace, on three floors: 1 - Ataturk Room, old ships' figureheads, Crimean Room etc.; 2 - WW1 Room, Mehmet II Room, Naval Uniforms,

Extra Visit continued

Ships' Models etc.; 3 - Basement - Battlecruiser *Yavuz*, Flags, Torpedoes and Mines etc.
Open Wednesday to Sunday, 0900-1200 and 1300-1700
6. Topkapi Palace
The famous Harem, the fabulous jewels and porcelain merit a visit. It takes a
half day to do justice to the collections.
Open 0930-1700 hours, closed Tuesday in winter.
Harem open 1000-1200, 1300-1600 hours.

THE JOURNEY TO THE PENINSULA

The best day to travel is Sunday, otherwise the traffic in the industrial outskirts of
Istanbul is daunting. Allow 4-5 hours driving time.

Take the D-100, which becomes the motorway E5, towards Tekirdag and Edirne.
Once clear of the city, the road skirts the Sea of Marmara through new developments,
which creep ever further out from Istanbul. En route there are frequent petrol stations/
'comfort stops', with a variety of restaurants/snack bars/provision shops and WCs,
at which you will need around 300,000 Lira, which qualifies you for a sheet of paper.

Continue along the road to the narrow neck of land at Kucukcekmece Bay.

*Kucukcekmece Koyu

Here the road runs near the railway which in 1915 was used by the Turks to
transport troops and supplies to Gallipoli. On 8 September 1915, Lieutenant-
Commander D. de B. Stocks of Submarine *E2* planned to destroy the railway with
explosives laid on the bridge by 1st Lieutenant Harold Vernon Lyon who swam
ashore early in the morning. Lyon did not return, although the explosives
detonated. He is commemorated on the Portsmouth Naval Memorial.

Continue to the junction of the E5 with the E25 and take the latter to Tekirdag.

* Tekirdag/RWC

This ancient town (established in 4,000BC) has been ruled by the Thracians, the
Greeks and the Byzantines and has undergone as many changes of names - from
Bianthe to Rodosto to Tekirdag. Today it is a popular seaside resort, famous for its
wines and its natural yoghurt. It is ideal for a refreshment break, being almost
halfway between Istanbul and Canakkale.

In 1915 there were some exciting submarine exploits in the waters off Tekirdag
and in the Sea of Marmara all the way to Constantinople, as well as up the Narrows.

Two VCs were won, the first by Lieutenant-Commander Edward Courtney Boyle of Submarine *E14*. Between 27 April and 18 May when he had run out of torpedoes, he sank two Turkish gunboats and a military transport which went down with 6,000 men.

Lieutenant-Commander Martin Nasmith of Submarine *E11* was also awarded the VC for actions between 20 May and 8 June 1915. Nasmith destroyed one large Turkish gunboat, two transports, one ammunition ship, three store ships and four other vessels. He began his adventures on 21 May when he lashed *E11* to a small sailing ship and accompanied her to Constantinople, where he cruised around all day. On 23 May he torpedoed a Turkish gunboat and then a large transport ship lying alongside the Arsenal. On 7 June *E11* got entangled with a large mine in the Narrows. It was too dangerous to surface to disengage it and the cool-headed Nasmith continued to Kumkale before he surfaced and manoeuvred free. Further exploits continued in August: in a 12-day campaign he torpedoed another gunboat, fired on Turkish troops marching down to the Peninsula, torpedoed the battleship *Harridin Narkaressa*, burnt six small sailing craft, sank a transport ship moored at Haidar Pasha railway pier, and bombarded a railway viaduct of the Bagdad Railway. Then *E11* had a tangle with a convoy of three tugs and some sailboats escorting a destroyer, inflicting much damage before it finally submerged. Several prisoners were taken, including a stout German bank-manager carrying a large sum of money to Chanak. Dressed only in a pink silk vest, the dismayed banker lost all his treasure. In her forty-five-day cruise, *E11* had accounted for eleven steamers, five large sailing vessels and thirty-five smaller ones. Then in November, *E11* torpedoed a steamer lying off Constantinople and sank a destroyer with a crew of eighty-five, rescuing two officers and forty men, including five Germans. The intrepid Nasmith went on to become Admiral Sir Martin Eric Dunbar-Nasmith, KCB, KCMG, served through WW2 and became Vice-Chairman of the Imperial War Graves Commission. He died in 1965. Boyle also became a Rear-Admiral and served as Flag Officer in Charge, London, 1939-42. He died in 1967.

Another casualty was *E20*, which was torpedoed by the German U-boat *U14* off Tekirdag trying to make a rendezvous with the French submarine *Turquoise*. The *Turquoise* had actually grounded on 30 October, she and her crew were captured and the rendezvous plan discovered.

Continue through the beautiful Thracian landscape to

Bulair and the Bay of Saros

This strategic narrow neck of the Peninsula, only 5 kilometres wide from the Aegean to the Sea of Marmara, has been strongly fortified by successive generations, notably by the Ottomans c1357 and the-then allies - the Turks, the French and the British - during the Crimean War of 1854-56, and known as the Lines of Bulair. *The Times* correspondent, W. H. Russell, described them as being 'the Chersonesian Torres Vedras' [the name of the defensive lines constructed in Portugal by Wellington's engineers in 1810/11]. They were 'about seven miles long, and about two and three-quarters or three miles are executed by our men' [the remainder being constructed by the French]. 'They consist of a trench seven feet deep; the bottom from scarp to counterscarp six feet broad; the top thirteen feet broad'. In 1915 the Turks dug a comprehensive system of trenches here in anticipation of an Allied landing.

The Gulf of Saros, where Freyberg performed his prodigious solo feat

Gelibolu from the Lapseki Ferry

When Hamilton arrived at Tenedos on 17 March 1915, he considered a landing at Bulair, but the marshy ground and Turkish trenches convinced him that, 'If Bulair had been the only way open to me and I had no alternative but to take it or wash my hands of the whole business, I should have to go right about turn and cable my master he had sent me on a fool's errand.' In the event he consulted with his commanders, Hunter-Weston of the 29th Division and Paris of the Royal Naval Division, and decided to 'land his whole force in one - like a hammer stroke - with the fullest violence of its mass effect - as close as I can to my objective, the Kilid Bahr plateau.' He would, however, make a feint landing with the RND at Bulair.

Memorial, French Crimean War
Cemetery, Gelibolu

Akbas Turkish Cemetery
and Memorial

Commemorative water fountain, Akbas Bay

On 24 April an impressive flotilla carried the three divisions of the RND to the Gulf of Saros and the next day HMS *Dartmouth* and HMS *Doris* bombarded the Lines of Bulair. Then five of the transports each deployed eight cutters containing twenty men. Finally, after dark, a small landing party from the Hood Battalion took off in a cutter but it was decided that only one man should actually land. Arthur Asquith, the Prime Minister's son, a keen swimmer, was anxious to go, but the choice fell on the instigator of the idea, Lieutenant-Commander Bernard Freyberg who had won the New Zealand Swimming Championships in 1906 and 1910. 'He was fighting as a mercenary for [Pancho] Villa when he heard of the outbreak of war in Europe. He deserted with a blood-price on his head, walked and hitch-hiked some three hundred miles.' [Violet Asquith, who met him in Egypt when he was convalescing from wounds sustained in Gallipoli.] In London he was gazetted as a temporary Lieutenant in the RNVR and given command of 'A' company of the RND, then in training at Betteshanger in Kent.

Detail of Archway at
entrance to National Park

On the night of 25 April Freyberg was covered in dark grease to protect him from the icy water and to camouflage him, and given a wood and canvas raft containing oil flares, calcium lights, a signalling light, a knife and a revolver. Five kms out he began swimming and an hour and a quarter later lit his first flare. Finding that the Turkish trenches were 'dummies' he lit more flares and swam back out in the dark, freezing water, with severe cramp, to be picked up by Lieutenant Nelson in the cutter. Freyberg, for all his strength and athletic prowess, was a sensitive man and well-loved by his fellow officers. They were all worried about his safety on this perilous adventure, reeling as they still were from the shattering death of their beloved Rupert Brooke (qv). Denis Browne (qv) wrote, 'Freyberg has just gone off on a flare-lighting expedition, swimming. We are all anxious about him. He has been wonderful the last few days. He loved and understood Rupert intuitively in spite of the differences in their temperaments; and last night when we were making the grave, he was as gentle as a woman, and as strong as a giant.' Freyberg was later awarded the DSO for his prodigious feat. The expedition – and its diversionary effect – was a complete success. Liman von Sanders was awoken in Gallipoli and told of the invasion. He immediately ordered his troops to march north, riding himself at once to the Gulf of Saros where he watched the diversionary fleet bombarding the coast. Part of it then sailed to Cape Helles where the Howe and Hood Battalions of the RND landed on 30 April and 1 May.

Von Sanders decided to stay in the area to assess the situation as the landings devolved. 'The success of the whole campaign, the existence of the whole Empire, hung upon his shoulders at that moment,' wrote Hans Kannengiesser Pasha, who, as a Colonel, was called for by von Sanders to command the southern portion of the Peninsula on 26 April 1915. Von Sanders concluded that the decisive action would take place in the southern portion of the Peninsula and moved the whole of his force from Saros to Maidos, leaving only a pioneer company to pitch tents on the heights in a deception exercise.

When Turkey was drawn into the war, Mustafa Kemal was offered the newly-formed 19th Division under Liman von Sanders. Early in 1915 he was sent to Tekirdag to train his new division and took them to Maidos on 25 February. His pre-war period on the Peninsula had convinced him that the terrain around Bulair was far too difficult for a serious invasion to take place there and he accurately predicted the actual intended locations of the 25 April landings. He resisted the German pressure to mass his troops at Bulair and insisted on putting them further down the Peninsula where he exercised them night and day on defence.

Continue to the road junction on the by-pass signed Gelibolu/Feribot/Lapseki.

* Gelibolu (Gallipoli)

This is the town and ferry port which gives the Peninsula its name. There are now three main choices for the continuation of the journey:-
  i. Asian Route: driving to the ferry and crossing the Dardanelles from Gelibolu to Lapseki on the Asian side and thence to Canakkale.
  ii. European Route: visiting Gelibolu and the French Cemetery and continuing to Eceabat on the European side.
  iii. The Quickest Route: missing out Gelibolu, continuing to Eceabat via the by-pass.
i. Asian Route

Take the turning to Feribot/Lapseki into the town and continue to the harbour.
The ferry takes about 35 minutes. The ticket booth is by the entrance and the ferry departs hourly. On board there are light refreshment facilities and, in an emergency, a WC.

Lapseki was the ancient port of Lampsakos, used by the Ionians in the 7th Century BC on their way to colonise the Black Sea area, and here Lysander scored a famous victory over the Athenians in 405 BC.

From Lapseki follow signs to Izmir.
The road is good and traffic moves fast. It takes about 30 minutes to Canakkale, which is well-signed from the main road. *Follow signs to Feribot to reach Canakkale town centre.*
Note - it is of course possible to visit the French cemetery in Gelibolu during this option.

ii. European Route
Follow signs to Feribot/Lapseki and drive to the harbour.
Gelibolu's most famous son is the Turkish Admiral, Piri Reis, c1465-1554, to whom there is a memorial bust on the seafront here and a small museum. He is remembered for his two world charts and his book *Pilot of the Mediterranean.*

In April 1915 Liman von Sanders had his headquarters in the former French Consulate (the building was also used by the 9th S. Lancs during the Occupation of 1919). From 0500 hours onwards on 25 April reports started to reach him of the threatened landings. 'My first feeling,' he wrote in *Five Years in Turkey,* 'was that there was nothing to alter in our dispositions. The enemy had selected for landing those places which we ourselves had considered would be the most probable and had defended with special care. Personally I had to remain for the present at Bulair, since it was of the utmost importance that the Peninsula should be kept open at that place.'

From the ferry terminal drive uphill past the military barracks.
There is a splendid statue of Kemal Ataturk in uniform on the left (but don't attempt to photograph it, it is in a restricted military area).

During the Crimean War of 1854-1857 Gelibolu was occupied by the British and the French. The *Times* correspondent, W. H. Russell, described how the vanguard of the British Expeditionary Army - the Rifle Brigade and two companies of Sappers and Miners, some 1,000 men - embarked from Malta on the appropriately named *Golden Fleece*. They entered the Dardanelles on Wednesday 5 April 1854, and anchored off Gallipoli. He found it 'a collection of red-roofed barns, with tall white minarets rising up among them... a wretched collection of hovels with 10,000 inhabitants, Turks, Jews, and Greeks.' He went on to say that 'an army encamped here commands the Aegean and the Sea of Marmora, and can be marched northwards to the Balkans, or sent across to Asia or up to Constantinople with equal facility.' The troops disembarked and encamped some eight and a half miles north of Gallipoli. There was much rivalry between the Allies for supplies and quarters, the British feeling particularly badly done by and up-staged by the French who quickly set up a well-equipped hospital for their men while the British made do with commandeered beds in a variety of houses 'with no medical comforts' available. A shipload of 97 women in *The Georgiana* lay off anchor at Gallipoli and were not given permission to land, though 'Lady Errol who accompanies her husband...was an object of great curiosity and wonder to the Turks as she rode off from the beach.' No lessons seem to have been learned in 1915 from the chaos caused by lack of 'commissary officers' in the 1850s, when bad staff work was to cause as much confusion and as many deprivations for the men.

Discussions then took place as to where to construct defensive positions. It was eventually decided that the neck of the isthmus at Bulair 'could more easily be defended' and teams of British and French worked alternately to dig 'Intrenchments and strong earthworks of a formidable nature'. At the end of April, by which time about 5,000 British soldiers and some 22,000 French had arrived at Gallipoli, 'splendid' quarters were prepared for the new arrivals in the barracks at Scutari, on the Asian side of Constantinople. Lord Raglan sailed in to Gallipoli on 2 May on the *Emeu* before continuing to the Bosphorus and the following day Prince Jerome Napoleon, the Emperor's stout and fussy cousin, nick-named 'Plon-Plon', arrived in Gallipoli and he and General Canrobert held a grand review of the troops - an awe-inspiring sight, accompanied by the Zouaves playing 'a wild and eccentric march'. There then followed a gradual move up to the barracks in Scutari, from where they embarked across the Black Sea to Varna at the beginning of June.

Continue till the road begins to descend and the Dardanelles are on the right.

French Crimean War Cemetery

To the left is the cemetery, enclosed by a whitewashed stone wall. Walk up the side of the cemetery to the entrance in the road above. Inside is the curator's cottage. The cemetery is in immaculate condition and contains some interesting Crimean War (*Guerre d'Orient*) period graves, including that of General Félix Ney and a mass grave (*ossuaire*) for 5,000 soldiers, with a memorial to the French soldiers who died at Nagara and were reburied here in 1886. There are also some 19th century consular burials. In the centre of the cemetery is an imposing memorial to the Senegalese soldiers who died for their country (*Mort Pour la France*) in the 1919-1923 Allied occupation of the area.

The British graves from this period were moved to Haidar Pasha (see above).

iii. The Quickest Route

Return to the D909 and continue towards Eceabat.

This coastal road was opened in 1986.

* *Akbas Bay (Akbas Limani)*

Here was the ancient Sestos, a Greek city founded in 700BC by the Aeolians. Because of its strategic position, on the second narrowest (11kms) point in the Straits and at the foot of an easily defendable mountain, and its plentiful fresh-water wells, the site has constantly been fought over, by the Spartans, the Persians, the Romans and the Byzantines. The crossing to Abydos (modern Nara) on the Asian side, known as the Hespastadion Ford, was one of the busiest trade routes from Asia to Europe. Here, too, was the setting of one of the most romantic legends of ancient times: the story of Hero and Leander. Hero was a priestess of Aphrodite (and therefore had to remain a virgin) who lived in a tower at Sestos. During the annual festival of Aphrodite, Leander came to Sestos from Abydos, saw Hero and fell madly in love with her. As their love had to remain a secret, he swam over the Hellespont each night to visit Hero, guided by a light in her tower. Finally, during a winter storm, the wind blew out the light. Leander battled against the rough waves and eventually drowned. Hero saw his body on the shore at dawn and in her despair fell from the tower and was also killed, thus reuniting with her lover in death.

Leander's nightly feat was attempted by Lord Byron in 1807. Despite being born lame, Byron was a strong swimmer and completed the difficult swim. In 1813 he set his verse tale, *The Bride of Abydos* here.

Herodotus recounts how the Persian King, Darius, ordered a bridge to be built over the Hellespont, thus joining Asia to Europe by lining up ships side by side over which he passed from Sestos to Abydos. This was then repeated, in 480 BC, by Xerxes, Darius's successor, using 300 boats, in the other direction. When a storm destroyed his bridge he commanded that the Hellespont should receive 300 lashes and decapitated the bridge builders. The next conqueror to cross here was Alexander the Great in 334 BC - from Europe to Asia.

During the Gallipoli campaign Akbas Bay again became an important Turkish military port, where many troops and supplies were landed. It was, therefore, bombarded by the Allies by air, naval guns and submarines. In the valley behind the bay were the main Turkish Army field hospitals. A WW1 ship-wreck is visible just offshore.

At 32km from Gelibolu, turn right, opposite the Marsan Canning Factory on the left, following sign to Akbas Sehitligi and continue some 300 metres. On the left is

* Akbas Sehitligi ve Aniti (Turkish Military Cemetery and Memorial) (Map P4/5)

The cemetery is enclosed by a stone wall with cannon balls at the corners – a traditional style for Turkish military cemeteries. In the centre is a 6metre-high stone pylon memorial.

To the west of the cemetery, on the slopes of Uluflu Tepe, are the ruins of Akbas Castle, a Byzantine structure, with nearby evidences of much earlier settlements and the remains of a necropolis, much disturbed by local villagers quarrying for stone.

Extra Visit to Tombs of Erika (Alman Hemsire Erika'ninmezan) and Major (Bimbasi) Cirpanli Ali Zeynel Abidin, Yalova Cemetery (Map P2/3)

Round trip: 10 kilometres. Approximate time: 30 minutes

Continue along the road signed to Yalova. Drive through the village to the local cemetery at the outskirts. Continue along the road, with the cemetery to the right and stop at the enclosed area with its own gate towards the end.

The tomb of the Major is in the right-hand top corner of the overgrown enclosure.

Continue along the road to the corner of the cemetery wall. Park and walk up the path and steps to the wall-enclosed tomb at the top.

This is the grave of the German nurse, now only known as Erika.

Return to the main road and turn right.

Tomb of German Nurse 'Erika', with local guardian, Yalova

Continue towards Eceabat to the fountain on the right.

* Water Fountain dedicated to Gallipoli Martyrs

Many of the road-side water fountains are so dedicated by various organisations. This is a particularly handsome one.

Continue towards Eceabat.

* Kilye Bay

There have been settlements here from ancient times, notably the Athenian walled town of Kelius, established in 400BC. The Romans subsequently occupied the site and named it Coela. In the 1820s a fort named Boghali Kale was built here, which housed fifty guns. In 1915 the Turks built a harbour here to take supply ships from Constantinople and in July the Germans strung an anti-submarine net between here and Nara Burnu on the opposite shore where it was secured on an anchored steamer. It was a formidable steel mesh of two-and-a-half-inch wire which reached 220 feet down to the bottom of the Narrows. To complete the barrier, Turkish motorboats loaded with bombs patrolled the surface and guns were sited on the land at each side. Searchlights aided them at night. This was the net that snagged the *E14* on 21 July when she missed the one narrow gate in the centre, but which she managed to pierce.

On 4 September *E7* was also trapped by this net. She, however, was unable to struggle free and after twelve hours her Commander, Lieutenant-Commander Cochrane, burned his papers and ordered his crew to abandon her. They were picked up by the Turks and became prisoners-of-war. It was the end of an eventful saga for the submarine, which had started on 30 June when she made her way up the Narrows to the Sea of Marmara. By 17 July she reached the entrance to Constantinople and proceeded to cause panic by firing the six-pounder guns fitted to her decks. On the return journey Commander Cochrane was warned by Commander Boyle of the *E14* about the new nets and this time managed to negotiate them, although with difficulty, and return to Mudros.

In 1919 The Graves Registration and Enquiries Unit set up their headquarters here, under Director of Works Lieutenant Cyril Hughes (qv), within reach of the quarry at Ilgadere where the stone for the cemeteries and memorials was cut. During the 1922-23 British occupation the 28th Division camped here in Nissen huts and tarmaced the road which leads to Gaba Tepe.

It is here that the administrative offices of the new Peace Park, the existing Milli Park and the Commonwealth War Graves Commission are planned to be sited.

A large coloured archway indicates the entrance to the memorial area of the National Park.

Continue to

*** Eceabat** and thence, if staying on the Asian side, take the ferry (see Itinerary One below), to*

*** Canakkale***

ITINERARY ONE

HELLES AND KRITHIA

* **Itinerary One** starts at the Canakkale Ferry Port or at Eceabat, and covers the British and French Beaches at Helles and Seddulbahir and the area around Alcitepe (Krithia). It ends at Eceabat. **Refer throughout to Holts' Map 5 (H).**

* **The Route:** Canakkale; Eceabat - National Park Centre/Camburnu Fort/Eceabat Turkish Captain's Cemetery; Turkish Balkan/Gallipoli Campaign Memorial; Military Engineer Captain Tahir Bey Memorial; Unknown Turkish Artillery Captain's Cemetery; Kilitbahir Fort; Namazgah and Rumeli Ramparts; Mecidiye Cemetery and Memorial; Corporal Seyit Memorial (Man with the Shell); Havuzlar Cemetery and Memorial; Military Museum, Krithia; Twelve Tree Copse CWGC Cemetery and New Zealand Memorial; Pink Farm CWGC Cemetery; Gully Beach/Ravine; Lancashire Landing CWGC Cemetery; Helles Memorial/Hawick Memorial; Ertugrul Fort No 1 - Gun Emplacements/Grave of Private Halil Ibrahim/Sergeant Yahya Cemetery; V Beach CWGC Cemetery; Site of *River Clyde*; Ruins of Seddulbahir Castle; Ilk Sehitler Aniti; Seddulbahir Cephanlik Cemetery; Grave of Lieutenant-Colonel Doughty-Wylie, VC; Morto Bay/S Beach; French National Cemetery and Memorial; French Guns; Canakkale Sehitleri Memorial Area: Main Turkish Memorial/Museum/Memorial Garden/Outdoor Mosque/Wounded Soldier Statue/Kemal Ataturk Bas Relief/Memorial Wall/Symbolic Cemetery; Skew Bridge CWGC Cemetery; Redoubt CWGC Cemetery/Lieutenant Duckworth Memorial.

* **Extra Visits** are suggested to Grave of 1st Lieutenant Mustafa Efendi; Isimiz Topcu Cemetery; Brigadier-General Fevzi Cakmak's Monument; Lieutenant-Colonel Hasan Bey Memorial; Son Ok Turkish Memorial and Cemetery; Turkish Soldier; Zigindere (Gully Ravine) Field Dressing Station Memorial and Cemetery; Nuri Yamut Turkish Memorial and Cemetery; Lancashire Landing/W Beach; Turkish Guns; French Memorial, Zimmerman's Farm area; Gozetleme Tepe Cemetery and Memorial.

* **Planned Duration**, without stops for refreshment or Extra Visits: 7 hours 15 minutes.

* **Total distance: 73 kilometres.**

* *Canakkale Ferry/0 kilometres/RWC/Map*

There is a PTT (Post/Telegram/Telegraph) kiosk at the terminus where one can change money, travellers cheques, buy stamps, post letters and telephone.

Tickets for the ferry are available at the ticket office to the left of the entrance. A fee for parking is also charged for waiting cars - even if you don't actually park! On board there are light refreshment facilities and a WC for emergencies. Ferries leave every hour on the hour and take about 30 minutes. The same applies to the return crossing.

From the ferry looking north on the Asian side can be seen

* Turkish Memorial, Hillside above Canakkale/Map

This large sign commemorates the Turkish victory over the Allied Fleet of 18 March 1915. *Straight ahead across the Dardanelles to the left of Eceabat is*

* Turkish Dur Yolcu Memorial, Hillside above Kilitbahir /Map P14

The large inscription is a verse by the poet Necmettin Halil Onan which translates,

Traveller, halt!
The soil you tread
Once witnessed the end of an era.

Dur Yolcu Memorial, Kilitbahir hillside

Eceabat Ferry Terminal

National Park Centre entrance
Eceabat Yuzbasi Cemetery

* Eceabat/0 kilometres/RWC/Map P

Now - and at the beginning of every Itinerary - you should put your trip to Zero. There is also a PTT kiosk at the Eceabat Ferry Terminus amongst the row of souvenir and snack kiosks to the left of the promenade.

Eceabat, originally a fortified Greek colony, named Madytos was renamed Maidos during the Byzantine period. It was conquered by the Ottomans in 1354 and the modern name of Eceabat is in honour of Ece Bey, the conquering Ottoman general. Today it is the main town in the Peninsula, containing half the population of the National Park (c4,000), which is a mixture of Albanian, Bulgarian, Greek, Rumanian and Serbs. Because of the ferry which crosses the Dardanelles, it is a busy transit centre, the link between Istanbul and the tourist areas of Troy and Izmir, with many workers and schoolchildren commuting to Canakkale each day. Hotels are springing up along the front here, mostly of the one/two star variety, and there are several restaurants which serve good, simple meals, especially fish (though be careful to establish the price, which depends on weight and quality, when ordering). Staying on the Peninsula can save a good hour each day of touring, but there are better quality hotels and more shops and facilities in Canakkale (see **Tourist Information** below).

During the campaign the small village of Maidos was heavily bombarded by the guns from the Allied battleships and only half a dozen houses remained standing. *Turn left on leaving the ferry and drive along the front, taking the first turn left following signs to Kilitbahir. Continue past the Vegamite Bar on the left (.9kms) to*

* The Gallipoli National Park Centre/Camburnu Fort/Museum/Eceabat Yuzbasi (Captain's) Cemetery/1.7 kilometres/10 minutes/Map P7,8,9

The modern building houses the administrative offices of the National Park and contains a small **Museum, open during office hours**, with some guns and battlefield artefacts. Adjoining it are staff houses and in the park that surround it is a variety of guns, reached by walking along the path parallel to the sea. To the left of the path are the ruins of **Camburnu Fort**, built between 1807 and 1820 by the order of Sultan Mahmut II to strengthen the defences of the Narrows. Up steps at the end is the trapezoid-shaped **Eceabat Yuzbasi Cemetery** with a grave-like memorial to an Unknown Artillery Lieutenant just within the complex wall. In 1915 there was a Turkish hospital in the fort. In this area in the winter of 1918/1919 the Australian 7th Light Horse and the Canterbury Mounted Rifles camped in old Turkish huts until replaced by French forces.

Continue towards Kilitbahir to the memorial in the high bank on the right and stop in the nearby parking bay. Climb up the steps to

* Camburnu (Pine Cape) Balkan War Martyrs' Memorial/2.5 kilometres/10 minutes/Map P10

The local stone memorial with marble plaques was erected by the 'Aid the Canakkale Martyrs Memorials Society' in memory of Turkish soldiers who died in the Balkan Wars as well as in the Gallipoli campaign. On one of the plaques is a

quotation from the Turkish poet, Necmettin Halil Onan, which translates, 'This earth you tread unawares is where an age sank. Bow and listen. This quiet mound is where the heart of a nation throbs.'
Continue to the cemetery in the bank on the right

* Isimsiz Topcu Yuzbasi Sehitligi (Unknown Artillery Captain's Cemetery)/3.5 kilometres/5 minutes/Map P11

The grave is enclosed by a stone wall and surrounded by cypress trees.
Continue, with a view over the Straits now to your left, to the 'Dikkat' (restricted military area) sign and on the left, opposite the entrance to the Degirmen Burnu Rampart barracks, is

* Istihkam Yuzbasi (Military Engineer Captain) Tahir Bey Memorial/Degirman Burnu Rampart/3.7 kilometres/Map P12,13

As the brick memorial, surrounded by cannon balls and shells, is in a restricted area, photographs are not permitted. It commemorates Captain Tahir Bey and four soldiers who were killed when their ship was hit by a Turkish mine on 15 May 1915.

In the barracks across the road, also in a prohibited area, are fortifications built in 1884 during the reign of Sultan Abdulhamit II. They comprise seven ammunition bunkers and in 1915 were armed with Krupp flintlock guns.
Continue to the fishing village and ferry port

* Kilitbahir Ferry/4.7 kilometres/Map P

The Kilitbahir-Canakkale Ferry is a good alternative to the Eceabat-Canakkale Ferry. It is smaller, so cannot take a full-sized coach, but is quicker and cheaper. It departs when it is deemed full enough to go, has a rapid turn-around time and a crossing of about 15 minutes. Basic refreshment and WC facilities on board. There are several small shops, cafés and fish stalls in the vicinity and a motel. The village is an interesting and bustling area, with a good deal of local traffic.
Continue through the stone archway to

* Kilitbahir Fort/5.0 kilometres/15 minutes/Map P15

The fort was built in 1452 by Mehmet II the Conqueror. It has outer and inner walls and a seven-story triangular tower in the inner courtyard. It was restored in 1541 by Suleiman the Magnificent and again in 1870 by Sultan Abdulaziz. Further rebuilding and additions were undertaken in 1893 by Sultan Abdulhamid II, when eight artillery batteries were installed behind embrasures. This impressive and well-built defensive structure is open to the public.

A series of fortified ramparts continue along the coast from the fort, so interjoined that it is not feasible to give a separate distance/timing for each. Fortifications enthusiasts should allow at least 20 minutes for clambering over them.
Continue to the next complex of ramparts on the left.

Camburnu Balkan War Memorial

Captain Tahir Bey Memorial with the Dardanelles in the background

Kilitbahir Fort

Kilitbahir Harbour

Steps inside Kilitbahir Fort

* Namazgah Rampart/Map P16

This fortification, on the left, was built on the orders of Sultan Abdulaziz. During the 1915 campaign it was armed with sixteen heavy artillery guns, two of 28cm, eleven of 24cm and three of 21cm calibre. The complex comprises fourteen ammunition bunkers built of hewn stone, half submerged and covered with earth on top, giving the impression of small hillocks.

Continue past the next complex of ramparts on the right.

* Rumeli Hamadiye Rampart/Map P17

This is to the right of the road, 10m above sea level and masked by pine trees. It was built in the reign of Sultan Abdulhamit II in 1896 to fill the gap in the Dardanelles defensive line between the forts to the north and south. It comprises three ammunition bunkers, built in the same style as the adjoining fortifications, and in 1915 there were two Krupp 35cm guns in the emplacements, which still exist.

Continue to the cemetery and memorial on the bank to the right, opposite a statue on the left.

* Mecidiye Cemetery and Artillery Memorial/5.6 kilometres/10 minutes/Map P18,19

The cemetery, surrounded by a brick wall topped with traditional cannon balls, contains the graves of Sergeant Ali, Mehmet son of Ismail, Suleyman son of Mustafa and thirteen artillerymen killed on the Mecidiye Rampart on 18 March 1915. On the rear of the memorial is a plaque to Corporal Seyit. Outside the cemetery wall is a single tomb.

Continue to the statue opposite.

* Corporal Seyit, the Man With Shell, Statue/5.7 kilometres/5 minutes/Map P20

The statue was commissioned by the Turkish Ministry of Culture and sculpted by Huseyin Anka Ozkan in 1992. It depicts the hero, artillery Corporal Seyit, who, on 18 March 1915, when sixty-one of his comrades were killed by Allied naval shells, carried the last 275 kilogram shell to his gun in the Rumeli Mecidiye Ramparts and fired it himself. The shot hit the battleship *Ocean*, damaging her rudders, and she then ran into mines and sank.

Continue past the ramparts on the right.

* Rumeli Mecidiye Rampart/5.9 kilometres/10 minutes/Map P21

These fortifications were built on the orders of Asaf Pasa during the reign of Sultan Abdulhamit II. They comprise eight ammunition bunkers and six artillery batteries. The stone structures are sunk into the ground and topped with earth. Steps lead down from the entrances to the barrel-vaulted rooms. In 1915 six artillery pieces were in use here, four of 24cm calibre and two of 28cm. It was here that Corporal Seyit performed his heroic action.

Continue to the cemetery and memorial on the left.

* Havuzlar Cemetery and Memorial/7.9 kilometres/5 minutes/Map P22,23

The obelisk memorial at Havuzlar was erected in 1960/61 by the 'Aid the Canakkale Martyrs' Memorial Society'. It marks the site of four 12cm siege guns which bombarded the Allied ships during their 18 March 1915 attack. It commemorates two officers – Captain Kemal Bey of 2nd Division and Lieutenant Ismail Efendi, aide-de-camp to the commander of 126th Regiment, and eight private soldiers who died during the combat against the French at Kereves Dere on 21 June 1915. The memorial bears a poem by Nail Memik, former governor of Canakkale, and an extract from Captain Kemal Bey's divisional order of 20 June 1915. The cemetery is bordered by a stone wall, with traditional cannon balls at each corner, and trees (*Platanus Orientalis*).

Continue along the coast past the Huzur Motel on the right (8.8kms) and after 1.7kms on the right is

The brown Milli Park sign, **Cocuklarimza Birakabilecegimis En Buyuk Miras Temiz Temiz Bir Cevredir**, translates as, 'The most valuable heritage that we can give to our children is a clean, clean environment.'

Continue 1.4kms to the lighthouse on the left.

There is parking 100 metres beyond on the left.

The **lighthouse**, which is on the seashore below the cliff, is an excellent Reference Point **[RP]** which can clearly be seen from the mine rails by the Military and Naval Museum in Canakkale on the Asian side of the Straits. Looking straight across the Straits here, the Dardanos (Kephes) lighthouse opposite and the battery above it (see Itinerary Five) can be seen with binoculars.

Follow the road inland towards Alcitepe through a beautiful agricultural area, passing a sign to the village of Behramli to the right (16.2kms). Continue 3 kilometres towards Alcitepe to a cancellation of a non-overtaking sign on the left.

Extra Visit to Mulazim Ustegmen (Grave of First Lieutenant) Mustafa Efendi'nin Mezari (Map P24)

Round trip: approx 500 metres. Approximate time: 15 minutes

Stop on the left by an unmarked track leading down and then uphill. Park and walk up the track which bends right and some 20 metres later turn left across a field and climb uphill over a second field and go through a large tractor access in the high hedge on the left.

The field ahead of you was a Turkish soldiers' cemetery from 1915. Scattered across the field are at least three neglected graves (one of which is under a tree), which may be seen or not according to the crops currently growing. To the right of the field is an area of trees and bushes. In this area is the **grave of the**

Mecidye Cemetery and Memorial

'The Man with the Shell'

Havuzlar Cemetery and Memorial

Extra Visit continued

Lieutenant Mustafa Efendi, killed on 18 September. Around the Lieutenant's grave are many other broken graves. This neglected cemetery is little-known and was shown to the authors in October 1998 by an ancient goat-herd from Behramli who had himself not visited it for at least 10 years. At that time he recalled iron railings round one of the graves in the centre of the field.

Return to the road and pick up the main itinerary.

Grave of Mustafa Efendi'nin

View over lighthouse on Peninsula shore towards Canakkale

Continue to a road junction (22.6kms) to the right signed Kabatepe/Anafartalar. Stop.
Look back down the road you have just driven up and take that direction as 12 o' clock. At 1 o' clock with a white building (water station) and lone tree is the summit of Achi Baba, with its deceptively gentle-looking slopes. In his sensitive 'factional' account of the Gallipoli campaign, *The Secret Battle*, A.P. Herbert, who served with the Hawke Battalion of the RND, and who arrived at Helles on the night of 28-29 May, described it thus: 'We saw at last the little sugarloaf peak of Achi Baba, absurdly pink and diminutive in the distance. A man's first frontal impression of that great

rampart, with the outlying slopes masking the summit, was that it was disappointingly small; but when he had lived under and upon it for a while, day by day, it seemed to grow in menace and in bulk, and ultimately became an overpowering monster pervading all his life; so that it worked upon men's nerves, and almost everywhere in the Peninsula they were painfully conscious that every movement they made could be watched from somewhere on that massive hill.'

In another of the many similarities between the Gallipoli campaign and the WW2 Italian campaign of 1944, the journalist Fred Majdalany (who, like Herbert, had also been an active participant in the actions he later described) wrote in similar terms of the Abbey of Monte Cassino, perched atop a high hill: 'Because of the extraordinary extent to which the summit of Monte Cassino dominated the valleys: ... because of the obsessive theatrical manner in which it towered over the scene, searching every inch of it ...[it] had become the embodiment of resistance and its tangible symbol.... Hostile eyes can be sensed without being seen, and the soldier develops an exceptional awareness of this. Monte Cassino projected this feeling over an entire valley'. Coincidentally, the man on whose advice the controversial decision to bomb the historic Abbey was made was none other than Lieutenant-General Sir Bernard Freyberg, then commanding the New Zealand Division. In 1915 he served with the Hood Battalion of the RND and on 7 May, during the Second Battle of Krithia, whose object was yet again to take Achi Baba, Freyberg received a serious abdominal wound. He was evacuated to Egypt on the *Grantully Castle*, the ship that had borne 'The New Argonauts' (qv) to the Dardanelles. On the nightmare journey to Egypt there were 'no nurses, and one over-worked doctor and two medical orderlies to 800 serious cases' [Freyberg, 1951].

Bernard's eldest brother, Oscar, serving with the Collingwood Battalion RND, was killed in the Third Battle of Krithia and last seen in a Turkish trench with a pistol in each hand. He is commemorated on the Helles Memorial. His second oldest brother, Paul, was mortally wounded at Basseville and on 18 June 1917, died in hospital at Boulogne where he is buried in the CWGC Cemetery. Just as Bernard was looking forward to seeing Oscar on his return from Egypt in June 1915, only to find that he had been killed, so he looked forward to meeting Paul in France in June 1917 with the same sad disappointment.

Continue to Alcitepe.

* Alcitepe (Krithia)/23 kilometres/Map H

On the left as one enters the village are the old barracks and just within the perimeter there was until 1998 a memorial.

Turkish Garrison Memorial. The white marble memorial bore a bust of and a quotation from Mustafa Kemal. It was within the old barracks perimeter. Its present whereabouts are unknown.

Continue to the outskirts of the village.

The town of Krithia was completely destroyed in 1915 and the present settlement was constructed by Rumanian and Bulgarian immigrants in 1934. Today its 1,000 or so population depend on agriculture and olive oil production and the raising of livestock.

Extra Visits to Turkish Isimsiz Topcu Cemetery (Map H9)/Summit of Achi Baba/Yarbay (Lieutenant-Colonel) Hasan Bey Memorial (Map H16) /Maresal (Brigadier-General, later Marshal) Fevzi Cakmak HQ/Monument (Map H12)

Round trip: 12.3 kilometres. Approximate time: 40 minutes

On entering the village, immediately turn left (before the Museum) along a narrow road which deteriorates to an unmade track. Continue 900 metres to a cemetery on the right.

Turkish Isimsiz Topcu Cemetery
The small cemetery, enclosed by a white wall with the traditional cannon balls around and with cypress trees within, contains the grave of some unknown artilleryman. This area was immediately behind the Turkish lines during the battles for Krithia in 1915, and from the cemetery are views over the Turkish Memorial and the British Memorial at Helles.

Continue across a flat plain, passing on the left an old quarry used by the CWGC for stone. From now on the going becomes very difficult and, especially if wet, would only be negotiable with four-wheel-drive.

Turn left up a very rough track to the second white water station (3.4kms).
Summit of Achi Baba/OP. Considering the apparent gentleness of the ascent, the views from the top are breathtaking in their scope and one is vividly made to understand the importance of this dominating feature to defenders and attackers alike. It gives a complete 360° view over the Peninsula, with the Sari Bair Ridge, Nibrunesi Point and Suvla to the north and Helles and Kumkale, on the Asian coast, to the south. There are the remains of trenches and defensive positions around.

Return to the junction (3.8kms) and turn left. Continue to a memorial on the right (4.8kms).
The obelisk memorial, surmounted by a shell, is to **Mustafa Fevzi Cakmak** (1876-1940), the General Officer Commanding Gelibolu V Corps, Southern Group, from 10 July 1915, until the Allied Evacuation, whose headquarters were nearby. It was erected in 1941.

Continue through fields of olive groves to a T-junction (7.6kms). Turn left and a further 700m on turn left along a very rough track through an olive grove and then across a field to a large fig tree with a fir tree beside it (8.5kms) and continue a further 300m to a memorial.
The two-metre-high concrete pylon commemorates the commander of the Turkish 5th Division, 17th Regiment, **Lieutenant-Colonel Hasan Bey.** He was killed here on 11 July 1915, the day before the last major attack by the French, by a wounded French soldier. His last words were purported to be, 'Don't kill the Frenchman; he did his duty'.

Turn round and return to the junction. Keep right and continue into Alcitepe.
Pick up the main itinerary.

Isimsiz Topcu Cemetery

Marshal Fevzi Cakmak Memorial

On the left, just before the crossroads, is the

* Military Museum, Krithia/24.3 kilometres/15 minutes/Map H8/RWC

This private museum is owned by villager Salim Mutlu and comprises his personal collection, supplemented by local people, of artefacts found on the surrounding battlefields, plus some ephemera and documentation. It is in two large rooms. Part One contains artefacts, some with English and Turkish captions, and a picture of Kemal Ataturk. Part Two has more artefacts, books, letters etc. Open all day, every day. **There is a small shop with drinks and snacks inside and a WC.**

There is no formal entrance fee, but a box for voluntary contributions.

Continue to the crossroads with CWGC Cemetery signs pointing in each direction.
Turn right signed towards Twelve Tree Copse and other CWGC cemeteries.

Military Museum, Krithia (Alcitepe)
Roadsigns, Alcitepe

Extra Visit to Son Ok Turkish Cemetery and Memorial/Turkish Soldier Statue/Turkish Sargiyere (Dressing Station)Cemetery and Memorial/Turkish Nuri Yamut Cemetery and Memorial, Fusilier Bluff (Map H6,7,5,3,4,1,2)

Round trip: 4.6 kilometres. Approximate time: 40 minutes.

Continue to a fork and turn right signed 'Son Ok Sargiyeri'. Continue to the cemetery on the left.

Son Ok Turkish Memorial and Cemetery

Built in 1948 by the Turkish Government to commemorate the dead of the Battles of Krithia, the obelisk-type memorial recalls the action of 4 June 1915, when Turkish victory was only achieved after the third charge. Son Ok means 'Last Arrow'. The inscription translates, 'The gunners of a 12cm siege battery defeated the enemy at this point by a bayonet charge and so secured the Third Victory of Kirte (Krithia), 7 June 1915.' Beside it is a cemetery surrounded by trees.

Continue over the crest and on the next rise, on the left, is a

Turkish Soldier Statue

Continue to the bottom of the valley

Turkish Cemetery and Memorials, Zigindere Field Dressing Post

The Field Dressing Station was in the upper reaches of Gully Ravine (Zigindere) and the group of statues sculpted by Professor Tankut Oktem (who also sculpted the massive soldier) represents wounded soldiers from the 25th and 26th Infantry Regiments. The memorial commemorates them and Captain Kemal Bey, Staff Commander of 2nd Division, killed here by British artillery.

A bridge leads over the Zigin stream, on either side of which are tablets describing the Allied bombardments of the Dressing Station, to the cemetery and main memorial, which were built in 1943 and renovated in 1992.

Continue along the track to the cliff top overlooking Fusilier Bluff to the

Turkish Cemetery/ Nuri Yamut Memorial/OP

On Gully Spur (Zigindere Vadisi), and overlooking Fusilier Bluff (Silahendaz Yamaci) on the old Turkish front line, is the memorial erected by Lieutenant-General Nuri Yamut, Commanding Officer of the Gelibolu II Corps. It commemorates the 10,000 Turkish soldiers who died on the Gully Ravine front from June 26 to July 12 1915. Beside it is a cemetery with, on the wall, a **Memorial plaque marking the Turkish right wing.**

With one's back to the cemetery entrance, the Turkish Memorial at Helles can be seen at 12 o' clock. At 9 o' clock is the outline of Achi Baba. Clockwise just before it in the depression can be seen the head of the soldier statue and just past it the cemetery. The British Memorial at Helles is at 10 o' clock and Imbros can be discerned on a clear day at 3 o' clock.

It is possible to enter the ravine from here, but great caution should be taken. *Return to Alcitepe and pick up the main itinerary.*

Follow signs towards Twelve Tree Copse CWGC and continue 1.5kms. Park on the left and look straight ahead.
The Helles Memorial can be seen on the horizon (say at 12 o' clock) and the Turkish Memorial is at 10 o' clock.

* Twelve Tree Copse CWGC Cemetery/New Zealand Memorial/25 kilometres/15 minutes/Map H11,10

This large (covering 7,817 square metres) cemetery, built on three terraces, was made after the Armistice by concentrating several smaller cemeteries, notably 925 burials from Geogheghan's Bluff (qv), from the Gully Ravine action of June-July 1915, 522 burials from Clunes Vennel Cemetery on the south of Krithia and some from Fir Tree Wood Cemetery, south of this site where the 29th Division and New Zealand Infantry Brigade fought in May 1915, and from isolated graves. The cemetery was designed by Sir John Burnet, principal architect of the CWGC memorials and cemeteries on the Peninsula. It contains the graves of 462 soldiers, sailors and marines of the RND and the RNAS from the UK, 13 from New Zealand, 2 from Australia, and 1,953 whose unit could not be ascertained. There are 2,226 unnamed graves and 644 special memorials to soldiers from the UK, 10 from New Zealand, 1 from Australia and 2 from India. They include 142 officers and men of the 1st Essex of 6 August and 47 of the 1/7th Scottish Rifles of 28 June. The special memorials are in alphabetical order, starting from the bottom. Inside the cemetery gate is a metal plaque describing the action in the area, which is also reproduced at Skew Bridge and Redoubt Cemeteries.

The cemetery was named after a group of pines which were somewhat south of the present cemetery and the area was named by the 86th and 87th Brigades who reached it on 28 April. The original trees were destroyed by shellfire, their stumps used to reinforce trenches, but twelve pine trees have been planted in the cemetery to represent them.

Buried here are:- among the Royal Inniskilling Fusiliers an American, **CQMS Michael Joseph D'Arcy**, age 29, of Omaha, Nebraska [Sp Mem B 28]; **Lieutenant-Colonel W.J. Law** of the 7th Battalion Lancashire Fusiliers, age 38, who died on 19 December during the preparations for the detonation of a mine, part of the diversionary action for the Evacuation, was Mentioned in Despatches and awarded the *Croix de Guerre* with Palm. He was one of the few who reached The Vineyard in the 7 August attack [Sp Mem C 305]; **Captain Keith Maurice Levi**, of No 1 General Hospital Australian Army Medical Corps and Regimental Medical Officer to the 2nd Hampshire, died 7 August, was Mentioned in Despatches [1 E 20]. **Private Henry Morton** of the Sussex Yeomanry, age 48, who died on 13 November, had the Long Service and Good Conduct Medal, served in South Africa and had 20 years' service in the 3rd Battalion the Grenadier Guards [Sp Mem C 165]; the **brothers Lance Corporal Arthur and Private Frederick Roper** of the 1st Battalion Essex Regiment, age 24 and 25 respectively, were both killed on 6 August [Sp Mems C II and C257]; three senior officers of the 156th Brigade, veterans of the South African Campaign - **Brigadier-General William Scott-Moncrieff** (qv) of the

Nuri Yamut Cemetery and
Memorial

Detail of Memorial

Son Ok Cemetery and Memorial

*Turkish Soldier overlooking
Zigindere Field Dressing
Station*

*Wounded Soldiers,
Zigindere Dressing Station*

*Symbolic Cemetery
Zigindere Dressing Station*

1st/7th Battalion the Cameronians, age 57, who commanded 156th Brigade [Sp Mem C 132], **Lieutenant- Colonel Henry Hannan**, 8th Battalion the Cameronians, age 41 [VII A 7], and **Lieutenant-Colonel John Boyd Wilson**, 7th Battalion the Cameronians, age 40 [Sp Mem C 406], all killed in the Battle of Gully Ravine (qv) on 28 June; **2nd Lieutenant Alfred Victor Smith, VC, of D Company 1/5th Battalion East Lancashire Regiment**, *Croix de Guerre*, age 24, [Sp Mem C 358] who was in the act of throwing a grenade when it slipped from his hand and fell to the bottom of the trench, close to several of our officers and men. He immediately shouted out a warning, and himself jumped clear and into safety, but seeing that the officers and men were unable to get into cover, and knowing well that the grenade was due to explode, he returned without any hesitation and flung himself down on it. He was instantly killed by the explosion. His magnificent act of self-sacrifice undoubtedly saved many lives.' This act of heroism was to be repeated by Private Billy McFadzean of the 14th RIR on 1 July 1916, on the Somme and by Pfc Joe Mann of the 101st US Airborne on 18 September 1944, at Best in Holland (where there is a memorial to him). Some men served under assumed names: Private S. Vagg of the 1st/7th Battalion Lancashire Fusiliers, died 21 December age 18, served as 'Bagg'; and Private Harry Smith of the 1st Battalion, died 4 June age 26, served as 'Fisher'. There were many reasons for men to serve under an alias. Often it was so that under-age enlistees could not be found by their families or to conceal a criminal record or, in the anti-German climate of the beginning of the war, to lose a Teutonic-sounding name.

In bitter contrast is the grave of a man described as Private J. Robins, 5th Wilts, [Sp Mem C 259]. At 0800 hours on 2 January on the beach at Helles Robins, who had landed in August as a corporal and who had been promoted to sergeant, was executed for 'Wilfully disobeying an order given by a superior officer in the execution of his duty.' Robins maintained that he was too unwell to go on a patrol. The inadequacy of his defence is described by Putowski and Sykes in *Shot at Dawn*.

The New Zealand Memorial is one of four of that country's in the Peninsula. It flanks the Cross at the top of the cemetery and is inscribed with the names of 59 of the Auckland Battalion, 49 of the Canterbury Battalion, 21 of the Otago Battalion and 48 of the Wellington Battalion who fell in the Second Battle of Krithia, May 1915. *Continue to the cemetery sign on the left.*

* Pink Farm CWGC Cemetery/28 kilometres/15 minutes/Map H15

Originally called Sotiri Farm, it was renamed by the Allies for the red soil in the area. Here Brigadier-General W.R. Marshall (later Sir William Marshall, GCMG, KCB, KCSI) commanding the 87th (Union) Brigade, who landed at X Beach between 0800 and 0900 hours on 25 April, set up Brigade HQ. Marshall, who had trained the brigade from its inception, was shot in the leg above the knee during the landings but refused to go sick. On 27 April he had command of all British troops on shore and his brigade continued to be a model, incurring few losses in the attack of 4 June. In August Marshall replaced General de Lisle as G.O.C. when the 29th Division moved to the Suvla sector.

The foundations, well and an old water pump belonging to the original farm, together with the traces of trench lines, can still be seen among the trees, about 50 metres to the north-east of the cemetery. Several battle cemeteries were started round the farm after the First Battle of Krithia on 18 April 1915. Designed by Sir John Burnet, the cemetery is on two levels, most of the identified graves being on the lower level with the un-named graves on the upper level. Pine trees form a dark and dramatic screen to the back wall with the white Cross of Sacrifice and the cemetery is surrounded by beautiful tamarisk trees. It contains 209 UK burials, 3 New Zealand, 2 Australian, 5 Indian Army and 164 totally unidentified. There are 250 unnamed graves, and 212 sailors or soldiers from the UK, 2 New Zealand, 1 Australian and 4 Indian Army are commemorated on special tablets.

Buried here are **Lance Corporal Frederick William Birch** of the 2nd Hampshires, died 17 October, age 32, who has the poignant personal message to 'Our Fred' [IV D I]; **Major George Cecil Brooke** of the 1st Border Regiment, died 28 April, age 44, Mentioned in Despatches, served in the Waziristan Expedition 1895 (Medal with Clasp), the Malakand Expedition 1897-8 (Medal with Clasp), the Siege of Tientsin and the Relief of Pekin (Medal with Clasp), was attached as Adjutant to the Chinese Regiment and was Adjutant of Militia and Special Reserve of the Lancashire Fusiliers Depot 1907-10 [Sp Mem 127]; **Private T.H. Bull**, 8th Battalion RWF, died 7 January, age 16 [Sp Mem 12]; **PO Mechanic Ernest Robert Scott**, Armoured Car Division, RNAS, died 25 September, age 32 [Sp Mem 91].

Continue along the road. After some 500 metres, and just past a lone tree to the right, and before the group of trees on the left, park and walk to the track which starts in the bushes on the right. Continue down the path to the beach.
The walk takes 7 minutes down and slightly longer back up.

* Gully Beach and Ravine/28.5 kilometres/20 minutes/Map H

This small beach was known as 'Y2', but no landing was planned here as the inland mouth of the ravine was thought to be too well fortified. It was actually held by just two platoons of the Turkish 2/26th Regiment who on 25 April mounted a spirited attack on the Royal Fusiliers who had landed at X Beach. On 26 April the Turks were pushed back towards Gully Ravine and, with severe losses, eventually withdrew to their second line of defence round Krithia. The ensuing Battles of Krithia are described in the *Historical Summary.*

On 28 June, in what became known as 'The Battle of Gully Ravine', an intensive artillery bombardment was the prelude to 'an advance with limited objectives' [*29th Division History*]. 'In my nine years of war', recalled the G.O.C., General de Lisle, 'I have seen many thrilling sights but not one compared to the 28th June. Its success was well-nigh complete, and the troops appeared to move with the assurance of victory.' Each man had a triangle of biscuit tin attached to his back which glinted 'like heliographs in the sun' [de Lisle] and which helped the artillery to range. Supported by HMS *Talbot*, 87th Brigade on the left beside the sea eventually took the entire Turkish first system - three lines of trenches. Then 86th

Twelve Tree Copse CWGC
Cemetery with NZ
Memorial at the top

Headstone of Brigadier Scott-Moncrieff

Headstone of 2nd
Lieutenant A.V. Smith VC

Brigade passed through them to take the second line and the Fusiliers reached the high ground that would become known as Fusilier Bluff (where today the Turkish Nuri Yamit Memorial stands - see *Extra Visit* above). The attack had started well, but on the right the bombardment, lacking HE shells, had scarcely damaged the Turkish trenches and the fighting continued for three days.

During the attack Lieutenant Herbert James of the 4th Worcestershires, attached to the 5th Royal Scots, earned the VC. His citation reads, 'When the advance of part of the regiment had been checked, Second Lieutenant James, from a neighbouring unit, gathered together a body of men and led them forward under heavy fire. He then returned, organised a second party and again advanced, putting fresh life into the attack. On 3 July [it was actually the 2nd] he headed a party of bomb throwers up a Turkish communication trench and when all his party had been killed or wounded, he remained alone, under

Headstone in Pink Farm

Pink Farm CWGC Cemetery

murderous fire and kept back the enemy until a barrier had been built behind him and the trench secured.'

James's was the first VC of the Regiment and his feat was immortalised in a painting by Gilbert Holiday. It shows him using a 'jam pot' bomb as he held the trench single-handed with just his sack of bombs and two rifles. James, who joined the regiment in 1909 and served with them in Egypt and India, was commissioned in November 1914. He survived the war and died in August 1958 after lying alone for five days following a heart attack.

When it was obvious that things were not going well with the 1/4th and 1/7th Royal Scots to the east of Gully Ravine (most of their officers had been killed in the attack), Scott-Moncrieff, commanding 156th Brigade, ordered two companies of the 1/7th Scottish Rifles from the reserve to renew the attack and rushed forward to see the situation for himself. He found that a few men had actually reached the Turkish front line and ordered his last two companies to support them. Leading this last reserve, the gallant 57-year-old officer, who had served in the Zulu and Boer Wars (where he was badly wounded in the leg and thereafter limped), was killed as he reached the end of a forward sap. Killed with him was Lieutenant-Colonel John Boyd Wilson, commanding officer of the Scottish Rifles, and both officers are buried in Twelve Tree Copse CWGC Cemetery. The attack petered out, but the battle was deemed a success by Sir Ian Hamilton who informed 29th Division that in it they had 'added fresh lustre to British arms all the world over'.

Here on Gully Beach the 29th Division moved their HQ from their original position on the slopes of Hill 138 (see Holts' Map 5) captured by the Worcesters on 25 April, when de Lisle took over as G.O.C. The area was then filled with tents, dugouts, sand-bagged shelters, stone sangars, supply dumps, horses, mules and donkeys. When Compton Mackenzie [the author of the superb account, *Gallipoli Memories*, who served as an Intelligence Officer on Hamilton's Staff] visited Divisional Headquarters on 'the lower part of the notorious Gully Ravine' in June it was 'singing with spent bullets'. He found 'The sea was thronged with bathers in spite of the shrapnel which continually burst over them. Sitting with their backs to the cliff were men brewing tea and eating away at bread and jam exactly as they would have done at Margate.'

In the centre of the shore a pier was built at which the supply trawlers which plied from beach to beach called. A few remains can be seen today in the sea, together with the remnants of a boat grounded in 1915. The concrete well which supplied water to the division can also still be seen near the entrance to the Gully. It was built by Joseph Murray of the Hood Battalion, RND, on 21 July, when water was struck at a depth of only 4 feet, as described in his book, *Gallipoli As I Saw It*. There is still an iron ladder in the well and the faint words 'RE 135 Company'.

On this beach Private Thomas Davis of the 1st R Munster Fusiliers was shot at 0500 hours on 2 July for 'quitting his post'. In his diary for 1 July Private Atkinson (qv) recorded, 'Guard doesn't wake S. Major to call us, we are late, but get job done in time. Find it is platform for shooting man who is sentenced to death. First uncomfortable job but he had three chances, and deserted in each action in the advance.' Davis is commemorated on the Helles Memorial.

Extra Visit: A Climb up Gully Ravine (Map H)
One-way trip: Approximately 2.5 kilometres. Approximate time: 3 hours 30 minutes

Walk up the beach to the entrance to the ravine.

Make sure you are well-equipped against hot/cold/wet weather as the case may be, with stout walking shoes, drinking water and dog-appeasing or discouraging material. A companion is recommmended.

Known by the Turks as Zighin or Saghir Dere, the ravine is the pathway of a stream, normally dry, or no more than a trickle, except in periods of heavy rain. At its mouth it is 100 yards wide, but as it narrows the cliffs on either side rise to menacing heights. It was, as the 29th Division History says, 'a formidable military obstacle', separating X and Y Beaches, with Gully Spur to the left and Fir Tree Spur to the right. Within the protection afforded by the steep cliffs on the left, terraces were built and a new camp formed where waggons and kitchens were based. Here the 88th Field Ambulance moved from W Beach. On the right is the entrance to a smaller ravine. Today the area is covered by the ubiquitous scrub. In 1915 the gully, being comparatively well-protected from all but stray shells and bullets, was a busy thoroughfare to and from the trenches in Gully and Fir Tree Spurs, home to many and burial place to others. It had a unique atmosphere, part foreboding, part reassuring and those who lived beneath the shelter of its high cliffs remembered it with a mixtue of dread and affection. Here they made their dugouts, filled their water bottles from the streams and springs, queued for food at the cook-houses, were carried to first aid posts when wounded, rested after spells in the trenches, and dug graves for their lost comrades. Here the Indians and the Zion Corps sheltered their mules and Field Ambulances set up dressing stations. Today many evidences of their occupation remain in the ravine and it is hoped that souvenir-hunting (and remember that it is illegal to export battlefield artefacts) will not deprive future visitors from the thrill of seeing a shard of rum jar, the remains of a water bottle or ration tin...and the opportunity to reflect on the men who used them in 1915.

Continue up the sandy gully through pine trees for approximately 1.7 kilometres, passing side gullies (such as Artillery Row and Aberdeen Gully) running off to the left to Gully Spur.

The sides of the gully become very steep as one climbs and turns and at this stage to the right is the site of Gully Farm, the extreme left of the Eski Line (see Holts' Map).

Continue along the twisting path some 500 metres.

On the right the flat area known as the 'Football Field' and the Zig Zag (a route to Fir Tree Spur, Twelve Tree Copse and Pink Farm) are passed.

Continue to the flat slope from Gully Spur known as Geogheghan's Bluff.

Here was the main cemetery in Gully Ravine and after the war the bodies were

Gully Beach,
1915 wreck

View up the
Ravine

Extra Visit continued

moved from it to Twelve Tree Copse CWGC Cemetery.

On 18 June, the 100th Anniversary of the Battle of Waterloo, an event marked by Sir Ian Hamilton and his Staff by a special dinner of crayfish on Imbros, the Turks mounted a strong attack on the British trenches to the east of Gully Ravine. To the right of where you now are was Turkey Trench, taken from the Turks on 11 June and this is where they put down an unusually heavy shelling barrage (estimated at 500 HE shells in 30 minutes) at 1830 hours. It was followed by an attack which, on the second attempt, succeeded in retaking Turkey Trench, held by the 2nd South Wales Borderers (SWB). Bombs rained on the nearby 1st Royal Inniskilling Fusiliers and a 30-yard gap in the line was created. Captain Gerald O'Sullivan then led A Company and a platoon from C Company into the threatened areas. Armed with jam-tin bombs he regained part of his trench and, with some SWBs, bombed his way along the trench against counter-bombing Turks. The battle raged backwards and forwards along the trench. O'Sullivan held on, waiting for a renewed attack by the SWBs which started at about 1530 hours. It was repulsed, then Brigadier-General Marshall ordered another combined attack by the Borderers and Inniskillings. At 1630 hours Captain O'Sullivan took half a dozen SWB bombers and led the way down the Turkish sap, driving the Turks out but it was not until 1000 hours the following day that the 60 metres of Turkey Trench were once again completely in British hands. O'Sullivan, who always had the reputation of an

Well dug by Joseph Murray

Extra Visit continued

impetuous dare-devil, joined the Inniskillings in 1909 and served with them in China and India. Ever since the landings of 25 April he had shown himself capable, brave and resourceful as a company commander. His outstanding soldiership was to continue after the Turkey Trench episode (for which he was recommended for the VC) in the Battle of Gully Ravine (see above) which started on 28 June. Once again O'Sullivan stormed a Turkish trench with jam-pot bombs. This time he was supported by Corporal James Somers, a prodigious bomb-thrower who reckoned to have personally put eighty Turks out of action, and who continued alone through the night when O'Sullivan was wounded in the leg. The next day Somers managed to get out of the trench and bring up a bombing party. The desperate fight continued throughout the day and although the struggle ended with limited success, both O'Sullivan (for the second time) and Somers were recommended for the VC for their determination. Somers was promoted to Sergeant and O'Sullivan was evacuated to hospital in Egypt. He returned on 11 August in time to move with his battalion to Suvla and to take part in the attack on Scimitar Hill on 21 August. Exhorting his band of fifty men to make 'one more charge for the honour of the Old Regiment', he led them through a hail of fire. Only one man came back from the charge. O' Sullivan's body was never found and he is commemorated on the Helles Memorial. Somers died in Tipperary on 7 May 1918 of gas poisoning.

Below to the left are **Y Ravine and Y Beach**, the latter marked as Pinarici Koyu (Little Fountain Cove) on local maps.

Today it is extremely difficult to reach. The 2.5 kilometre coast-line round the base of the cliffs from Gully Beach is virtually un-walkable. It is possible, but not advised, to reach it from Gurkha Bluff (see Holts' Map) a few hundred metres further on to the left in the ravine. Alternatively it may be approached from the Nuri Yamut Memorial (at the end of this walk) by walking just over 1 kilometre along the cliff top to Gurkha Bluff and then climbing down.

Y Beach was considered 'an unexpected spot' [*Official History*], because of its steep, scrubby cliffs, from which ran two ravines - Y Ravine to the north and Gurkha Ravine to the south. Here some 2,000 men of the 1st King's Own Scottish Borderers, a company of the 2nd South Wales Borderers and the Plymouth Battalion, RMLI, landed without opposition. They duly scaled the cliff or scrambled up the gullies and Winston Churchill's brother, Jack, a Major serving on Ian Hamilton's Staff, wrote,

Y Beach, the Scottish Borderer cried,
While panting up the steep hillside,
Y Beach!
To call this thing a beach is stiff,
It's nothing but a bloody cliff.
Why beach?

Extra Visit continued

The news that troops were observed sitting on top of the cliffs and nonchalantly carrying cans of water up from the beach was passed to a delighted Ian Hamilton on board the *Queen Elizabeth* and the landing of more men at this unopposed landing site was briefly considered. Colonel Matthews of the Plymouth Battalion and two companies of Marines made forays out towards Krithia, looking in vain for a Turkish gun that was supposed to be in the vicinity. A message was sent to X Beach at 1145 confirming that the KOSBs were established at Y. But disappointment soon set in as the expected advance from Helles did not materialise and Colonel Matthews decided to withdraw to the edge of the cliff top and dig in. His position was hidden from the watching ships. The decision to entrench rather than to advance gave the Turks time to bring up three reserve battalions with a field battery and a machine-gun section. By nightfall the British troops were subjected to wave after wave of attacks with bayonet and bomb. They sustained heavy casualties and almost ran out of ammunition. Matthews signalled for reinforcements. It was not until early the next morning that 30,000 rounds of ammunition were sent from the *Sapphire*. But the inexperienced troops were beginning to be alarmed and a young KOSB officer sent a signal asking for help as 'we are cut off, and have no ammunition and also a number of wounded'.The navy immediately sent boats to take them off, unbeknown to Colonel Matthews on the cliff top. He called for supporting fire from the ships, withstood a strong Turkish attack with the bayonet and the Turks, who had also lost heavily, turned tail and fled. But the panic on the beach spread and more messages asking for help were sent to the ships. Eventually Colonel Matthews, seeing that his right-flank trenches were empty, realised what was happening and allowed the re-embarkation to continue. The landing that had started with such promise ended in disaster. At the Dardanelles Commission Enquiry (qv) Colonel Matthews took full responsibility for the withdrawal. It is typical of Sir Ian Hamilton's command style that, seeing the evacuation in progress, he concluded that it 'had been sanctioned by General Hunter-Weston, and that, not knowing the situation, it would be dangerous to interfere' [*Official History*]!

Continue up the ravine.
You will next pass the remains of two earth barricades, as the cliffs on each side diminish, and the stone remains of the old British front line. Just beyond was the Turkish front line.

Avoiding any crops, proceed round the field ahead to the Nuri Zamit Memorial (qv). Return to Gully Beach and pick up the main itinerary or have a car meet you at the Memorial.

Walk back to your transport and continue along the road.

Parallel to the road, to the right, is **X Beach** [see **Historical Summary**]. Here the Turks and the Germans considered the steepness of the cliffs to be a sufficient deterrent to a landing here and there were, consequently, few other defences. Having successfully scaled the cliffs with the support of HMS *Implacable*, the 2nd Royal Fusiliers were to proceed southwards towards W Beach and link up with the Lancashire Fusiliers. This their forward parties did by about 1100 hours. But the Lancashire Fusiliers, whose aim was to attack the heavy defences on Hill 138 and Gozcu Baba Tepe (where the Helles Memorial stands today) became confused about the identification of the three hills in the area. Hill 138 was taken by about 1500 hours, then, believing they were attacking Hill 141, the Lancashires actually moved on Gozcu Baba Tepe and an incorrect message stating that 141 had been taken was despatched to the *Clyde* at 1600 hours. The advance was stopped at nightfall short of Hill 141 by strong Turkish counter-attacks and by the sheer exhaustion of the men. Progress was slow the following day and the link was not made with V Beach until about 1430 hours. Only then could the main thrust towards Achi Baba begin.

Continue along the road.

Parallel to the road beyond X Beach was **Bakery Beach**, so named because the ASC set up a most welcome bakery here on 21 May. In 1915 a road was built under the cliff by Turkish prisoners and Egyptian labourers which joined Gully Beach and Lancashire Landing. Returning along it in June Compton Mackenzie (qv) described the cosmopolitan nature of the road as being 'thronged with promenaders of every kind - tall grave Sikhs, charming dapper little Gurkhas, button-headed Egyptians, Zionist muleteers, Greek hawkers, Scottish Borderers, Irish Fusiliers, Welshmen, men from Lancashire, Hampshire, Essex, and Worcestershire, Cockney Royals, Gunners, Sappers, and as many different types besides.' He remembered 'The laughter and shouting and babble' and that 'Occasionally stretcher-bearers would pass with a man who had been hit, as you may see stretcher-bearers jostle through the crowds at Margate with a woman who had fainted on a torrid August Bank Holiday.' Vivid contemporary eye-witness cameos such as these are the only conduit we have today to the surreal landscape of 1915 Gallipoli.

Continue along the road to

* *Lancashire Landing CWGC Cemetery*/31.1 *kilometres* /15*minutes*/Map H21/OP

Situated on Hill 114, the Karacaoglan (meaning son of Karaja) Ridge, the cemetery was started after the landing of 25 April 1915. Later, Dr William Ewing, the Chaplain of the 4th Royal Scots, laid out the lines of graves in regular rows, surrounding them with a barbed wire fence. Each grave was marked with a little cross and a careful record was kept. A broad trench was dug round the cemetery with a view to planting trees around it, but this work had not been completed before the Evacuation. Dr Ewing also fenced in an old Turkish cemetery that was being destroyed by the traffic passing through.

Headstone of Lance-Sergeant Kenealy, VC, Lancashire Landing CWGC Cemetery

Headstone of Private Bergman, Zion Mule Corps, Lancashire Landing CWGC Cemetery

Rows A to J and part of Row L are of burials made before the Evacuation of January 1916. In Row I are 86 men of the 1st Lancashire Fusiliers who fell in the first two days. The rest of Row L and Row K were made after the Armistice by graves brought from the islands of Imbros and Tenedos, including 45 officers and men from the Monitors *Raglan* and *M28*, sunk by the German Battle Cruisers *Goeben* and *Breslau* on 20 January 1918. There are 1,171 burials from the UK, 27 from Australia, 15 from New Zealand, 2 from Canada, 1 of the Zion Mule Corps, 1 of the local Mule Corps and 17 Greek Labourers. There are 135 unidentified graves and 11 special memorials. The cemetery is enclosed by a stone wall, has a screen of pine trees behind the gently curving wall that incorporates the Cross, with tamarisk and evergreen oaks on the other sides. The flowers here are always spectacularly beautiful in April.

On the right hand gateway pillar are the words: 'The 29th Division landed along the coast on the morning of April 25th, 1915.' Inside the entrance is a plaque which reads: 'Lancashire Landing Cemetery stands on a cliff overlooking the beach on which the 1st Lancashire Fusiliers landed on 25th April. In this operation, carried out under heavy fire through wire entanglements and at great sacrifice, the Regiment was awarded six Victoria Crosses and on that and the following day the Royal Navy was also awarded six Victoria Crosses. The Lancashire Fusiliers and the other battalions of the 88th Brigade went on to storm the cliffs and establish a line on the hills beyond.' One of those Lancashire Fusiliers **VCs, Lance Serjeant William Stephen Kenealy** [or Keneally], age 29, is buried here [C104]. His citation reads: 'On 25th April 1915, three companies, and the Headquarters of the 1st Bn. Lancashire Fusiliers, in effecting a landing on the Gallipoli Peninsula to the West of Cape Helles, were met by a very deadly fire from hidden machine guns which caused a great number of casualties. The survivors, however, rushed up to and cut the wire entanglements, notwithstanding the terrific fire from the enemy, and after overcoming supreme difficulties, the cliffs were gained and the position maintained. Amongst the many very gallant officers and men engaged in this most hazardous undertaking, Captain Willis, Sergeant Richards and Private Kenealy have been selected by their comrades as having performed the most signal acts of bravery and devotion to duty.' Kenealy was killed on 29 June in the Battle of Gully Ravine. Captain (later Major) Willis VC survived the war and died on 9 February 1966 in Cheltenham. Sergeant Richards VC, whose right leg was almost severed by a burst of fire as he reached the beach, but who continued to crawl through the wire, shouting encouragement as he advanced, was evacuated as soon as the beach was secured. One of the battalion's best footballers, his leg was amputated in Egypt a month later. He served in the Home Guard in WW2 and died on 21 May 1953, in Southfields, London, holder of the Long Service and Good Conduct Medal. The other three VCs were Corporal John Elisha Grimshaw, who died on 20 July 1980, in Isleworth, and Major Cuthbert Bromley and Sergeant Frank Edward Stubbs, both commemorated on the Helles Memorial.

There are several Boer War veterans buried here, including **Private Thomas Fay** of the 8th Battalion the Manchester Regiment, died 25 June, who had the Long Service and Good Conduct Medal and who had served in Jamaica, the British West Indies, as well as in the South African Campaign. He was 54 [C 72]. In contrast is **Private Robert Steel** of the 1st/8th Battalion, Lancashire Fusiliers who died on 2 November and whose parents lived in Maine, U.S.A. He was just 16 [H 18]. **Captain Harold Thomas Cawley** of the 6th Battalion Manchester Regiment, killed by a sniper on 23 September, age 37, was the Member of Parliament for Heywood, and second son of Sir Frederick and Lady Cawley. [A 76]. **Sub-Lieutenant Francis Henry James Startin** of Nelson Battalion, RND, died of wounds on 19 July, age 24. The son of Admiral Sir James and Lady Startin, he was Mentioned in Despatches for his action on 13 July in the attack on Kanli Dere when, mortally wounded, he lay for 36 hours in an area swept by Turkish fire, encouraging other wounded and refusing aid until they were rescued [A 53].

Of the Airmen buried here, **Flight Sub-Lieutenant Sidney Arthur Black** of 3rd Wing, RNAS, was killed on Imbros in an accident the night before the Evacuation on 8 January 1916 [K 60]; **Flight Sub-Lieutenant Cecil Horace Brinsmead** of 3rd Wing, RNAS, age 22, was killed 'in aerial combat' [K 67] and **Lieutenant Noel Henry Boles** of 2nd Battalion Dorsetshire Regiment, attd. RNAS, age 23, was killed in action both on 11 January 1916 [K68]. **Flight Commander Charles Herbert Collett**, DSO, 3rd Wing RNAS, age 27, 'Twice Mentioned in Despatches', died of injuries 'received through engine failure when flying a strange machine' on 19 August 1915. He had successfully carried out the first long-distance air raid into enemy territory of the war, when he bombed the Zeppelin sheds at Düsseldorf on 22 September 1914 [K49]. Chaplain Ewing recorded that **Lieutenant Bennett Burleigh**, 'a son of the famous war correspondent, came in, fatally wounded. I buried him in the afternoon' [A 50]. Bennett Burleigh senior, the eccentric correspondent of the *Daily Telegraph*, was shot in the neck by the Dervishes in the Sudan, and was famous for his scoops in the Boer War. Ewing was also upset by the death of **Lance-Sergeant Austin Dent** who, as he was going to bathe, 'was caught by a splinter of shell. He was carried back to the camp, and in spite of the most careful and skilful attention he sank and died the following day. The son of my old friend, Mr. J. M. Dent, the publisher, he was a young man of refined nature and attractive disposition. His untimely death cast a gloom over the Ambulance - the 88th - to which, on volunteering for foreign service, he was attached.' He was 23 [F 96]. Of the 1st Mule Corps was **Driver Abdullah** who died on 2 January 1916 [J 93], and Private Bergman, of the Zion Mule Corps, died 7 June, at age 60 - probably the oldest Allied combatant to die on the Peninsula [B74]. The Corps, numbering 737 men and 750 mules, was raised in Alexandria, with mostly Russian-speaking, educated professionals, refugees expelled from Palestine by the Turks. It was thought to be the first Jewish military unit to be formed in 2,000 years. Under their five British and eight Jewish officers they trained in Egypt and on 7 April Sir Ian Hamilton inspected them just before he left on SS *Arcadian* for the Dardanelles. In his diary, with no heed for political correctness, he recorded, 'I overhauled the Assyrian Jewish Refugee Mule Corps at the Wardian Camp. Their Commander, (Colonel John Patterson), author of the thrilling shocker, "The Man-Eaters of Tsavo", finds Assyrians and mules rather a mouthful and is going to tabloid bipeds and quadrupeds into "The Zion Corps". The mules look very fit; so do the Assyrians and ... they may, in fact, serve as ground bait to entice the big Jew journalists and bankers towards our cause; the former will lend us the colour, the latter the coin. Anyway, so far as I can, I mean to give the chosen people a chance.' When Colonel Patterson was invalided out, the Corps was commanded by an equally colourful character, Joseph Trumpledor, a Trotskyite Russian who lost his left arm in the Russo-Japanese War. In 1914 he attempted to form a Jewish Volunteer unit in Alexandria to fight with the British Army. This unit became the Zion Mule Corps. It landed on Lemnos on 20 April where, under protest, it was divided in two - 300 or so men accompanied 29th Division and the remainder were attached to the ANZACs. Both groups acted with exceptional bravery during their time on the Peninsula: occasionaly they joined, quite unofficially, in assaults. By the end of July the Corps was reduced to half its original strength and Colonel Patterson was sent to Egypt to recruit reinforcements. In December they were down again to five British and 2 Jewish officers and 126 men. When they evacuated the Peninsula in January 1916 the Jews paid tribute to their dead and slashed the throats of their remaining mules (100 of whom had already been killed in action). Having declined to go to Ireland to quell the rebellion, the Corps was disbanded on 26 May 1916. There is a memorial to them at Chatby CWGC Cemetery, Alexandria. Trumpledor persuaded Lord Derby to establish the Jewish Legion which fought with Allenby in Palestine.

With your back to the gate, face the British Memorial at Helles and take that direction as 12 o' clock. At 2 o' clock is the lighthouse. Lancashire Landing ('W' Beach) is at 3 o' clock. At 9 o' clock on the horizon is Achi Baba. Just before 10 o' clock is the white tower of the French Cemetery and just after 10 o' clock is the Turkish Memorial above de Tott's Battery. At 11 o' clock a tall tree to the left of the water tower marks the grave of Lieutenant-Colonel Doughty-Wylie.

Continue to a fork (31.9kms).

W Beach looking towards Tekke Burnu

Extra Visit to Lancashire Landing, W Beach (Map H) Round trip: 2.4 kilometres. Approximate time: 45 minutes.

Until 1995 Lancashire Landing was a military restricted area but is now freely visitable.

Turn sharp right at the fork and drive as far as possible along the track, turning left at the sentry box, then park and walk down the rough track to the beach.

En route a neglected Ottoman cemetery and the concrete remains of the old military camp are passed.

Because the beach was until recently in a forbidden zone, it has been little visited and so retains much of its original character. The low scrub is interspersed with young pines and some spectacular wild flowers as the path descends through a gully to the sandy beach which is bounded by steep cliffs with the Cape Tekke headland running into the sea to the west. The atmosphere on this quiet and secluded beach, with spectacular view towards Achi Baba, X and V Beaches, enables one to time-travel back in a powerful way and to try and comprehend what happened here in 1915.

The Turks had strongly defended what was obviously one of the few feasible landing areas on the Peninsula with broad wire entanglements and a further barbed network under the sea in the shallows. The high ground was fortified with trenches and machine guns were concealed in the cliff, protected from the Allied Naval bombardment.

After the Landings [see *W Beach, Historical Summary*] were established, W Beach became the main British camp area at Helles (the French moving to take over the Seddulbahir area round V Beach). Within 24 hours the beach was filled with all manner of supplies (water, boxes or tins of beef, jam, cheese, vegetables), weapons and ammunition and various forms of transport (horses, mules, bikes, motorbikes, carts, wagons and limbers). Later came hospital tents, field kitchens, roads and telegraph posts and lines, 'bomb-proof' shelters, POW cages and a light railway (constructed at most beach-heads, the railway carriages were mostly horse-drawn). Army Service Corps wagons pelted at speed up and down the road to Krithia, shells bursting around them. Piers to facilitate the bringing in of supplies were built. A breakwater was made from scuttled ships (a forerunner of the 'Gooseberries' in 1944 Normandy). Headquarters were established and the area became a vast, bustling tented city which later spread along the clifftops towards Helles on one side and towards Tekke Burnu on the other. A 'Wireless Station' was established on the heights above the beach; the RE set up a forge. Tractors were landed in pieces and re-assembled. Army Corps Headquarters were set up by Lieutenant-General Sir Aylmer Hunter-Weston on the Helles side of the gully, next door to the aerodrome, in a dugout he called The Baronial Hall. It was not immune from the Turkish shelling and the day after joining in the 18 June Waterloo Centenary dinner on Imbros, Hunter-Weston returned to Lancashire Landing to receive eighty-seven large Turkish shells in thirty-five minutes.

In a vivid evocation, Hamilton called the beach area 'An ant's nest in revolution. Five hundred of our fighting men are running to and fro between the cliffs and sea carrying stones wherewith to improve our pier. On to this pier, picket boats, launches, dinghies, barges, all converging through the heavy swell with shouts and curses, bumps and hair's-breadth escapes. Other swarms of half-naked soldiers are sweating, hauling, unloading, loading, road-marking; dragging mules up the cliff, pushing mules down the cliff; hundreds more are bathing, and through this pandemonium pass the quiet stretchers bearing pale, blood-stained, smiling burdens.'

The Turks soon disrupted the regime that was becoming established by setting up two powerful guns behind Achi Baba ranged on the beach and there

Sunset over Imbros from North Beach

Extra Visit continued

was a scurry to dig in below or in the protection of the cliffs. The beach was also shelled from the Asian side.

W Beach was the main evacuation point for the British and the remnants of the French on 7/8 January 1916 [see *The Evacuation* above].

Geoffrey Dearmer, last survivor of the WW1 poets (he died in 1996 at the age of 103) served with the Royal Fusiliers in Gallipoli from September 1915 to January 1916. He wrote a poem which starts,

From 'W' Beach
The Isle of Imbros, set in turquoise blue
Lies to the westward on the eastern side
The purple hills of Asia fade from view,
And rolling battleships at anchor ride.

Dearmer's younger brother, Christopher, a Lieutenant with the RNAS, was wounded at Suvla and died on 6 October. He is commemorated on the Chatham Naval Memorial and it is thought he was serving with the RNAS Armoured Car Squadron and died either on a hospital ship or in Malta. In July their mother, Mabel, serving with the Ambulance Unit, had died of enteric fever in Serbia.

Return to your transport.

To the right of the road here, though no signs of it remain today, was the emergency **RNAS airstrip** set up after the Landings by Commander Charles ('Sammy') Samson on scrubby but relatively flat land [see *Aerial Activity* above]. *Continue to a a small tree, just before the second track to the left, some 50m before the right-hand turn to the Helles Memorial. Park.*

Extra Visit to Turkish Guns (Map H22) Round trip: Approximately 800 metres. Approximate time: 45 minutes.

Walk along the small and partly overgrown track for approximately 400 metres. At this point the land becomes rough and the path takes a bend to the left. *Walk into the scrubby field ahead and to the right.*

In a patch of thick brambles several guns may be found. The most accessible is in its overgrown emplacement, on its carriage and on its track, made in Nantes

in 1884 by Desbois et Boussechausse. There are three similar guns nearby, but because the undergrowth is so thick they are not easy to find. The intrepid may be rewarded by finding a fifth gun, some 400 metres further on up the track. This is a Krupp with a 9-metre-long barrel also in its own

Turkish gun near Lancashire Landing.
Courtesy of John Price

Extra Visit continued

gunpit. According to Kieran Hegarty, writing in *The Gallipolian*, these guns were spiked by the raiding party of the Royal Marines in March 1915 (qv) and there are photographs of the French guns in the museum at Krithia, taken shortly after the Evacuation in January 1916.

Return to the road.

Continue to the right turn and follow it to the parking area by the large white obelisk.

* Helles Memorial/Hawick Memorial/32.8 kilometres/20 minutes/Map H23 /OP

The site chosen for the main British Memorial on the Peninsula is on the small hill (50 metres above sea level) Gozcu Baba Tepe, because 'It was here that the original British landing was made; it was here that the greatest amount of Turkish territory was occupied; it was from here that the last troops were evacuated,' to quote from the Committee of Selection's Report of June 1921. The 32.9-metre-high obelisk is based on a raised platform enclosed by a low stone wall and is approached by steps. It was designed by Sir John Burnet who sought 'a great rocky cliff' for its site, wished it to be 'simple and even austere ... and be easily seen from vessels passing through the Dardanelles' (as it was mistakenly felt that few pilgrims would ever visit it from the land). It looked over the Dardanelles to the Plain of Troy, scene of the ancient battles that were so awe-inspiring to many of the young men of 1915. General Hunter-Weston, who was the National Battlefields Memorials Committee's Dardanelles adviser, approved of the choice. Although the ANZACs shared in the Helles project, the Australians required their own memorial at Lone Pine, and the New Zealanders (who have no names on this memorial) theirs at Hill 60, Twelve Tree Copse and Chunuk Bair. The memorial has two functions: it is a Battle Memorial, and it is a memorial to the individual dead over whose bodies headstones could not be erected. It is constructed with similar rough-hewn stone to the walls of Troy, quarried at Ilgardere (qv). The stone was shipped to the site, then dressed by stonemasons. On a panel on one face of the obelisk are inscribed the names of the battleships, battle cruisers and cruisers which fought in the Dardanelles, and facing that panel on the low wall opposite are the names of the other vessels which took part in the fighting. On the other three sides of the obelisk are inscribed the Divisions and Brigades which fought on the Peninsula, arranged under the words HELLES, ANZAC and SUVLA, and on the wall opposite each is the detailed composition of these larger units: the GHQ and Lines of Communication units are named on either side of the Suvla units. On the outer face of the surrounding wall, and on the greater part of its inner face, are carved the names of the officers and men from the United Kingdom and India who fell on the Peninsula and whose graves are not known; those of the Australian soldiers who fell at the Second Battle of Krithia and whose graves are not known; and those of the soldiers who were lost or buried in Gallipoli waters. Of these,1,825 officers

The Hawick Memorial

Name of 2nd Lieutenant Hamo Sassoon

CAMPBELL T. C.
COLVER E. W.
REES-MOGG L. L.
WARD W. A. B. K.

SECOND LIEUT.

ALLAN G. M.
BOGLE G. S.
JAMESON H. C.
JOHNSON C. C.
MOSELEY H. G. J.
PRETYMAN M. W.
RAMSEY G. B.
RICHARDSON E. B.
SASSOON H.

COY. QMR. SERJT.

MARYGOLD J.

ROYAL NAVAL VOL. RESERVE
LT. COMMANDER
ANNAND W. M.
GIBSON M. C.

LIEUTENANT
ANDERSON C. C.
BROWN W. H.
COKE HON. A. G.
DUNCAN R.
EDGAR H. J. M.
FERGUSON J. W.
GARNHAM P. C.
HAYES W. F.
HOOD HON. M. H. N.
LOWE F. A.
McINTOSH H. B.
MILLER N. H.
MORGAN W. W.
RAMSEY E. B.
SPENCER-WARWICK J. C.

SUB LIEUTENANT
BAGSHAWE A. G.
BOLTON W.
BOOKLESS J. H.
BROWNE W. D.
CHERRY L. A.
CLIFFORD E. A.
COOKE G. P.
CROWE T. M.
DAVIES J. E.
DICKSON J. M. F.
EDWARDS W. H.

SUB LIEUTENANT
RICHMOND J. A. H.
ROSS G. W.
SMYTH B. C.
STACEY F. W.
V. C. TISDALL A. W. StC.
TREMAYNE J. A. E.
TUCKER L. E.
WEIGHTMAN J.
WHITAKER H. J.

CHIEF P. O.
CHARLES F. G.
McLAUGHLIN T.
SKELTON W.
WALKER R.

PETTY OFFICER
ANDERSON A. W.
BALBIRNIE W.
BIRCH E.
BIRNIE R.
BRIDGER A. G.
CAIRNS R. P.
CARRIER S.
CHRISTIE J.
CRIPPS S. H.
CRONE W. L.
DAVY B. J.
ERRIDGE W. L.
FLEMING E.
HACKNEY C. S.
HORRELL P.
HUGHES E.
HUTCHESON G.

The RNVR Panel, showing the names of
Lieutenant-Commander W.M. Annand and
Sub-Lieutenant Denis Browne

The Helles Memorial

and men were buried at sea from Hospital Ships, 1,048 men fell in four vessels - The *Royal Edward*, torpedoed on 13 August with 861 men from the UK, the *Southland*, torpedoed on 2 September with 15 Australians, the minesweeper *Hythe*, sunk by collision on 28 October with 143 from the UK, and the *Mercian*, attacked by submarine on 3 November with 29 from the UK.

Of all the regiments commemorated on the memorial, the Lancashire Fusiliers with 1,246 names and the Manchester Regiment with 1,086, sustained the heaviest losses. Also inscribed on the Memorial [Panels 42-44] are the names of 167 members of the **1/5th Battalion Norfolk Regiment (the 'Sandringham Company')** (qv), including their commanding officer, **Lieutenant-Colonel Proctor-Beauchamp,** and his nephew, **2nd Lieutenant M.B.G Proctor-Beauchamp,** their Adjutant, **Captain Arthur Edward Martyr Ward, Captain Frank Beck,** the King's Estate Manager, and his nephews **Lieutenant A.E.A. Beck** and **Private L.E. Beck,** who all disappeared on 12 August 1915. Many of the Norfolks' bodies were later discovered near Tekke Tepe and reburied in Azmak Cemetery.

The CWGC Introduction to the Memorial Register ends with the memorable words, 'By the Treaty of Lausanne (qv), the Helles Memorial is established in perpetuity to overlook the land and the seas on which, for three thousand years, Europe and Asia have fought, and on which, twelve years ago, the fiercest conflict of all began and ended. It is in no disparagement of the stubborn and successful valour of the Turks that its inscriptions recall the self-sacrifice of men from Western Europe, from Australia and New Zealand, from Asia and from Africa, who fought under the British flag. It is a memorial to the dead of an unsuccessful but a supremely glorious campaign.'

Inside the Memorial gate is a marble **plaque** to the soldiers from **Hawick** who fell in Gallipoli. It was taken out to the Peninsula during the Pilgrimage organised by the St. Barnabas Association (who had arranged a massive Pilgrimge to Ypres in 1923) on 4 September 1926, and laid on the Memorial to the Missing by Mrs Patrick from Hawick, whose son, **2nd Lieutenant J. B. Patrick** of the 1/4th (Border) Battalion the KOSB [commemorated on Panels 84-89], was reported missing on 12 July 1915. The plaque had been displayed in the window of Messrs G. Sutherland & Sons, sculptors of Hawick, so that relatives and friends could view it before it left for Gallipoli. It was originally intended to be erected at the entrance to Twelve Tree Copse, the nearest cemetery to the action of that day. On 12 July 1988, a plaque was unveiled in Hawick High Street 'In Recognition of the Loyalty of the Members of the Hawick Gallipoli Comrades Association Who Met Here Annually on 12 July to Remember Those Who Fell on That Date in 1915.' On that day over 300 men from the 1/4th (Border) Battalion the KOSBs were killed and 200 were wounded in an action before Achi Baba that became known as 'The Charge'. The losses were so heavy that the battalion never again attained full strength for the duration of the war.

There are four Victoria Cross holders commemorated on the Memorial, all posthumous:

T/Major Cuthbert Bromley, VC, age 36, of the 1st Battalion, Lancashire Fusiliers, one of the six VCs elected for the award by his regiment for gallantry during the landing of 25 April when he was one of the first men to reach the top of the cliff. The Battalion's adjutant, Bromley was a professional soldier, gaining his commission in 1898. He was a popular officer and outstanding sportsman. Although wounded in the back during the landing, he refused to leave the unit until he was again wounded on 28 April and had to be hospitalised. During the Third Battle of Krithia on 4 June he made a gallant attempt to save the wounded lying in no-man's-land. Although a truce was refused, a stretcher party was given permission to go out on the morning of 6 June under the Red Cross flag but a British battery fired unwittingly on them. When the firing ceased, Bromley mounted the parapet and stood fully exposed in front of it. On 13 June he was promoted to Major and became Battalion CO, leading it in the Battle of Gully Ravine on 28 June. He was wounded in the head during the advance but again refused to leave, working through the night to consolidate the Battalion's gains. Eventually evacuated to Egypt, he recovered, but was drowned on 13 August when the troopship *Royal Edward* was torpedoed by the submarine *U14* off the island of Andileousa during his return to the Peninsula [Panel 218].

Sergeant Frank Edward Stubbs, VC, age 27, another of the Lancashire Fusiliers six. His platoon objective on 25 April had been the solitary tree on Hill 114 (see Holts' Map) and he was killed as he reached it. Stubbs enlisted as a boy soldier and served with the Battalion in India [Panel 218].

Captain Gerald Robert O'Sullivan, VC, age 26, of the 1st Battalion, the Royal Inniskilling Fusiliers, who died on 1/2 July (see Gully Ravine entry above) [Panel 97].

Sub-Lieutenant Arthur Walderne St Clair Tisdall, VC, age 26, of the Anson Battalion, RND [Panel 8]. On 25 April, during the landing from the *River Clyde*, Tisdall, who commanded 13th Platoon, hearing wounded men on the beach calling for help, jumped into the water and, pushing a boat in front of him, went to their rescue. He found, however, that he could not manage alone, but with help from other naval personnel, he made four or five trips from the ship to the shore and was responsible for rescuing several wounded men under heavy and accurate fire. Tisdall was shot through the chest whilst standing on the parapet of a trench where he was making his men take temporary cover during the 6 May attack on Achi Baba, and he was buried nearby. His body was subsequently lost. He is also commemorated in St George's Church, Deal, where his father was then Vicar and where an impressive memorial service, with music by the Royal Marines band, was held on 13 May 1915. Tisdall, a Scholar of Trinity College, Cambridge, and Chancellor's Gold Medallist (1913), was born in Bombay in 1890, where his father was a missionary, was educated at Bedford School, where he distinguished himself academically, going up to Trinity in 1909, where he rowed for his college and joined the OTC. Destined for a career in the Civil Service, he became an Able Seaman in the RNVR in May 1914 and went with it to Walmer, near Deal. He took part in the Antwerp Raid and received his commission in the Anson Battalion, RND, on his return on 11 October. Moving to Chatham he met Rupert Brooke, whose work he knew and admired, and was on the *Grantully Castle* en route with him to Gallipoli on 28 February. He was a well-loved young officer, 'All his men cried about him when he went, because all the boys thought the world of him,' wrote his Chaplain,

the Rev. C. Foster, calling him 'The bravest man I ever knew.' On 27 April he had
sent a postcard to his parents which made no reference to his own bravery, 'Have
been under fire and are now ashore; all day spent in burying soldiers. Some of my
men are killed. We are all happy and fit. Plenty of hard work and enemy shells and
a smell of dead men...' His exploits were, however, the subject of letters from 'R.N.
D.S.O.' and 'Surgeon, R.N.' published in *The Times* on 6 and 8 December 1915, the
former maintaining that 'I have never seen more daring and gallant things
performed by any man, naval or military' than the actions that he had witnessed
by what was at the time an unknown officer. Tisdall loved writing poetry, though
sadly all his verses and his diary from his Gallipoli period were lost. In 1911 he
wrote a prophetic poem to the goddesses who inspired 'my maiden aunt' which
ends

> Muse of my aunt, give lightning-fame I pray
> Bright and shortlived; that is my heart's desire:
> I would not weary men of future day;
> O make me not a Homer or Isaiah!

Other names of note on the RND panel are:

Lieutenant-Commander W.M. Annand, father of 2nd Lieutenant Richard
(Dickie) Annand, 2nd Battalion The Durham Light Infantry, the first military VC of
WW2 (15 May 1940), the Adjutant of Collingwood Battalion, was killed in the first
moments of the costly and unsuccessful attack of 4 June on the Turkish third line
on Kereves Dere Ridge [Panel 173].

Sub-Lieutenant W. Denis Browne, Hood Battalion, RND, one of the 'New
Argonauts' (qv) beloved of Eddie Marsh (Churchill's Secretary), was killed in the
same attack. On reaching the enemy trench, Browne jumped in and bayonetted a
Turk. Shot in the shoulder, he bayonetted another Turk before being shot again, this
time the bullet driving his belt buckle into his body. A petty officer bound up his
wounds, but had to retreat as he was under fire, carrying Browne's pocket book
with him, which he gave to Patrick Shaw-Stewart. It contained a message to Eddie
Marsh, 'I've gone now, too. Not too badly, I hope. I'm luckier than Rupert, because
I've fought. But there's no-one to bury me as I buried him, so perhaps he's better
off in the long run.' [Leonard Sellers, *The Hood Battalion.*] His body was never
recovered. Shaw-Stewart wrote to Lady Desborough (mother of the poet Julian
Grenfell), 'I was forced to think very hard about my own battalion, who suffered
cruelly in a charge on a Turkish trench on the Fourth of June, in which out of fifteen
officers left six were killed, including Denis Browne, and five wounded, leaving me
and only three others now. I was filled with disgust and rage at the crushing folly
of it for a time.' A friend of Rupert Brooke's from Rugby days, then at Cambridge,
Browne had trained under the musician Busoni in Berlin, was a talented composer
and when the war broke out was organist at Guy's Hospital. Through his
association with Marsh, he was commissioned in the RND in September 1914 and
took part in the Antwerp Raid in October. He transferred to the Hood Battalion in
December 1914, sailed with the Battalion on the *Grantully Castle* and during the
voyage often attempted to get the rather unwilling stokers to sing folk songs,
which he accompanied. When Rupert Brooke was suffering from dysentery in

Egypt at the beginning of April, he wrote a down-to-earth ballad for Browne to set to music,

My first was in the night at one;
At half past five, I had to run.
At 8.15 I fairly flew;
At noon a swift compulsion grew.
I ran a dead-heat all the way;
I lost by yards at ten to two.
This is the seventh time today...

Denis Browne was with Rupert Brooke when he died and was part of his burial party on Skyros. He took part in the attack of 6 May, a sniper's bullet passing through his coat collar, slightly injuring his neck. He convalesced from the wound in Egypt, leaving for the Peninsula at the end of May, arriving in time for the fatal battle of 4 June [Panels 8-15].

Able Seaman T. Houghton of the Hood Battalion was killed in the 5/6 May attack on Achi Baba when he crawled forward to help a wounded comrade, Yates. 'While comforting him', wrote Joseph Murray of the Battalion, 'he was shot through the head.... Poor Houghton died crying for his mother. He said he was 17, but if he was 16 he would be lucky. Totally unsuited for this rough life, he never once complained. Always willing and eager to help, he himself was now beyond help' [8-15].

Sub-Lieutenant Oscar Freyberg (qv), Hood Battalion, killed on 4 June, the brother of Bernard Freyberg, VC, (qv) [Panels 8-15].

2nd Lieutenant Hamo Sassoon, RGA, the brother of the poet Siegfried Sassoon was working with Thorneycroft, the family business, in Argentina when war broke out, but he returned to enlist in May 1915. In August 1915 he was gazetted a 2nd Lieutenant and sent to Gallipoli. In late October he was wounded and died on a hospital ship on 1 November. He was buried at sea. Siegfried was distraught at his brother's death and wrote the poem,

To My Brother
Give me your hand, my brother, search my face;
Look in these eyes lest I should think of shame;
For we have made an end of all things base.
We are returning by the road we came.

Your lot is with the hosts of soldiers dead,
And I am in the field where men must fight.
But in the gloom I see your laurell'd head
And through your victory I shall win the light.

Siegfried Sassoon, 18 December 1915.

It is also thought that Hamo was the model for Stephen Colwood in *Memoirs of a Fox-Hunting Man*, and whose death, 'killed in action', hit the narrator, George Sherston (Siegfried) hard [Panel 325].

Two senior officers are commemorated on Panel 16: **Brigadier-General Henry Napier** (qv), age 53, commanding 88th Brigade, killed on 25 April during the landing at V Beach. Napier, his staff and a few soldiers were the only men to come ashore in the small number of watertight boats. Officers on the *Clyde* yelled at them that it would be impossible to land from the boats but Napier shouted, 'I'll have a damned good try' before he and most of the others in the boats were killed. **Brigadier-General Anthony Baldwin** (qv), age 51, commanding 38th Brigade, was killed on 10 August at The Farm in the assault on the Sari Bair Ridge. In the same attack was **Lieutenant J. W. J. Le Marchand** (qv) of the 56th Rifles Indian Army (Gurkhas), killed on 9 August [Panels 269-272].

One of the last senior officers to be killed on the Peninsula - in the final Turkish attack on Gully Spur of 7 January 1916 - was **Lieutenant-Colonel Hercules Frank Walker** (qv), age 46, commanding the 7th Battalion N Staffs [Panels 170/171].

Private Thomas Davis of the 1st R Munster Fusiliers, executed at Gully Beach on 2 July, is commemorated on the Addenda Panel.

Looking for a name on the Memorial is like looking for a needle in a haystack unless the panel location of the name is known. It is therefore essential if you are looking for a particular individual to obtain the location from the Commonwealth War Graves Commission (see below for contact numbers in the UK, Australia, New Zealand and Canakkale) before you arrive, as, apart from the days of official ceremonies, the registers are not available at the Memorial. As an elementary aid, a plan of the Memorial and the panel numbers of the various regiments as listed in the register are given below.

UNITED KINGDOM UNITS
Army Cyclist Corps 199
Argyll & Sutherland Highlanders 183,184
Ayrshire Yeomanry (Earl of Carrick's Own) 16
Bedfordshire Regiment 54/At Sea 218
Berkshire Yeomanry 18, 19
Black Watch. The (Royal Highlanders) 144
Border Regiment 119-125/At Sea 222, 223
Cameron Highlanders, Queen's Own 177
Cameronians, The (Scottish Rifles) 92-97
1st Reserve Regiment of Cavalry at Sea 325
Cheshire Regiment 75-77
City of London Yeomanry 20
Commands and Staff 16
Connaught Rangers 181-183
2nd/3rd County of London Yeomanry (Westminster
    Dragoons) 19
Derbyshire Yeomanry 17
Dorsetshire Regiment 136-139
5th Dragoon Guards (Princess Charlotte of Wales's) 16
Duke of Cornwall's Light Infantry 117
Durham Light Infantry 173
East Kent Regiment (The Buffs) 113-117
East Lancashire Regiment 113-117
East Surrey Regiment 117
East Yorkshire Regiment 51-54
Essex Regiment 144-150/At Sea 229-233
Fife and Forfar Yeomanry 20
General List 201
Glasgow Yeomanry (Queen's Own Royal) 19
Gloucestershire Regiment 101-104
Hampshire Regiment 125-134/At Sea 223-226, 228-229, 328

CSM Bernard Steven, 1/Essex, killed in the Third Battle of Krithia, 4 June 1915. Courtesy of his grandson, Derek Pheasant

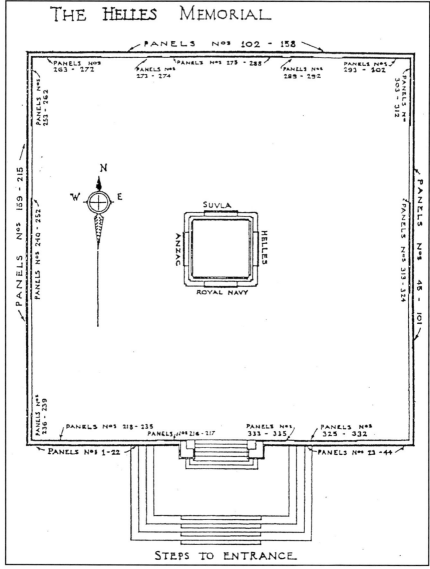

THE HELLES MEMORIAL

PANELS N°S 102 - 158

PANELS N°S 263 - 272

PANELS N°S 273 - 274

PANELS N°S 275 - 288

PANELS N°S 289 - 292

PANELS N°S 293 - 302

PANELS N° 303 - 312

PANELS N°S 253 - 262

PANELS N°S 159 - 215

PANELS N°S 240 - 252

N
W · E

SUVLA

ANZAC

HELLES

ROYAL NAVY

PANELS N°S 313 - 324

PANELS N°S 45 - 101

PANELS N°S 236 - 239

PANELS N°S 218 - 235

PANELS N°S 216 - 217

PANELS N°S 333 - 315

PANELS N°S 325 - 332

PANELS N°S 1-22

PANELS N°S 23 - 44

STEPS TO ENTRANCE

Herefordshire Regiment 198
Hertfordshire Regiment 18
Highland Light Infantry 173-177
King's Own Royal Lancaster Regiment 31-32
King's Own Scottish Borderers 84-92/At Sea 220-222
Kings, The (Liverpool) Regiment 42
King's Royal Rifle Corps 156
King's Shropshire Light Infantry155
Lanarkshire Yeomanry, The 16
Lancashire Fusiliers 58-72/At Sea 218-219
Leicestershire Regiment 54
Leinster Regiment, Prince of Wales's (Royal Canadians) 184-185

Lincolnshire Regiment 44-46/At Sea 331
London Regiment (Royal Fusiliers) 1st, 2nd, 3rd, 4th
 Battalions 196
 10th Battalion (Hackney) 196-197
 11th Battalion (Finsbury Rifles) 197-198
Lovat's Scouts 20
Loyal North Lancashire Regiment 152-154
Manchester Regiment 158-170
Middlesex Regiment (Duke of Cambridge's Own) 155-156
Middlesex Yeomanry 19
Military Police Corps 200/At Sea 330
Norfolk Regiment 42-44

Continue downhill following signs to V Beach CWGC Cemetery/Yahya Cavus Sehitligi.

Fort Ertugrul: Ramparts and gun, with the Asian shore beyond

Grave of Private Halil

12/26th Regiment Symbolic Cemetery

Statue of Sergeant Yahya and recreated trenches

View over V Beach from Fort Ertugrul with gun emplacements in foreground, V Beach CWGC Cemetery, Seddulbahir village and old Castle. The water tower on the left marks the area of Doughty-Wylie's grave

View along V Beach showing the cemetery entrance, the Helles Memorial and the lighthouse

*Ertugrul Fort No 1/Gun Emplacements/Grave of Private (Er) Halil Ibrahim/Sergeant Yahya, 12/26th Regiment Cemetery and Memorial/ Recreated Trenches/33.1 kilometres/10 minutes/ Map H25,24,26, 27 /OP

The fort was built by Asaf Pasa during the reign of Sultan Abdulhamit II in the 1890s. Like the Rumeli Ramparts at Kilitbahir, the stone structures of the fort are half-submerged in the ground and covered by earth. They comprise three ammunition bunkers, between which are two Krupp 24cm artillery pieces, dated 1883.

To the right is the grave of Private Halil Ibrahim who was killed by the allied bombardment on the fort. On the edge of the cliff are gun emplacements and earthworks and 50 metres further on and to the left is a group of sculptures showing Sergeant Yahya and his comrades charging over V Beach. When his company commander, Lieutenant Abdurrahim, was killed, the Sergeant and sixty-seven Privates of the 10th Company, 3/26th Regiment, charged the 1st Royal Dublin Fusiliers, the 1st Royal Munster Fusiliers and the 2nd Hampshires as they landed on V Beach from the *River Clyde* in the early morning of 25 April 1915. They held on until reinforced late in the day by two battalions, including one from the 2/26th Regiment. Marble plaques describe the company's heroic feats. Behind is a symbolic cemetery and there are recreated trenches around the area. The memorial, which was originally built in 1962 by the 'Society to Assist the Memorials of the Canakkale Martyrs', was renovated in 1992 by the Turkish Ministry of Culture.

From the cliff top there is a magnificent view over V Beach Cemetery, with two gun emplacements in the ground before it, one of which still has its gun, and the Seddulbahir Fort beyond. The *River Clyde* was beached by the second outcrop of rocks that can still be seen in the bay.

The SS River Clyde

The idea of constructing a modern version of the Trojan Wooden Horse to run men ashore in comparative safety, and thereby to double the number who could be landed in the first wave, was that of Commander Unwin (qv). He

The SS River Clyde on V Beach. IWM Q.13,319

View from the SS River Clyde showing the French Depot at Seddulbahir. IWM Q.13859

chose the innocent-looking ten-year-old collier, the *River Clyde*. She carried two thousand men who were to emerge from 'sally ports' - holes cut into her side - and then run down gangways to a bridge of lighters. They in turn were linked to the shore by a steam hopper. Wemyss supported Unwin's idea and the various Staffs involved agreed to the plan.

The *Clyde* remained in situ in use as an ammunition store, shelter, field dressing facility, breakwater and pier throughout the duration of the campaign, its condensers supplying fresh water. The French incorporated it into the dock they constructed here and the Turkish guns on the Asian coast used it to register their aim on W Beach.

In June 1919 the historic old ship was refloated by a salvage company and taken to Malta. Under the names *Maruja* and then *Aurora* (she was resold at least twice to Spanish shipping companies) she plied the Mediterranean until she was sold for scrap in March 1966 and was broken up in Aviles in Spain.

This ignominious end to her career greatly upset Compton Mackenzie (qv). On hearing the news, he recalled seeing her as he scrambled up the cliff at V Beach in May 1915 in search of a supposed rare orchid, passing four dead horses whose stench 'would have made even a bomb bounce back from it like a tennis ball'. He mused on her past 'when she has steamed past Sedd-el-Bahr, carrying coals for her Greek owner up the Dardanelles to Constantinople, she who once anchored off here with a cargo of heroes, they too bound for Constantinople. But they sold her, and I would that the man who signed the

Orchids at Helles, as searched for by Compton Mackenzie in May 1915

order might carry in his nose till death the stench of those four horses.'

The anecdote illustrates two aspects of the campaign: the high awareness of many of the men of the beauty of the flora that surrounded them and, in contrast, the appalling smell of death - human and animal - that perpetually hung over the Peninsula.

The old French battleship *Massena* was sunk and attached to a transport to form the northern arm of the breakwater here.

The story of the landing here is told in the **V Beach** section, *Historical Summary.*

In this area was **11th Casualty Clearing Station** (CCS), to which the Chaplain Dr. Ewing (qv) was assigned in May. The tented hospital wards formed three sides of a square, with administrative offices in the middle. In *From Gallipoli to Baghdad,* he wrote, 'The C.C.S. is one link in the chain of agencies by which the men wounded or fallen sick at the front find their way to the great hospitals at the base. To the wounded soldier, wherever possible, first aid is rendered by his comrades, using the field dressing which is part of every man's equipment. If unable to walk, he is carried to the spot where the regimental MO waits to give such further assistance as may be necessary and practicable before he is taken down the lines to the Dressing Station. This is an outpost of the Field Ambulance. The MOs in charge see that dressings, bandages, etc., are in order, take any emergency measures called for, and forward the patient by ambulance waggon or car to the Field Ambulance. The regulation establishment provides three Field Ambulances to each Division. Here is accommodation for considerable numbers. Those who are but slightly wounded who will soon be fit for duty again, may not need to go farther. Those whose injuries are dangerous may be kept for a time until, if they survive, it is safe to move them. Others are sent on to the CCS where they are once more carefully examined, dressings are approved or renewed, operations are performed where these have become urgently necessary, and patients are assigned to different wards according to the degree or kind of their injuries or sickness. Provision is made to keep for a time those whom it would be dangerous to move, and such as may be able for light duty, although unfit for full work. The others are put on the way as soon as possible for the more distant base hospitals, which are equipped with every convenience to secure the comfort and proper treatment of the men. Those who are specially fortunate may even make a voyage to dear old "Blighty" itself.'

Also serving with No 11 CCS was the young Edgar Banner of the RAMC who would go on to found the Gallipoli Association (qv).

Continue down the track, which, unless very wet, should be driveable, to

* V Beach/Site of River Clyde/V Beach CWGC Cemetery/33.5 kilometres/15 minutes/RWC/Map H28

This beautiful cemetery is planted with tamarisk bushes, Japanese laurels and rosemary. Behind the white screen and Cross, in front of which is the Stone of Remembrance, is a dark row of trees. The cemetery was started on the first day of the landings and burials ended in May when there were two long graves at the head of which a painted board commemorated: *'Gallant dead of the Munsters and others'.* It now contains 480 unmarked graves. After the Armistice the graves were concentrated in Row O. There are fifteen rows of headstones, only twenty of which are named. A further 196 men are marked with special memorials, arranged in semi-circles facing the Cross and in four rows to the left of the entrance.

In early May 1915 Compton Mackenzie (qv) visited V Beach and 'knelt for a few moments by those two long graves'. Among the named burials is **Captain Garth Neville Walford**, VC, Royal Artillery, age 32 [O 1]. His citation reads, 'On 26th April, 1915, subsequent to a landing having been effected on the beach at a point on the Gallipoli Peninsula, during which both Brigadier-General and Brigade-Major had been killed, Lieutenant-Colonel Doughty-Wylie (qv) and Captain Walford organised and led an attack through and on both sides of the village of Seddulbahir on the Old Castle at the top of the hill inland. The enemy's position was very strongly held and entrenched, and defended with concealed machine-guns and pom-poms. It was mainly due to the initiative, skill and great gallantry of these two Officers that the attack was a complete success. Both were killed in the moment of victory.' After graduating from Balliol College, Oxford, Walford, never strong nor interested in sport, joined the RA in 1902. At Staff College when war broke out, he fought at Mons and on the Aisne, being evacuated sick at the end of September. Promoted to Captain on 30 October, he served at Ypres and in January 1915 was recalled to take up the appointment of Brigade-Major RA with the newly formed 29th Division. Like so many of his contemporaries, conscious of the historical significance of the area, he wrote a poem, *The Last Crusade*, which began

> Once more revives the never-dying war
> Of East and West: through this one entry gate
> Between two worlds have armies alternate
> Swept forth to conquest on an alien shore.

On 21 April he wrote home, 'Well we are off in a day or two if the weather stays fine: just like the Greek fleet going to Troy, people collected from all over the known world; we have even got our wooden horse [the *River Clyde*]. Walford is also commemorated in Chagford Church, Devon, and in the Regent Hotel, Royal Leamington Spa, his base in early 1915.

CSM David Danagher of the 1st Munsters a Boer War veteran, age 37, is in A 32. **The Rev William Finn**, Chaplain to the Forces, 4th Class, Catholic Padre of the 1st RDF was the first Chaplain of the war to be killed, ironically on a Sunday [F 4]. Though badly wounded himself during the landing of 25 April, he attended to other wounded before collapsing. Also killed was the commanding officer of the RDF, **Lieutenant-Colonel Richard Rooth**, age 49, [F 4].

Other Victoria Crosses won here on that bloody day of 25 April were:

Commander Edward Unwin of HMS *River Clyde* who 'left the ship and under murderous fire attempted, with the help of four other men* to get the lighters into position. He worked until, suffering from the effects of cold and immersion, he was obliged to return to the ship for treatment. He then went back to his work against the doctor's orders and completed it. He was later attended by the doctor for three wounds, but once more left the ship, this time in a life-boat and rescued three men, wounded, in the shallow water. He continued at this heroic labour under continuous fire, until forced to stop through pure physical exhaustion.' Unwin, a 51-year-old former Merchant Navy Officer, was brought out of retirement in 1914. An extraordinarily strong character, his leadership was selfless and inspirational on the day of the landings and throughout the campaign. He was the last man to leave Suvla on 20 December, and as his crowded lighter neared the troop ship a man fell overboard. Unwin immediately dived overboard to rescue him. Admiral Wemyss recommended him for the Royal Humane Society Medal. This was not awarded, but Unwin was later created CB and CMG and received the Order of the Nile. He died in Grayshott in 1950.

* **Midshipman George Leslie Drewry** 'assisted the commander of the ship at the work of securing the lighters under a very heavy rifle and Maxim fire. He was wounded in the head, but continued his work and twice subsequently attempted to swim from lighter to lighter with a line.' The 20-year-old Drewry had been hand-picked by Unwin to serve under him on the *Clyde* and more than fulfilled all his Commander's expectations. He survived the Gallipoli Campaign only to be killed accidentally in Scapa Flow on 3 August 1918.

* **Midshipman Wilfred St Aubyn Malleson** also helped Unwin to secure the lighters under heavy fire. 'When the other midshipman with the party had failed, through sheer exhaustion, to get a line from lighter to lighter, Midshipman Malleson swam with it himself and succeeded. The line subsequently broke and he afterwards made two further unsuccessful attempts at his self-imposed task.' At 19, Malleson was the youngest recipient of the Victoria Cross at Gallipoli. He served on HMS *Cornwallis* which survived the naval assault of 18 March and was assigned to cover the landings at S Beach. Malleson was one of a party from her detailed to ferry troops ashore at V Beach on 25 April. Miraculously he survived, completely unwounded, the curtain of fire under which his act of gallantry was performed. It left him exhausted, however, and he contracted rheumatic fever and was evacuated to Malta. His brother, 15-year-old Rupert, was serving as a Midshipman on the *Lord Nelson* in support at Gallipoli. Malleson went on to serve in WW2, first as a Commander at Devonport. Retired in 1941, he was then appointed Assistant Captain of Malta Dockyard. After the war he became King's Harbour Master and died in 1975, the oldest survivor of the V Beach VCs.

* **Seaman George McKenzie Samson** also assisted in securing the lighters. 'He worked all day under very heavy fire, attending wounded and getting out lines. He was eventually dangerously wounded by Maxim fire.' Samson was working on a railroad in Smyrna when war broke out. He left Turkey, sailed to Malta, joined HMS *Hussar* and was thence detailed to the *River Clyde*. He was the most injured of the V Beach VCs,

receiving seventeen separate injuries. He was evacuated to Egypt and then to England, still with thirteen pieces of shrapnel in his body. Like Sergeant Dwyer, the young Western Front VC, Samson was used in the recruiting drive. He recovered sufficiently after the war to join the Merchant Navy and on 23 February 1923, was taken ill off Bermuda. He died in hospital there and was buried with full military honours in the military cemetery.

Commander Unwin and Midshipman Drewry were treated by the indefatigable Surgeon P. Burrowes Kelly on the *Clyde* which acted as a collecting and dressing station. Though wounded, he remained on duty until the 27th, during which time he attended 750 men. He received the DSO [*Official History*].

Buried in the cemetery are the brothers **Privates John**, age 19, and **Samuel**, age 21, **Mallaghan** of the 1st RDF, both killed on 25 April (Sp Mems 46 and 47). Until 1998, when a descendant visited their graves and pointed out the error, both brothers were recorded as being 19, but the CWGC will alter Samuel's headstone to read 'age 21'.

*Able Seaman William Charles Williams, whilst helping to secure the lighters, 'held on to a line in the water for over an hour under heavy fire until killed.' The first member of the Royal Navy to be awarded a posthumous VC in the War, Williams joined the Boys' Service of the RN in 1895, aged 15. He served in the Boer War and the Boxer Rebellion and was recalled to active service in August 1914 and, like Samson, served on HMS *Hussar* under Commander Unwin. He worked closely with his Commander as he attempted to secure the lighters and, after being mortally wounded by a shell, died in his arms. Unwin described him as 'the man above all others who deserved the VC at the landing'. He is commemorated on the Naval Memorial at Portsmouth and by a gun from a German submarine presented in his memory by King George V which stands in the centre of Chepstow.

The bare words of the citations in the *London Gazette,* quoted above, give little impression of the enormity of the acts which won these men their country's most prestigious gallantry award. They worked in a fury of desperation and determination to fulfil their impossible tasks, enraged, distraught and superhumanly strengthened at seeing comrades slaughtered at their sides.

V Beach was one of the three embarkation beaches for the 8/9 January 1916 Evacuation (see above). A total of 7,606 men, 1,611 on the last trip alone, were taken off from here. Among the last to go were the RND, and Patrick Shaw-Stewart (qv) of the Hood Battalion described passing the afternoon with the last Frenchman on the Peninsula, the French artillery commander, on the beach, making small bonfires: 'I have burnt a nice suit of khaki drill, a bowler hat, and about twenty books, resolved not to leave the Turks even any intellectual pabulum.' Though 'almost sorry to leave Seddul Bahr... it's nothing to be proud of for the British Army or the French either - nine months here, and pretty heavy losses, and now nothing for it but to clear out.'

Beyond the cemetery is the **Mocamp Seddulbar, open for refreshments/WC in the season.**

Drive past the Motel along the beach track and continue round the walls of the fort. Turn right at the track crossroads at the end of the wall and continue to the Turkish memorial, signed Ilk Sehitler Aniti.

Headstones of the Mallaghan Brothers, V Beach CWGC Cemtery

First Martyrs' Memorial

Grave of George Samson, VC, in Bermuda

Detail of Memorial

The Camber

Cephanlik Cemetery, Seddulbahir Fort

View to Helles Memorial from within
Seddulbahir Fort.

* Seddulbahir/Ruins of Old Castle/Guns/First Martyrs (Ilk Sehitler) Memorial/Seddulbahir Magazine (Cephanlik) Cemetery/34 kilometres/10 minutes/Map H29,30,32,31

The memorial resembles a symbolic castle with stone bastions. A plaque describes the first British-French Naval attack by six cruisers at a range of 16,000 yards on Seddulbahir and Kumkale Forts on 3 November 1914, which did more damage to the castle than any subsequent attacks. One explosion killed five officers and eighty-one men when a shell detonated the magazine. A memorial, surmounted by a shell, was first erected here in 1915 but was destroyed during the subsequent fighting. The present memorial was erected in 1986.

Walk to the edge of the memorial grassed area and look down to the sea.

Immediately below, attached to the north-east wall of the castle, by the road which leads to a small jetty, is the **Seddulbahir Magazine (Cephanlik) Cemetery**. On the cemetery wall are inscribed the names of the five officers killed by Allied bombardment on 3 November 1914, the first Turkish martyrs to be killed in the Dardanelles Campaign: Captain Sevki, fort Commander; 1st Lieutenant Cevdet, Deputy Commander; 1st Lieutenant Hasan Pala, 1st Lieutenant Riza and 1st Lieutenant Esref, Squad Commanders, and eighty-one Privates. Adjacent to the cemetery is an historic fountain. The small harbour below, with a small jetty, is on the site of **The Camber**. It was the scene of several raids by the Royal Marines in February and March 1915. Between 27 February and 3 March they put thirty guns out of action. On 4 March, meeting fierce resistance, they withdrew under cover of fire from the *Majestic*, which in mid-May became the third capital ship to be sunk in a fortnight (see entries for *Triumph* and *Goliath*). She was the second major victim of Commander Otto Hersing in the German U21 (qv). His torpedo penetrated the battleship's protective screen and scored a mortal hit. Sailors leaped off the sinking ship as nearby boats rushed to pick them up. She went down with forty-nine men still on board, her keel protruding above the water as a dreadful reminder to the soldiers struggling to survive on shore. During the great storm of 17-18 November she finally submerged and today lies off W Beach (see Holts' Map) and is accessible to the adventurous diver.

Walk down into the ruined shell of the fort.

Within the fort are some **gun remains (Map H30)**

The fort, with its commanding views over the entrance to the Dardanelles, was built of roughly-dressed stone veneer and rubble stone walls infilled with earth in 1659 by Grand Vizier Koprulu Mehmet Pasa's military architect, Mustafa Aga. By 1827 there were seventy guns and four mortars in the fort and in 1915 it contained ten guns, including two 28cm Krupps, and a powerful searchlight. On 19 February 1915 the fort was badly damaged by Allied bombardment and naval raids and by 18 March its threat to the Allied naval attack was much reduced.

On 25 April a Maxim machine gun and snipers hidden in the rubble caused much damage to the Allies landing from the *River Clyde*. Captured the following day, it was then occupied by the French and here General d'Amade had his headquarters. Hamilton called it 'the noisiest spot on God's earth' as the French battery of the famous 75s blazed away nearby. On an energetic visit on 30 April to the French lines - 'Had a real good sweat. Must have walked at least a dozen miles' - he commented, 'The French trenches are not as good as ours by a long chalk, and bullets keep coming through the joints of the badly built sandbag revetment.' With d'Amade was Capitaine Reginald Kahn, who had fought with Hamilton in Manchuria and with the Boers in S. Africa and who was detailed to write the French *Official History of the Dardanelles Campaign*. The fort was also used by the French as a hospital and for ceremonial decorations: 'Hollow square: rolling drums: bayonets flashing in the moonlight: the Legion pinned on the warrior's breast and kisses pinned on his cheeks by his General's prickly moustache' [Mackenzie].

To the west of the fort are the ruins of the old Ottoman baths.

In his superb account, *Gallipoli*, written in 1965, Rhodes James was still able to report that 'Near Sedd-el-Bahr a light railway, complete with trucks built in Birmingham, is piled into a hollow.' [Sir Robert Rhodes James died in May 1999.]

Return to the junction, turn right towards the Mosque and continue to the junction by the bust of Kemal Ataturk.

The village of Seddulbahir was first settled by the soldiers and masons who built the fort c1659. The name means 'Barrier of the Sea'. The local inhabitants were evacuated in 1915 and never returned. The site remained uninhabited until 1934 when over the next four years Rumanian settlers moved in and rebuilt the village. Apart from Eceabat it has the most tourist facilities on the Peninsula, with six bed and breakfast establishments as well as the motel and camping site. Further development is currently prohibited as it is an area of historical conservation - a source of discontent to the local population.

Turn left uphill to the two cypress trees on the crest to the right.

[Just before is a sign to the right to the Pansiyon Helles Panorama - see **Tourist Information** below.]

* Grave of Lieutenant-Colonel Charles Hotham Montagu Doughty-Wylie, VC, CB, CMG/34.8 kilometres/5 minutes/Map H33

This is on Hill 141, the site of Eskitabya, the Old Fort, at the top of the hill now called Doughty-Wylie Hill or Fort. A standard CWGC marker surmounts the flat tomb. Doughty-Wylie is the most senior recipient of the Victoria Cross on the Peninsula and probably the most famous. His citation in the *London Gazette* is identical to Walford's. 'Dick' Doughty-Wylie was a fascinating personality and had achieved much and was well-known before the war. A career soldier, he had served in the Egyptian Army, in China and in South and East Africa. He had a long association with Turkey and in 1907 was the British Military Consul in Konya. There he and his devoted wife, Lilian, met the extraordinary Gertrude Bell - intellectual, intrepid explorer, mountaineer, archeologist, linguist, writer, orientalist and, later in the War, intelligence officer - and formed a relationship with her. In April 1909 he had halted the massacre of Armenian Christians in Adana by riding at the head of 50 Turkish soldiers and restoring order, despite being shot in the arm. For his cool bravery he was awarded the CMG. During the Balkan Wars of 1912-3 Doughty-Wylie commanded a Red Cross Unit serving with the Turks and was awarded the Imperial Ottoman Order of Medjidieh, 2nd Class, for his work. In February 1915 he was promoted

Grave of Doughty-Wylie, VC,
with photo of Gertrude Bell

Lieutenant-Colonel and, because of his great knowledge and understanding of the Turks, removed from his consulate at Addis Ababa and employed by Hamilton as an Intelligence Officer. On 24 March Hamilton sent him to Athens 'to do "Intelligence"' and on 25 April 1915, he was on board the *River Clyde*, acting as Liaison Officer.

The landing of 25 April had ended in chaos with hundreds of men lying on the beach in the shadow of Turkish fire, apparently leaderless. During the night Captain Walford arrived with a message from General Hunter-Weston ordering the advance to continue. Doughty-Wylie had already visited the beach and discussed the idea of another attack with Major Beckwith of the 2nd Hampshires. It was now decided that Beckwith would assault to the right and clear the fort and village, the Dubsters (qv) under Lieutenant-Colonel Weir de Lancy Williams, a member of Hamilton's staff, would move left in an attempt to join up with support from W Beach, and another force later to be led by Captain G. D. Stoney, the military landing officer, would drive through the centre to take the entrenched Turkish position on Hill 141. Following a bombardment from *HMS Albion*, Major Beckwith and Captain Walford led the assault on the fort. Beckwith appears to have cleared the Fort promptly and Walford drove on into the village via a small gateway in the walls (it is still there, just below the Turkish memorial) running into determined opposition and hand-to-hand fighting in the narrow streets and small houses. About 0845 a report arrived on the *River Clyde* from Walford stating that he was unsupported on his left and that he was making little progress. Doughty-Wylie determined that something must be done and went ashore with Captain Stoney moving, apparently unconcerned, up to the fort, despite having his hat shot off his head. Walford, the driving force of the attack on the village, had been killed leading yet another group forward, and Doughty-Wylie continued on into the village leading the struggle from house to house until, shortly after midday, the village was cleared. The central force, meanwhile, had not moved and knowing that, even though the fort and village had been taken, the beach would not be secure until Hill 141 was taken, Doughty-Wylie arranged a naval bombardment on the Hill and led a co-ordinated bayonet charge from the centre of the village on the Turkish position - a redoubt guarded by a 20ft-deep moat and barbed wire. The cheering, charging soldiers won the position in minutes, but Doughty-Wylie, the inspiration for the victorious assault, standing on the edge of the moat, was shot in the head and killed. He was buried on the spot shortly afterwards by Colonel Williams.

Doughty-Wylie had continued his liaison with Gertrude Bell. They had spent some time together in 1913 and then exchanged love letters (which were published after Lilian Doughty-Wylie's death). Their last meeting was in London in February 1915 when Doughty-Wylie was en route for Gallipoli. The letters show the guilt the lovers felt and also Doughty-Wylie's premonition of his death. There is an extraordinary legend that in November 1915 a mysterious woman visited Doughty-Wylie's grave and placed upon it a wreath of flowers. Gertrude Bell was sent to Egypt that month to work with T.E. Lawrence in the Arab Bureau, as her knowledge of desert tribes was considered of value so she was within reach. Lilian Doughty-Wylie was serving with a hospital unit in St Valéry-sur-Somme when she learned of his death, but later moved to Tenedos to work with the Red Cross so she was also within reach. Both women were devastated by the death of the man they loved. Both had vowed to commit suicide if he should be killed. Gertrude Bell never married and in 1926 died from an overdose of sleeping pills. Lilian Doughty-Wylie lived on until 1960. Chaplain Ewing (qv) wrote that 'Two ladies...did land [on the Peninsula] - one by special permission to visit her husband's grave', giving credence to the fact that it was Lilian who visited Doughty-Wylie, but in all probability we shall never know the truth of the matter.

'The death of a hero strips victory of her wings. Alas, for Doughty-Wylie!... Doughty-Wylie was no flash-in-the-pan VC winner. He was a steadfast hero. Now as he would have wished to die, so he died,' wrote Hamilton. 'Killed like Wolfe in the moment of victory,' wrote Winston Churchill. The hero's fame spread. His deeds were heralded in the press; the King wrote to his widow when she was sent his Victoria Cross; his is the only lone marked Allied grave to remain on the Peninsula, so respected was he by the Turks for whom he, too, had so much affection that he led his charge against them unarmed, carrying only a stick.

Turn round and return to the junction. Turn left, continue to the fork and follow signs to the right to the Canakkale Sehitligi. After 500m, there is a junction to the left opposite a water fountain, signed to the Kereves Dere.

Extra Visit to probable site of Zimmerman's Farm and French Memorial (Map H18) Round trip: 1.8 kilometres. Approximate time: 25 minutes.

Take the left turn signed to Kereves Dere. The Deres run down from the heights of Achi Baba and, apart from Gully Ravine (Saghir or Zigin Dere to the Turks) which is in places over 30 metres deep, they are in general about 6 metres deep. The others are Kirte Dere (Krithia Nullah), Kanli Dere (Achi Baba Nullah) and, in the east, Kereves Dere, which runs directly into the Dardanelles and which to a first approximation formed the eastern boundary of the French forces.

Continue until you come to a No Entry sign on the right (600 metres). This leads to the top of the French Cemetery (see below). Take the track on the left that enters the wood (driveable if not too wet).

Remains of French Memorial near Zimmerman's Farm

Extra Visit continued

After some 300 metres the ruins of a farm, with trench lines around, can be seen in the woods. In all probability this was the site of Zimmerman's Farm, known in Turkish as Hadji Husseinar Ciftlik. After the war a cemetery was created here, but the remains buried in it were moved to the new French cemetery (qv) when it was created in 1923. There is another ruined farm at the bottom of the small hill and at one time there were two neglected French memorials which have now disappeared.

Return to the main track and continue 50 metres to a track to the left through the woods. Stop and walk up the path. Turn left at the first branch and after some 50m turn right.

In the woods is a concrete **French Memorial** with four pillars (some broken) around. The obelisk has lost its plaque and is sadly neglected.

Return to the main track. (It is possible to continue in the direction of the Kereves Dere until the track joins the road at a point which leads to Alcitepe to the left, to the Kereves Dere straight ahead, and the Turkish Memorial at Helles to the right. By turning right one would come out between the French gun and the cafe on the road leading down from the memorial to Morto Bay (see below). This circuit is sometimes used by the authorities during large ceremonies to relieve congestion on the main road.)

Turn round, return to the fork and pick up the main itinerary.

Continue along the road towards the Turkish Memorial.
You will pass on the right **The Abide Motel, open in the season for refreshments (and accommodation).** In the fields behind the Motel was Orchard Gully, a comparatively protected rest area, where the RND set up 3rd Field Ambulance and where a small cemetery was made. The bodies from it were later moved to Skew Bridge CWGC Cemetery. You are now driving along S Beach.

Morto Bay/ S Beach *(38.2kms)*

In this area the French (nicknamed 'Tangos' by the Turks, after the flamboyant dance) set up their headquarters when they crossed the Straits after their successful diversionary attack at Kumkale. Four battalions had also landed at V Beach after dark on 25 April and later rapidly moved along the coast to Morto Bay. On 30 April the French authorised a second division to prepare for the Dardanelles and on that day General d'Amade, who was described by Hamilton as 'one of the most charming gentlemen in the world', but as being overwrought at the recent death of his son, pessimistic and appealing for help 'on the very smallest provocation', was recalled. He was replaced by the ebullient 48-year-old Henri Gouraud, the youngest general in the French army, known as the 'Lion of the Argonne' where he had commanded a corps of the Colonial Army in 1914/1915. Gouraud arrived at Helles on 14 May and d'Amade left two days later.

It was a time of upheaval for the French on the naval command front as well. A sense of purposelessness and lack of unison had infected the Allied fleet after the landings. Once it became obvious that the landings had not achieved the desired effect, the enthusiastic Keyes pressed for another naval attempt to force the Straits, endorsed by the French Naval Commander, Guépratte, who felt that to do so would be 'immortalité'. His Parisian political masters considered the idea foolhardy, and felt that Guépratte was becoming mentally unstable. He was replaced by Vice-Admiral Nicol but allowed, at Churchill's request, to remain as second-in-command. The distraught Guépratte heard that his demotion was due to rumours that he was a 'daredevil and dangerous visionary' [L'Expédition des Dardanelles by P.E. Guépratte].

Apart from Keyes, the British tended to agree with the French as to the inadvisability of mounting another naval attack. The fleet now had the support of the ground forces to worry about. As Admiral Oliver (Chief of the Naval Staff) put it, 'On March 18 the Fleet was single, now it has a wife on shore.' The situation was aggravated by the arrival of German submarines in the Aegean and, finally, about 1,000 metres offshore here in the early hours of 12 May the battleship *Goliath* was sunk by three torpedoes from the Turkish destroyer *Muavenet-i Millet* as she lay anchored alongside the battleship *Cornwallis*. Her Captain, Thomas Lawrie Shelford, age 43, and 570 members of her crew were lost. Shelford is commemorated on the Chatham Naval Memorial. The German Commander, Rudolf Firle, was awarded the Iron Cross (First Class), the Austrian Iron Cross and the Turkish Order of Privilege. The sinking caused an end to the policy of stationing ships of the fleet off the tip of the Peninsula and Lord Fisher decided to recall the *Queen Elizabeth*. Winston Churchill approved, but Lord Kitchener 'became extremely angry. His habitual composure in trying ordeals left him. He protested vehemently against what he considered the desertion of the Army at its most critical moment. On the other side Lord Fisher flew into an even greater fury,' wrote Churchill and it was Fisher, not Kitchener, who won the acrimonious battle. Admiral de Robeck received a telegram from the Admiralty saying. '*Queen Elizabeth* is to sail for home at once with all despatch and utmost secrecy.' Knowing what alarm and despondency that would cause, the words 'You should make out she has gone to Malta for a few days and will return' were added. Fisher's triumph was short-lived. The War Council of 14 May 'was sulphurous' and on 15 May he resigned, pretending that 'I am off to Scotland at once to avoid all questionings'.

The wreck of the *Goliath*, which had triggered such momentous events, lay off Morto Bay intact until broken up by Turkish salvage teams. Now only a few remains are left.

On his arrival on the Peninsula General Gouraud was quick to recognise the stalemate that existed and the desperate need to take Achi Baba. His idea was to attack it from the Anzac area with two new divisions to cut off the Turkish defenders at the waist and open the way for the fleet. Hamilton agreed on the urgency of taking Achi Baba and the Third Battle of Krithia was launched. Its failure confirmed Gouraud's fears of unresolvable stalemate. More and more Hamilton was relying on the moral support of the Frenchman whom he regarded 'more as a coadjudicator than as a subordinate'. When it was known that three British divisions were on their way to Gallipoli, Hamilton conferred with Gouraud on their use but before any concrete plans could be made Gouraud was injured and returned to France.

Gouraud was replaced by General Maurice Bailloud who, at the age of 67, had been recalled from retirement to command the 156th Division. He was described by Lieutenant-Colonel Maurice Hankey, Secretary to the War Council, as 'the most confirmed pessimist I have met since the war began... He is a stupid old man and ought to be superseded.' Nevertheless he came into the thick of the fierce struggles for the redoubts known as the *Haricot* (bean), the *Rognon* (kidney) and the Quadrilateral and spirited Turkish counter-attacks.

When the Junior British Liaison Officer with the French was wounded in July, he was replaced by Lieutenant Patrick Shaw-Stewart (qv), a position he described as being 'in inglorious safety on the gilded Staff and speaking French for dear life' [*Shaw-Stewart Letters*]. In October, then a Captain, he was promoted to Senior Liaison Officer. When he left the French during the Evacuation on 8 January 1916, he was awarded the *Légion d'Honneur* for his services by General Brulard, 'which is very sweet of him, and great fun', commented Shaw-Stewart. He went on to serve again with the French in Salonika and was awarded the *Croix de Guerre* for his work during the French advance of August 1916.

Continue to the sign to the left to the French cemetery and drive up the path to the parking area.

* French National Cemetery and Memorial/38.5 kilometres/30 minutes/Map H20,19

Steps lead up to this dramatic cemetery, one of the largest in the Peninsula, with a burial area of 76 metres wide and 140 metres long, built on a slope which leads up to the impressive Memorial. The total land given to France for the cemetery under the Treaty of Lausanne of 24 July 1923, is 28,000 square metres. Water runs down the slope, is collected in a cistern and pumped up to irrigate the plants in the cemetery which is surrounded by dark trees. To the right and left of the central avenue are rows of stark black metal crosses, their tips shaped like *fleur de lys*. The names are inscribed on diamond-shaped metal plaques with the legend *Mort Pour La France*, service number and name. Non-Christian soldiers either have a crossed stake without the fleur de lys or a vertical stake. The burials are graded in ranks: officers, NCOs and private soldiers. Inside the entrance to the right is the Kilitbahir Ossuary, containing the remains of twenty-two soldiers and sailors, to the left is the superintendent's cottage, where the registers and visitor's book are kept. They list the 2,235 names of the identified burials in alphabetical order, then numerically according to their place in the cemetery. The name, rank, grave inscription and place of

The dramatic French cemetery, Morto Bay

Detail of the Memorial

original burial are given. Among them are **Brigadier-General Ganeval** of the Metropolitan Brigade who was killed on 7 June 1915, at Seddulbahir (Grave no 36), the poets: **Marcel Houin** and **Edouard Ciesa**, who both died on 7 August, the writer **Jean Loew**, died 21 June and the editor, biographer, journalist and poet **Leon Adolphe Gauthier-Ferrieres**, died 17 July. In 1922 some bodies were taken back to France for reburial.

Around the lantern tower Memorial there are **4 sarcophagus-shaped Mass Graves,** planted with flowers, containing a total of 15,000 burials. The brilliant white obelisk Memorial is itself an ossuary. It is over 15 metres high, rises from a platform and is inscribed *Ave Gallis Immortalis* (Hail, Immortal France). Below is a verse by Victor Hugo,

Gloire à notre France éternelle.	Glory to our eternal France.
Gloire à ceux qui sont morts pour elle:	Glory to those who died for her:
Aux martyrs, aux vaillants, aux forts,	To the martyrs, the brave, the strong,
A ceux qui enflamme leur exemple	To those who are inspired by them
Qui veulent place dans le temple	Who wish a place in the temple
Et qui mourront comme ils sont morts.	And who will die as they died.

There are plaques from the original French cemeteries, and stones from individual original battlefield graves, several regimental and naval plaques, including one to the sailors who died in the submarines *Joule, Mariotte, Saphir* and *Turquoise*, the battleship *Bouvet*, the phrase *Paix à ses Glorieux Morts* (Peace to her Glorious Dead), the insignia of the *Croix de Guerre* and another couplet by Victor Hugo,

Ceux qui sont pieusement morts pour la Patrie
Ont droit qu'à leur cerceuil la foule vienne et prie.
(To those who died piously for the Fatherland
Is the right that the crowd should come and pray at their tomb.)

To cope with the heavy French losses, four wartime cemeteries were created behind the front line. One, called Galinier, was in the interior of Seddulbahir fort, another was beside the Kilitbahir road. 1st Division had a cemetery at the foot of the Eski Hisarlik cliff and 2nd Division's was 300 metres to the north of Morto Bay. The sick and wounded were evacuated to hospitals at Mudros on Lemnos and to Chatby at Alexandria and the dead were buried in the nearest military hospital. After the war the bodies left on the battlefield were moved to the nécropoles created in 1915 and in new cemeteries made at Zimmerman's Farm and at the Kereves Dere (Celery Valley). Thousands of unidentified remains were placed in ossuaries called Masnou (Kereves Dere) and Ganeval (after commanding officers). In 1922 a mission was sent out from France to repatriate the identified bodies claimed by their families. After the Treaty of Lausanne of 24 July 1923 this vast cemetery was constructed and all the French dead on the Peninsula were reinterred in it. It was inaugurated on 9 June 1930, by General Gouraud.

Behind the memorial is a small path which leads to the area of Zimmerman's Farm (approximately 1 kilometre away) and a French memorial, (see Extra Visit above). The farm was named after **Commandant Charles Zimmerman** of the 175th Regiment, who is buried in grave no 32 in the cemetery.

Return to your car and continue to the sign to Canakkale Sehitligi.

Before 1998 there was a Turkish sign here which read, 'Dear Visitors, The place you are in lies within the grounds of the monument which was erected in memory of 250,000 martyrs who sacrificed their lives for their motherland and for Turkish honour. Let us commemorate those who gave us this beautiful country of ours.' On the reverse was a poem by M. Akif Ersoy,

> Do not ignore the ground on which you have walked,
> It is not ordinary soil.
> Reflect on the thousands of people who lie beneath
> Without a shroud.
> You are the son of a martyr -
> Do not hurt your ancestor,
> Do not give away this beautiful motherland,
> Even if you have the whole world.

The sign has been removed for refurbishment and, one hopes, will be replaced.

Continue uphill.

To the right, at the tip of the point, is the site of De Tott's Battery. The battery was constructed in 1770 during the Russo-Turkish War and is named after Baron François de Tott, a French consultant to the Ottoman forces who supervised the building. In 1915 the Turks used the old fort as an observation post and established a torpedo station on the shore below. On the evening of 25 April the French battalions who had landed at Helles made contact with the South Wales Borderers who held the area after their landing. When the French took over the area the fort was in ruins. This was the area of Anit-Eski Hisarlik (the ancient Elaius - see below) . Opposite is a café, with a picnic area on the edge of the bay.

Halfway up the hill, in a clearing to the left (and therefore more safely visited on the way down) is a

French Gun/39.8 kilometres/5 minutes/Map H36

A plaque in front of the gun states that French soldiers reached this point, then retired, leaving their guns here.

Continue to the

* Canakkale Turkish Martyrs' Memorial Complex/Memorial/40.1 kilometres/40 minutes/Map H35,34, 37,38 /WC/OP

There is a large parking area and helicopter pads.

The massive **Main Memorial** is built on Eskihisarlik Burnu (Old Fortress Point) on the site of the ancient Athenian settlement of Elaius. During the 1915 campaign keen archeologists amongst the French soldiers undertook excavations making several significant finds, including many pots of the 4th and 3rd centuries BC. In the settlement's necropolis at Seddulbahir funeral urns and sarcophagi were found and the Director of the French Inscription Academy, Edmond Pottier, was sent out to catalogue them.

The design of the monument, by the architects Feridun Kip, Ismail Utkular and Dogan Erginbas, mainly because of its striking simplicity, was the winner of a national competition held in March 1944. The first stone was laid on 19 April 1954, and the building was completed on 21 August 1960. The monument is in the form of stone-veneered concrete pylons covered by a flat roof, which rise 40 metres above the 48-metre-high promontory on which it is erected, giving it a dramatic dominance over the mouth of the Dardanelles. It is 7 metres higher than the Helles Memorial. At night it is flood-lit, adding to its majesty. Beneath the pylons is a commemorative stone inscribed with an extract from the poem *For Those Fallen at Gallipoli* by Mehmet Akif Ersoy (1873-1936),

Soldier, you have fallen for this earth
Your fathers may well lean down from heaven to kiss your brow.
Who can dig a grave that will not be too narrow for you?
If I say, "Let us enshrine you in history",
It will not contain you.

Such a symbol of Turkish victory has it become, that in 1990 it appeared, with a stylised dove of peace, on a 1,000 lira stamp and an engraving of it appears on the 500,000 lira bank note.

The Museum entrance is in the wall below the pylons. It is open 0900-1300 and 1400-1800. An entrance fee is payable. Opened in 1971 the museum contains a small display of battlefield artefacts and ephemera. A small selection of snacks is available. Opposite are WCs.

To the left of the large Ceremonial Terrace is

The Memorial garden with trees dedicated to the UK, New Zealand, Turkey, Australia, Germany, France, Canada and Pakistan and bearing plaques with their national flags

Wounded Soldier Group of Statues by sculptor Tankut Oktem

Open Air Fountain and Area for Worship

Group of Statues sculpted in 1992 by Metin Yurdanur **depicting the famous photograph of Kemal Ataturk** looking over the battlefield

Memorial Wall with names of the missing

Symbolic Cemetery. The names on the grave markers are of 100 officers and 500 soldiers who gave their lives in the Gallipoli Peninsula and who came from every Province of the Ottoman Empire. There is also a large stone memorial book.

French gun en route to the main Turkish Memorial

The Memorial with J-P Thierry of the Historial, Peronne and one of the authors

Sculpture of the famous picture of Mustafa Kemal with modern Turkish soldiers in the foreground

Symbolic Cemetery

Wounded soldiers statue

Headstone of Lieutenant-Colonel Quilter

Skew Bridge CWGC Cemetery

The avenue of trees leading to Redoubt CWGC Cemetery

2nd Lieutenant Duckworth Memorial Oak Tree with marker below

Return down the hill to the main fork and turn right towards Eceabat. Continue to the cemetery on the right.

* Skew Bridge CWGC Cemetery/43.4 kilometres/10 minutes/Map H17

The cemetery was named after a wooden 'skew' bridge which carried the Krithia road over the Kanli Dere. It was made after the Second Battle of Krithia of 6-8 May and used thereafter until the Evacuation. The original cemetery contained 53 graves, the remainder were concentrated here after the Armistice from small cemeteries and the surrounding battlefields. Now it contains 124 UK burials, 5 Australian, 2 New Zealand, 1 Indian and 345 unidentified. The majority of the latter are probably of the RND. There are 125 UK special memorials and 4 Australian to the left of the entrance.

Amongst those buried here is **Private J. Benjamin** of the Chatham Battalion, RMLI who died of wounds, age 19, on 12 July, and who served as 'Davis', probably for his own reasons choosing a less Jewish-sounding name [II E 14]; **QMS Charles Henry Rowed Henman** of No 1 Field Coy Div Engineers, RND, age 37, died 29 July, was 'an architect employed in the "Barracks" Construction Dept., War Office' [I B 1]; **Lieutenant-Colonel John Arnold Cuthbert Quilter**, age 40, was killed on 6 May whilst commanding the Hood Battalion, RND [II B 4]. Educated at Eton and Trinity Hall, Cambridge, Quilter was commissioned in 1897 into the Grenadier Guards, served in South Africa, was Mentioned in Despatches and was commended by Major-General Paris for his leadership of the Hood Battalion at Antwerp in October 1914. It was to Quilter that Ian Hamilton entrusted a sick Rupert Brooke on 2 April in Cairo - 'Mind you take care of him. His loss would be a national loss.' Sadly he was unable to fulfil this order and accompanied Brooke's coffin to Skyros. It was he who selected Freyberg for his dangerous diversionary mission near the Lines of Bulair (qv) and, once landed on the Peninsula, led his men with inspiration. On 6 May, in the attack on Krithia and Achi Baba, carrying an 'oversize walking stick', he was killed. He was buried near Backhouse Post (see Holts' Map). Three volleys were fired over the grave and the Last Post was sounded under a hail of shrapnel. A fellow officer penned this tribute to him:

IN MEMORY OF COLONEL QUILTER
...We honoured our gallant Colonel -
Quilter by name was he.
The deeds of the Hood Battalion,
Alas he lived not to see.

...His presence was a tonic
In the midst of danger and strife.
But in the hour of victory
A bullet took his life.

All honour to Colonel Quilter,
The Battalion mourns his loss.
The only things we could give him
Were a grave and a wooden cross.
[*Joseph Murray Papers*].

The equally popular commanding officer of the Nelson Battalion, **Lieutenant-Colonel Edmund George Eveleigh**, Twice Mentioned in Despatches, was killed on 13 July according to the RND History. The cemetery register omits the 'i' in his name and puts his death at 14 July [II E 13]. A third RND commander is buried here - **Colonel Frank William Luard** of the RM Portsmouth Battalion, age 50, [II B 3] who was also killed in the attack of 13 July on the enemy third line when the two battalions advanced alone 'with the greatest gallantry'. Ten other officers were killed in the attack.

Continue towards Eceabat to the cemetery on the left, which is up a long avenue of beautiful trees.

They were planted by the Commission when the cemetery was constructed and continue on the far side of the cemetery. In front of it is a bank of fragrant rosemary.

* Redoubt CWGC Cemetery/Lieutenant Duckworth Memorial/46.2 kilometres/15 minutes/Map H13,14

The cemetery was begun in May 1915 by the 2nd Australian Infantry Brigade after the Second Battle of Krithia and was used until the Evacuation. After the Armistice it was increased by the concentration of small cemeteries in the vicinity at Krithia Nullah, Brown House, White House and Clapham Junction and by bringing in battlefield burials. It now contains 375 UK burials, 16 Australian, 4 New Zealand, 1 Indian and 1,282 totally unidentified. There are 341 special UK memorials, 4 Australian and 4 New Zealand in the centre of the rectangular cemetery. In 1919 Bean described how the British 'eventually concentrated their many cemeteries into six; as it happened one of these had originally been established just behind the rearmost of the two Redoubt trenches dug by our 2nd Brigade in its famous advance.' In this beautiful scented burial ground, planted with tall cypress trees, pink-barked strawberry trees, iris, heather and lavender, is a solitary English oak tree. It was planted in 1922 by his father as a **Memorial to 2nd Lieutenant Eric Duckworth**, of 1/6th Lancashire Fusiliers who died here on 7 August, age 19, and who is commemorated on the Helles Memorial. At its foot is a memorial plaque.

Also buried here is **Lieutenant Leslie Phillips Jones** of the 9th Royal Berkshires, attd. 2nd Hampshires, age 20, who died on 6 June. He had just entered Oriel College Oxford and had published a book of poems entitled *Youth*. On his headstone is inscribed a line from it, 'We must keep our garden free from weeds'. [Sp Mem A 173]. The sedentary civilian occupations listed in the cemetery register, many of them showing academic achievement, contrast with the violence and deprivation of the harsh few weeks the men spent on the Peninsula, e.g. 'Director of Jonas Brook & Bros' (2nd Lieutenant A.C. Brook [XII A 20]); 'an artist' (Ldg. Smn, S.G. Dadd [XI D 13]); 'Apprentice Electrical Engineer' (Private E.D. Kelly [I C 16]); 'Educated at Harrow; and Trinity, Cambridge. B.A. with honours' (Lieutenant W.F.J. Maxwell, only son of Sir William Maxwell, 4th Bart. of Cardoness and Lady Maxwell [VI C 19]); 'H.M. Junior Inspector of Mines for Liverpool and North Wales District (Spr W.H. Murray [Sp Mem B 116]); 'An Assistant Manager of Taikoo Dockyard, Hong Kong (Spr T.E.S. Robson [Sp Mem B 136]).

Major Edward Leigh of the 2nd Hampshires, age 47, killed on 1 May, served for 29 years with the Regiment - in South Africa, India, Malta and BWI [I A 18]. Another South African veteran was 49-year-old **Lieutenant-Colonel Owen Godfrey-Faussett, DSO**, Twice Mentioned in Despatches, of the Essex Regiment, killed on 2 May [Sp Mem A 58]. His father had served in the Regiment before him. **2nd Lieutenant Frank Richards** of the 2nd Hampshires, age 28, killed on 14 May 'served with the regiment from 1903 until he fell in action only a few days after being promoted to commissioned rank' [X A 17]. **Private Cuthbert Lodington** of the 6th Battalion AIF, killed on 8 May, served as 'Williams' [I A 12], and **Corporal Archie Odgers** of the 7th Battalion, killed on the same day, served as 'Wraith', [I B13].

Continue.
You are now driving through the area known as **The Vineyard**. After the costly offensive of 4 June the line was withdrawn to the northern edge of The Vineyard

Graves at Gozetleme

Girl student statue

Gozetleme Memorial

but this position too was evacuated by 2130 hours and the greater portion of the ground gained by 42nd Division's attack was lost. The cost to VII Corps was 4,500 officers and men out of 16,000 engaged and the French lost 2,000. The enemy, however, had lost between 9,000 and 10,000 and were on the brink of collapse when the British attack ceased. General Kannengiesser, then with the Turkish 9th Division, later wrote, 'I felt that another energetic attack by the English would have the worst results.' The final attack on The Vineyard was made on 6 August by units of the 29th and 42nd Divisions (part of the feint to divert attention from the Suvla Landings) which merely resulted in more casualties. There was little further action here until in November the 52nd Division straightened out its line to the west of The Vineyard.

Continue through Krithia and along the road to Eceabat until you reach the left turn to Kabatepe/Anafartalar.

Extra Visit along road to Gaba Tepe, including the Gozetleme Tepe Cemetery and Memorial (Map P25,26)

One way trip: Appproximately 15.0 kilometres. Approximate time: 35 minutes

Turn left along the road.

This is the quickest way back to Eceabat at the end of Itinerary One. It leads eventually to the Information Centre at Gaba Tepe - see Itinerary Two below.

*Continue 2.4 kilometres to a track to the left to the Turkish **Gozetleme Tepe Cemetery and Memorial.***

The unmade road can be negotiated in a normal car when very dry and if due caution is taken.

Continue 700 metres to a T-junction and turn right. Turn right again at the crest (1.2kms) and continue along the clifftop.

Built in 1939, the tower-like memorial, with three anonymous graves behind, is painted white and is situated in pine trees on the site of a Turkish Observation Post which controlled the Kum Limani Beach and which has beautiful views to Saros. At the top of the cliffs in front of the memorial and in the pines that surround it (which suffered a major fire in 1999) are clearly discernible trench lines. The Turkish inscription reads:

TURKUM NE MUTLU TURKUM DIYENE
ULUSUMA YAN BAKTIRMAN TURK ELINE
BEN TURKUM GUVENIRIM SUNGUME GUCUME
DAHA OLMAZSA ATIMLA SAHLANIRIM UZERINE

This is a famous quotation from Ataturk, the gist of which is 'With pride, how happy is he who can say "I am a Turk"'.

Return to the main road, turn left and continue towards Gaba Tepe. Continue a further 3.5kms.

On the right is a **white stone statue (Map P27). It is of a girl student, one of the hundreds who planted trees in this area after the fire of 1994.**

Continue, passing the entrance to the Kum Motel complex after a further 800 metres.

This beautiful area around the existing Motel is designated by the Peace Park project as one of the few areas where tourist development will be permitted.

Continue to a junction. Take care here to take the right fork that leads to the Information Centre, not the left fork that leads to the harbour. Turn right to Eceabat.

Return to Eceabat.

* End of Itinerary One

ITINERARY TWO

ANZAC COASTLINE

* **Itinerary Two** starts at Eceabat, heads across the Peninsula to the Anzac Landing Beaches and either returns to Eceabat or continues on to **Itinerary Four** to Suvla. **Refer throughout to Holts' Map 4 (A).**
* **The Route:** Eceabat; Gaba Tepe Information Centre; Junction of Lower and Upper Routes; Brighton Beach; CWGC 'Start of Anzac Area' Sign; Beach CWGC Cemetery; Shrapnel Valley CWGC Cemetery; Ross Bastiaan Marker No 3; Turkish Monolith, 27th Infantry Regiment; Anzac Cove naming Memorial, Turkish Monolith, Ari Burnu Cove; Ari Burnu CWGC Cemetery; Ross Bastiaan Marker No 1; The Sphinx; North Beach; Canterbury CWGC Cemetery; CWGC Cottages; Fisherman's Hut; No 2 Outpost CWGC Cemetery; New Zealand No 2 Outpost CWGC Cemetery; Embarkation Pier CWGC Cemetery; CWGC 'End of Anzac Area' Sign.
* **Extra Visits** are suggested to: Ataturk Museum, Bigali; Gaba Tepe Harbour; Plugge's Plateau CWGC Cemetery;
* **Planned duration,** without stops for refreshment or Extra Visits: 2 hours 30 minutes.
* **Total distance: 15.5 Kilometres.**

* Eceabat Ferry Terminus/0 Kilometres/RWC/Map

Leave Eceabat by the main coastal road direction Gelibolu. If coming off the ferry from Canakkale, turn right following a green CWGC sign to Anzac/Suvla and continue through the town, passing a chemist on the left, then the Post Office (PTT) on the right. Join the dual carriage by-pass signed Istanbul to the right. A petrol station is to the left and the Boomerang Café to the right. Continue to a left turn (2.3kms) with prominent signs to Kabatepe/Kemalyeri, turn left and 100 metres later is a junction.

Extra Visit to Ataturk's House/Museum, Bigali (Map P6)
Round trip: 9.8 kilometres. Approximate time: 40 minutes

At the junction take the road signed Bigali Ataturk Evi and continue to a fork. Turn left as the main road goes straight on and after 4.4kms turn right still following Ataturk Evi signs to the village. Turn right again in the village and in the centre fork left uphill along an extremely narrow road. The house, No. 126, is at the top on the right.

Extra Visit continued

Here Kemal Ataturk had his base when commanding 19th Division. The house is in typical local architectural style, with services on the ground floor and living quarters on the upper level, with a garden protected by high walls. In 1973 it was restored and opened as a museum in which his personal belongings, uniforms and civilian clothes (including very smart pyjamas, shirt, waistcoat etc.) are displayed. There is a lady custodian who will politely ask you to remove your shoes.

There is an entrance fee (100,000TL in 1998) and postcards and Milli Park literature is on sale. There are WCs in the garden.

According to Zeki Bey, the Turkish officer interviewed by Bean on the Peninsula in February 1919, the battalion he commanded, the 1st of the 57th Regiment, was camped in Bigali on the night of 24 April, and the news arrived at dawn the following day that a landing had been made at Ari Burnu. Zeki thought that at that time there was only one battalion of the 27th Regiment between the Azmak (sometimes seen as 'Asmac') Dere and Kum Dere (six kilometres to the south of Gaba Tepe). Mustafa Kemal was then ordered to send one battalion to face the invaders, but decided personally to lead a complete regiment to Chunuk Bair. This was audacious initiative, as the 19th was firmly assigned to a reserve position, and Kemal, then the equivalent of a Lieutenant-Colonel, did not wait for Essad Pasha, the Commander of III Corps at Gelibolu, to bring his staff down to Maidos (he arrived at about 1000 hours). Liman von Sanders remained convinced that the main attack was coming at Bulair and made no orders for troops to move down the Peninsula. But without further orders, and no detailed maps, Kemal, accompanied by Zeki Bey, dashed forward at the head of the 57th, the 77th and 72nd Arab Regiments, until they met Turkish soldiers tumbling in panic down a valley to the south of Chunuk Bair. Kemal ordered Zeki to attack the advancing Australians and contact was made on Battleship Hill (qv), when Zeki was wounded in the arm and hospitalised. The attack, during which one battalion of the 27th had three of its company commanders killed and lost most of its junior officers, pressed on towards Fisherman's Hut (qv) to peter out by dusk with both sides exhausted.

Return to the junction and pick up the main itinerary. (The road through the village continues to the Anafartala villages and thence to Anzac.)

Bear left following green CWGC signs to Anzac and Suvla cemeteries and brown Milli Park Turkish signs with yellow lettering. Continue through the Kilye Plain to, on the right,

* Gaba Tepe Information Centre and Museum/Ross Bastiaan Plaque/9.4 kilometres/20 minutes/Map A1,2 /WC/OP

The design of the centre, the winner of an architectural competition, was by Ahmet Gulgonen. The museum contains some books, maps and postcards and displays of

The Boomerang Café, Eceabat

Interior, Ataturk's HQ, Bigali

Australlian Veterans, Privates Bob Ponsford (24th Bn AIF), Walter Parker (20th Bn AIF) and Ted Thompson (6th Field Ambulance) with the Anzac Area Ross Bastiaan Plaque at its dedication in Melbourne on the 75th Anniversary of the Evacuation 9 January 1991

Courtesy of Ross Bastiaan

Gaba Tepe Information Centre

Wounded Soldiers sculpture

Sari Bair Ridge OP from the rear of the platform with Lone Pine on the left (see text)

battlefield artefacts, uniforms and documents. To the right of the entrance is a bas relief plaque and map showing the location of the Ross Bastiaan Markers and their origination.

ROSS BASTIAAN AUSTRALIAN BRONZE COMMEMORATIVE PLAQUES

In 1990 Melbourne dentist Dr. Ross J. Bastiaan, OAM, RFD, born in 1951, embarked on an ambitious project to erect informative commemorative plaques on battlefields where Australians served and died - worldwide. He was inspired by his 1987 visit to Gallipoli where he was saddened to find hardly any information in English about what happened there in 1915. So started the "Plaques Project".

First Dr. Bastiaan designed the basic plaque. It is of bronze, usually one-metre square, weighing over 80kg and has to be set in 3 tonnes of concrete. Most are placed at sites of particular Australian gallantry and bear a bas-relief map of the region today with superimposed features of the battle commemorated. A multilingual text (English and the local language) describes the action. Bastiaan personally hand-sculpted each plaque and wrote the text, using the Official Histories as his reference, in language accessible to the layman. Lengthy and complicated negotiations had then to be undertaken with the appropriate foreign governments to permit the siting of the plaques. The large cost of each plaque (now totalling over a quarter of a million Australian dollars) has mainly been funded by private companies. Most have been unveiled by WW1 veterans or Australian dignitaries such as a Prime Minister, Governor-General or Ambassador, which is recorded at the base of the plaque with the date.

The plaques now stand in sixteen countries around the world, including Australia, Belgium, Burma, Egypt, England, France, Greece, Indonesia, Israel, Libya, Malaysia, New Zealand, Papua New Guinea, Singapore, Thailand, Turkey. Others are planned for Vietnam (the first Allied memorial to be erected there since the war) and in Syria. They record actions from Gallipoli (1915) to the Gulf (1990).

Dr. Bastiaan's private commitment to commemorating his country's service people has been recognised by the award of the Medal of Honour of Australia, 'Anzac of the Year' by the Returned Services League, and the appointment to the Council of the Australian War Memorial at Canberra. He is also a Colonel in the RAADC Reserve.

The conception and erection of these plaques is a marvellous act of dedication which all visitors to the battlefields should appreciate. They are the most suitable form of battlefield marker: durable, clear, informative and in harmony with their surroundings.

To the left of the main building, approached down some steps, are WCs. To their left is a large Ceremonial Terrace, on the edge of which is a group of sculptures with the figures of two wounded soldiers, one struggling to uphold the Turkish flag, the other holding an olive branch. Between the figures and the museum is a helicopter pad. At the far end of the platform are symbolic triangular sculptures reaching out to the battlefields. These, and the terraces and symbolic cemetery which fall down towards the battlefield, were designed by architects Metin Hepguler and Ilhan Sahin, winners of a further competition in November 1983. There are recreated trenches behind the complex.

Walk beyond the pad to the largest of the triangular structures and stand on its left hand side. Face the slope ahead taking the direction of the road that climbs it as 12 o'clock.

On the top of the heights at 12 o' clock is the Australian Memorial at Lone Pine. Just to its right is the Turkish Memorial to 57th Brigade, to the right of which is Baby 700 Cemetery on the skyline to the right of a lone tree. At 1 o' clock are the five finger monoliths at Chunuk Bair and in the foreground, straight ahead, is the Kanlisirt (Mustapha Kemal Place) Monolith. To the left in the sea is Nibrunesi Point and beyond it the Kirectepe Ridge.

Continue along the road towards Anzac Cove to a junction signed left to Kum Motel/Kabatepe Limani.

Extra Visit: Gaba Tepe Pier with options for ferry crossing to Gokceada (Imbros)/ privately arranged boat trip to Helles. Round trip to harbour: 1.1 kilometres. Approximate time (excluding boat trips): 15 minutes.

Take the left turn, passing the Milli Park Camping site on the left, and continue to the Port.

It is a well-developed and picturesque harbour with booking hall, cafés, and fishing port.

Boats leave from here for Gokceada every day at 1100 returning at 1800 (also from Canakkale at 1600, returning at 0800). The trip takes 2 hours 30 minutes. Fare in 2000 from Gaba Tepe: Car: 2.5 millionTL. Per Person: 500.000TL. from Canakkale: Car: 8 millionTL. Per Person: 800.000TL Contact: Turkish Maritime Lines Canakkale Ferry Counter Tel: 00 90 286 217 1815

Imbros, as it was known in 1915, is now called Imroz or Gokceada, after its main town. It has a large bay, known as Kefeles Limani (Kephalos Bay in 1915) on the south-east coast, in whose harbour the Allied ships were moored and around which the military camps were set up. It has a rugged interior that resembles the ground above Anzac Cove.

When the alarming news of the appearance of a German submarine heading for the Dardanelles broke on 17 May Admiral de Robeck insisted that the *Arcadian*, on which Hamilton had established his headquarters, should move from its anchorage off W Beach to Imbros. During the time that HQ was on board ship Compton Mackenzie (qv) arrived to join the Staff. At their first encounter he found a disturbed Commander-in-Chief: 'In one illuminated instant I divined with absolute certainty that we should never take Constantinople. It may be that Sir Ian's own brave hope had been shaken and that the doubt in his mind was conveyed to me. I had no reasonable grounds at that date for pessimism. I had not yet experienced that insurmountable mental barrier of

Extra Visit continued

which Mr Winston Churchill was one day to write. *A wall of crystal, utterly immovable, began to tower up in the Narrows, and against this wall of inhibition no weapon could be employed. The 'No' principle had become established in men's minds, and nothing could ever eradicate it.'* Mackenzie did not then know that Hamilton had that day exchanged cables with Kitchener in which the dread word 'withdrawal' had first been mentioned, or that Winston Churchill's brother Jack (qv), also on Hamilton's Staff, had just heard that his brother had been forced to leave the Admiralty - both reasons for Hamilton's pessimism.

Cables were laid from Helles, 29 kilometers distant, and Anzac, 82 kilometers away, to the *Arcadian*, but communications proved unsatisfactory and on 31 May the Staff moved into an unprepossessing tented camp on the beach near the mouth of the Degirman Dere. Hamilton was obsessed with being seen to share the privations and discomforts of his men and as a result frequently suffered from 'the prevalent complaint' – dysentery. Mackenzie found the ship divided into the following sections: 'O' for Operations commanded by General Braithwaite, the C.G.S. (His 19-year-old son, Valentine, who won one of the first MCs of the war with the SLI in the Retreat from Mons, was his ADC. He was killed on 1 July 1916, on the Somme and has one of the few Private Memorials remaining on the Western Front outside Serre Road No 2 Cemetery.) and under him served Guy Dawnay (later Major-General, D.S.O.) and Cecil Aspinall (later Brigadier-General, Aspinall-Oglander would become the British Official War Historian): 'A' for Administration under the Adjutant-General: 'Q', the Quartermaster-General's branch: 'I' for Intelligence, divided into Ia (information about the enemy) and Ib (security). The war correspondents, such as Ashmead-Bartlett (qv) who lived in luxury with a Parisian restaurant manager to do his catering, Malcolm Ross the official New Zealand Correspondent, Charles Bean the Official Australian Correspondent (but who spent most of his time on the Peninsula), were also stationed at Kephalos Bay, choosing what was considered to be the best spot. A Turkish prisoner of war camp was set up nearby.

On 6 August 10,000 troops embarked from Imbros on the new 'Beetles' armour-plated motor-lighters, bound for Suvla, leaving hundreds of empty tents. A fleet of ships, including the liner *Minneapolis* with newspaper correspondents on

Major-General W.F. Braithwaite, CIGS and his ADC and son, 'Val', at Imbros. IWM (Q13521)

Extra Visit continued

board, trawlers, destroyers and battleships, sailed out of the congested harbour at Kephalos. They left behind an anxious, frustrated staff, in particular the C-in-C, who could only impotently watch as a tragedy caused by delay and inaction unrolled before their eyes. News had been painfully slow in coming in to GHQ and eventually Hamilton decided he must go and see what was happening for himself. No transport could at first be found and eventually he made the crossing in the *Triad*, a yacht used by de Robeck.

In July 1915 the RNAS airfield had been moved to Imbros from Tenedos [see **Aerial Activity** above] as their supplies of petrol could be brought into Kephalos harbour. It then had to be carried five kilometers on loose sand to the mud airstrip which was next to a salt lake. Wind funnelled unpredictably between the nearby hills and the sand dunes, making it hazardous to land, resulting in several crashes. An airship station was set up on Imbros in September but was moved to Mudros on 21 October. On Christmas Day Samson organised an Officers versus Men's football match, during which a Turkish aircraft flew over. In gentlemanly fashion the pilot deposited his bombs in the sand dunes so as not to interrupt the game [King].

Imbros (together with Tenedos) was returned to Turkey under the terms of the Treaty of Lausanne of 1923. It had been seized by the Greeks during the Balkan Wars of 1912-13, and they offered Lemnos, Tenedos and Imbros to the British as bases in February 1915. The British war graves on Imbros - in Kephalos British Cemetery (84 British, Australian and New Zealand soldiers and sailors, three Greeks and one German prisoner), Kusu Bay Cemetery (forty-five officers and men, fourteen of them unidentified, of the monitors *Raglan* and *M28*, sunk by the German battle cruiser *Goeben* and cruiser *Breslau* on 20 January 1918) and Panaghia Churchyard Cemetery (one officer and five men from the monitors and four airmen of the 62nd Wing, RAF), were then removed to Lancashire Landing CWGC Cemetery at Helles. A brass plate was placed on the church wall of Panaghia to commemorate the six sailors.

It may be possible to hire a private boat for a trip to Helles and back. Enquire in the Booking Hall (which only has a skeleton staff off-season (October-April)).

Return to the junction and pick up the main itinerary.

Gaba Tepe Harbour with Gokceada Ferryboat

Continue to the large green CWGC board (10kms) giving the names of cemeteries on the lower and upper routes and then to the road junction, with a large car park to the left and signs to Kamalyeri /Kanlisirt/ Conkbayiri/ Anzakkoyu/ Kirectepe, Jandarma Sehitligi. Take the lower road, straight ahead, signed to Anzac Cove.

You are now driving along **Brighton Beach**. This is the area where the Anzac landings should have taken place. It is almost 2kms long, over twice the length of, and wider than Anzac, and sits at the end of a broad depression that runs from Gaba Tepe (i.e. this area) to Eceabat that would have enabled the assaulting troops to strike directly across the Peninsula. It was not to be - losing their way in the dark the tows of boats put the men ashore further north at Ari Burnu (Anzac), hemmed in by savage cliffs.

On 24 May the old battleship *Albion* ran aground on a sandbank off Gaba Tepe. The Turks fired over 100 shells into her as the Navy attempted to pull her off. In the end she fired all her heavy guns simultaneously and bounced off in the recoil. The next day HMS *Triumph*, a 12-year-old ship of 11,800 tons, was sunk by German *U21* under Commander Hersing. The torpedo passed through her protective nets and after eight minutes, during which her crew dived off, she capsized. The crew of her protective ring of destroyers stood to attention as she went down, to cheers from the Turkish trenches and dismay from the watching ANZACs. Most of the crew of the *Triumph* were picked up by the destroyers, the Turks holding their fire, but eighty-seven men were lost. 'Men sat on the hill that night, cursing the Hun and all his allies!' commented Major Fred Waite, the NZ and A Adjutant Engineer. The Staff on board the *Arcadian* watched survivors being taken aboard the *Lord Nelson*, lying in Kephalos Harbour. The wreck of the *Triumph* remains to this day off Gaba Tepe.

The presence of German submarines and their proven ability to strike caused what amounted to panic in the Fleet. An immediate retirement of other battleships was ordered by De Robeck. Only the *Majestic* (qv) remained off Helles until she, too, was sunk on 27 May. Private Edward Atkinson of 29 Division Cycle Company saw the sinking and recorded in his diary, ' 6.30 am see the most pathetic sight of my life, see explosion and gun fire at a torpedo, but missed and the Majestic, a beautiful battleship, done good work in the 'Nelles heels over... I saw all the men appear on deck and the water line showing...apparently order was given to 'abandon ship' then they ran down the side of the sinking ship...the propellor seemed to be still moving and pumps still going...one officer took it calm...he sat on the side and undressed and plunged in water...it makes one feel sad and as though we are going to lose the game.'

The bunkers along this stretch of beach date from **WW2**. They are on the site of **Dawkins Point**, named after Lieutenant W. H. Dawkins who immediately after the landings was sent by General Birdwood, worried that he was landing on 'the most waterless piece of the Peninsula', to find water. Dawkins 'sank twenty shallow wells here, which gave 20,000 gallons daily of good soakage water. Troughs were immediately erected there for 500 animals. Pipes had to be laid under fire. A most useful water service had been completed, when, on 12 May, the gallant Dawkins went out to cover one of his pipes. The first shell of the day burst low in front of him and he was killed' [Bean]. He is buried in Beach Cemetery.

Continue to the green CWGC sign (11.2kms).

This marks the beginning of the **Anzac Battlefield Commemorative Area** controlled by the CWGC according to the terms of the Treaty of Lausanne of 1923 (qv). To the right of this marker was the area known as **Chatham's Post**. This was established by Lieutenant W. Chatham of the 5th Light Horse on the night of 19 June when he led a party of twenty men, later joined by Major J. H. White with a further 200 men, to seize this seaside spur. Despite opposition from Turkish patrols, the party dug a redoubt which was maintained until the Evacuation and named after the Lieutenant. The ridge beyond Chatham's Post was known as **Bolton's Ridge**, named after 53-year-old Colonel William Bolton who commanded the 8th Battalion AIF and who established the front line here on 25 April. The area was called **Kel Tepe** - Bald Hill - by the Turks.

Continue to the cemetery signs on the right (12kms).

The sign indicates a rough track to **Lone Pine**, 1.5 kilometres distant, and, en route, **Shell Green CWGC Cemetery,** 510 metres distant. The track follows the path of **Artillery Road** which was built soon after the landings to haul guns up to their positions on the Ridge. It is a strenuous walk to the top, and Shell Green is more easily reached from the Upper Route. Local taxis have been seen driving up the complete track but it is not advisable to attempt it even in dry weather.

Continue round the bend with a bunker in the bank to the right to the sign to Beach CWGC Cemetery on the left. Stop.

The promontory here is **Hell Spit** which marks the beginning of the pitifully tiny cove, now known as **'Anzac'**, where the landings were mistakenly made [see **Anzac, Historical Summary**].

To the soldiers whose life-line it was throughout the eight months of the occupation it was simply known as **The Beach**. The first impression on rounding the curve of the spit is of total disbelief: that this strip of shingle, then only 25 metres wide and about 650 metres long, should have been the nerve-centre of the Anzac operation, teeming with bodies, materiel and activity, defies modern-day comprehension. Here men were landed, and evacuated, when wounded, from the small Red Cross wharves; exhausted stretcher bearers scurried repeatedly to the medical facilities where surgeons worked desperately, hour upon hour. Headquarters were established and stores piled up. Here was the 'Periscope Factory', which produced 3,000 instruments before the end of May and the famous 'Bomb Factory', which issued their first product one hour before the Third Battle of Krithia on 4 June and which was soon in full production of grenades - always known as 'bombs' in 1915 - made from packing empty jam tins or fuse tins from the 18-pounders, and fifty-four men were set to the task on the desperate day of 7 August. Barges and lighters crowded the shore-line, moored to the few short piers, unloading great stacks of bully beef cans, jam and biscuit tins, cheese, fodder for the mules and horses, and water. There were depots of Engineers' supplies of barbed wire, telegraph wire, explosives, timber, and sandbags. A light railway moved stores between Anzac and North Beach. Mules led by their patient Indian and Jewish drivers transported these supplies or pulled artillery pieces up the gullies to the Sari Bair Ridge and along the beach to the Outposts. In the evening the men risked the 'Evening Hate' to plunge into the inviting blue Aegean. On a visit to Anzac on 29 April Hamilton described how 'Swarms of bullets sang through the air, far overhead for the most part, to drop into the sea that lay around us. Yet all the time there were full five hundred

| Shell Green
Beach
Shrapnel Valley
Plugge's Plateau
Ari Burnu
Canterbury
No.2 Outpost
New Zealand No.2 Outpost
Embarkation Pier
7th Field Ambulance
Hill 60
Green Hill
Lala Baba
Hill 10
Azmak ⬆ | Lone Pine
Lone Pine Memorial
Johnston's Jolly
4th Battalion
Parade Ground
Courtney's & Steele's Post
Quinn's Post
Walker's Ridge
The Nek
Baby 700
Chunuk Bair
Chunuk Bair Memorial
The Farm ➡ |

CWGC signs to the 'Lower' and 'Upper' Routes

men fooling about stark naked on the water's edge or swimming, shouting and enjoying themselves as it might be at Margate. Not a sign to show that they possess the things called nerves...Birdie...tells me several men have already been shot whilst bathing but there is no use trying to stop it: they take the off chance.' Much has been written about the strength and beauty of the Anzac soldiers. Soon they became a unique race, their healthy disregard for conventional discipline and custom was legendary and, as the heat of the summer reached the mid-eighties Fahrenheit, they cut down their trousers to make shorts and abandoned all gear and equipment other than that deemed necessary for their own personal survival strategy. Often they went bare-chested and entered competitions for 'the brownest man on The Beach'. Water was scarce and 'washing became a lost art' as mirrors were converted into periscopes and the men went unshaven. In the summer their constant companions were flies, hideously bloated from gorging on corpses and in latrines, and which swarmed thickly over the men and their food - and the resultant dysentery. During the week of 21-27

The Bomb Factory in full production. IWM (Q13281)

Beach CWGC Cemetery
Headstone of 'The Man with the Donkey'

July alone 1,221 cases of acute dysentery were reported at Anzac. Persistent lice added to their torment, as did the many broken teeth they suffered from the iron-hard biscuits. The fit and handsome men, so admired as they trained in Egypt, became gaunt and skeletal. Add to this the incessant roar, whine, screech and ping of shell and bullet and the obscene, all-pervading stench of decaying flesh. Dante could have not invented such an Inferno - a veritable hell on earth. The rum ration was the greatest 'treat' of the inhabitants of this strange colony. It sustained them, gave them some warmth as winter approached and helped them to snatch a few hours of fitful sleep. This tiny cove, the murderous gullies and scrubland and the rarely attainable heights formed the territory of this newly-born race and they adapted to it. They were, for the most part, uncomplaining and cheerful. They lived, like primitive cave-men, in holes dug into the sand, the stone and the clay and the name of the race thus became 'Digger'. It came as a P.S. to a message of 26 April to General Birdwood, 'You have got through the difficult business, now you have only to dig, dig, dig, until you are safe. Ian H.'
  Walk to the cemetery.

* Beach CWGC Cemetery/12.4 kilometres/20 minutes/Map A3

The cemetery was used from the day of the landings at Anzac to the Evacuation. There are 285 Australian burials, 50 UK (including sailors and Marines of the RND and RNAS), 21 New Zealand, 3 from Ceylon and 21 unidentified. There are 10 Australian special memorials and 1 New Zealand. The curved plot faces the sea just above Hell Spit and a concrete retaining wall has been built to halt the erosion on the seaward slope.

It is interesting to note the diverse origins and varied achievements of these men who came so far to die, e.g: **Captain Edward Frederick Robert Bage** of the 3rd Australian Field Coy, Australian Engineers, age 27, killed on 7 May, was a member of the Mawson's 1911-1913 Expedition to Antarctica [I D 7]. **Private F. Barling** was from Wagga Wagga [II J 10]; **Private F. Bauer**, of the 1st Field Ambulance Aust AMC, age 48, from Grafton, NSW, who died of 'heart failure' on 20 September [II 1 19] was of obvious German roots, as was **Private Willen Broudus Behr**, killed on 2 May with the 16th Battalion, AIF [I A 37]. **Lieutenant-Colonel George Frederick Braund**, V.D., of the 2nd Battalion, AIF, accidentally killed on 4 May when, being somewhat deaf, he ignored the challenge of a sentry and was shot, was 'Born in England' [I A 40]. A Member of the New South Wales Legislative Assembly, Braund was a man of unusual convictions for 1915 - a theosophist, vegetarian and teetotaller. **Lance Corporal Thomas James Carey**, of the 15th Battalion, AIF, who was killed 9/10 May was the 'Father of Master E.C. Carey' and was 'Born in Belfast' [Sp Mem 1]. **Commander Edward Howell Cater**, RN, Naval Transport Officer of HMS *Lord Nelson*, was killed, according to the cemetery register, on 7 August. During the landings at Anzac he had directed the incoming barges to their designated piers with only the light of the stars and a megaphone through which he shouted until he was hoarse. Bean describes him as being killed on 5 August when he rushed out along the pier to steady the crew of a small steamboat which had been holed during a bombardment. The brave disregard for his own safety of this officer won the respect and affection of the Diggers who called him 'The Bloke with the Eye-Glass', because of his over-size monocle. [II G 5]. **Lieutenant-Colonel Lancelot Fox Clarke, D.S.O.** (qv) of the 12th Battalion, AIF, age 57, was killed on 25 April at the Nek [I B 13]. **Lieutenant William Henry Dawkins**, 2nd Field Coy, AASC, age 21, killed on 7 May, gave his name to Dawkins Point (qv) [I H 3]. **Private Joseph Gervasi** of the 3rd Battalion, AIF, served as 'Brennan' [I J 9]; **Rifleman Guy Middlemiss** of the Ceylon Planters Rifle Corps, killed 6 May, born in Rawalpindi and educated at St John's School, Leatherhead [I B 36], was one of three buried here of this unusual unit which served in the Peninsula as General Birdwood's personal escort and guard. He had served with them in India. **Lieutenant Brian Walton Onslow** of the 11th King Edward's Own Lancers (Probyn's Horse), Mentioned in Despatches, killed on 28 July age 22, was ADC to Lieutenant-General Sir William Birdwood. He had been involved in an incident on 6 May when the Turkish guns ranged accurately on the crowded Beach, scattering men, many of whom tried desperately to shift the potentially lethal stacks of ammunition. The Indian drivers were divided, some staying with their mules, others fleeing. Onslow and Foster, another of Birdwood's ADCs, together with an Indian Officer and some natives of the Cart Corps, tried to lead the terrified beasts to safety. Several officers and men were wounded in the attack, including Foster, and thirty-four mules and fourteen horses were killed. [II F 6]. **Major Sydney Beresford Robertson**, 9th Battalion, age 29, was killed on Baby 700 on 25 April [I A 39]. **Major Charles Herbert Villiers-Stuart** of the 56th Punjabi Rifles, attd. HQ Staff Aust & NZ Army Corps, age 40, had landed at Anzac at 0535 hours on 25 April, together with Major Glasfurd (qv). Designated as 'Guides', the two officers had to choose forming-up places on the beach and rendez-vous areas to the north and south of it. Villiers-Stuart was killed on 17 May, hit through the heart by a shrapnel pellet while correcting valley contours on a defective map [I H 4]. **Private John Simpson Kirkpatrick**, served as **Private John Simpson,** 3rd Field Ambulance, AIF, aged 22, killed on 19 May, is probably the most famous legendary hero of Gallipoli - 'The Man with the Donkey'. Kirkpatrick was born in South Shields in 1892 (and today there is a statue to him in the town near the Metro Station). He emigrated to Australia in 1909, working on a variety of merchant ships and as a farm labourer. On 25 August 1914 he enlisted, thinking it would be a way of getting home to see his widowed mother and his sister. To his disappointment he landed in Egypt, not the Western Front. During the voyage out and the training in Egypt, Simpson had shown a resistance to discipline, a freedom of mind and spirit. He was a lover of practical jokes, a sloppy dresser, but with a strong affinity with animals - he had a pet possum and any stray dog would attach itself to him. The 3rd Field Ambulance landed on Anzac at dawn on 25 April from the transport *Devanha* and, despite immediately sustaining three men killed and fourteen wounded, set to attending the wounded on the beach and establishing collecting posts. Simpson soon 'annexed' a donkey, whom he called Murphy, and started plying wounded men down the terrible, bullet-strafed slopes of what was christened Shrapnel Gully (known by the Turks as Kuruku Dere - Valley of Fear) and the Valley of Death, transporting water and supplies up it. Man and donkey worked as a lone unit, a Red Cross armlet tied round the donkey's head. When Major-General William Throsby Bridges, the 54-year-old commander of 1st Australian Division, was mortally wounded on 15 May in Monash Valley, Simpson, on hearing him say, "Don't carry me down - I don't want any of your stretcher-bearers hit", is reported to have said, "You'll be all right, Dig. I wish they'd let me take you down to the Beach on my donkey". Bridges had been hit through his thigh, severing both femoral artery and vein and, during a unnatural lull in the Turkish fire, was taken to the hospital ship *Gascon.* There he was visited by Hamilton who wrote sadly in his diary, 'He looked languid and pale. But his spirit was as high as ever and he smiled at a little joke I managed to make about the way someone had taken the shelling we had just gone through. The doctors, alas, give a bad, if not desperate, account of him. Were he a young man, they could save him by cutting off his leg high up, but as it is he would not stand the shock. On the other hand, his feet are so cold from the artery being severed that they anticipate mortification. I should have thought better have a try at cutting off the leg, but they are not for it. Bridges will be a real loss. He was a single-minded, upright, politics-despising soldier. With all her magnificent rank and file, Australia cannot afford to lose Bridges.' But lose him she did. Bridges died shortly after. 'Anyhow,' he said with pride just before he died, 'I have commanded an Australian Division for nine months.' His body was taken to Australia and buried on the hill above the military college at Duntroon which he had founded.

Of Simpson, General Brand, commanding 3rd Brigade, wrote, 'Almost every digger knew about him'. The question was often asked, 'Has the bloke with the donk stopped one yet?' It seemed incredible that anyone could make that trip up and down Monash Valley without being hit. Simpson escaped death so many times that he was completely fatalistic. He seemed to have a charmed life. His cheerfulness and courage made a profound impression on everyone who saw his dedicated work. 'If ever a man deserved a Victoria Cross it was Simpson,' declared the Padre George Green. But when his charmed life came to an end on 19 May, shot through the heart by a sniper at exactly the same spot as General Bridges, no posthumous decoration was awarded to this undoubted hero. His comrades buried him at Hell Spit that evening and marked his grave with a cross that said 'Pte Simpson 3 Aust Fld Amb'. Colonel Monash wrote to HQ, New Zealand and Australian Division commending his bravery and told C.E.W. Bean that Simpson was worth a hundred men to him. His CO, Lieutenant-Colonel Alfred Sutton, attended the funeral and recorded in his diary that Simpson would at least get the DCM but that 'It is difficult to get evidence of any one act to justify the V.C. The fact is he did so many.' Simpson was universally mourned, even by the Indian troops with whose mules he often camped. On 22 September he was mentioned in General Sir Ian Hamilton's Despatches. There is a bronze statue by Wallace Anderson of Simpson and Murphy in the Shrine of Remembrance at Melbourne and in 1965 three special postage stamps were issued to commemorate the 50th Anniversary of the Gallipoli Landings. The 5d stamp bears a picture of Simpson and Murphy transporting a wounded comrade. In 1967 a petition was sent to the War Office on behalf of the Australian people requesting a posthumous VC for Simpson. This was refused on the grounds that it might create a precedent. Simpson will, however, be honoured on the Millenium Year Anzac Day badges sold in Australia.

Continue to the sign to the right to

* Shrapnel Valley Cemetery/Ross Bastiaan Marker No 3/12.7 kilometres/ 20 minutes/Map A6,5

The cemetery is a few metres off the road. Over the period of the anniversary of the landings (25 April) it is spectacularly beautiful, with flaming Judas trees and banks of iris. By the entrance is **Ross Bastiaan Marker No 3** which describes the action here.

Made shortly after the landings, the cemetery was enlarged by concentration of isolated graves in the Valley after the Armistice. There are 527 Australian burials, 56 New Zealand, 28 UK and 72 unidentified. There are 21 Australian special memorials and 2 UK.

Among the burials is **Private Abraham Levene** of the 4th Battalion AIF. Age 20, he served as 'Conroy' and was a 'Native of Russia' [I C 12]. **Captain Walter Lloyd** of B Coy, 8th Battalion RWF, age 41, Mentioned in Despatches, was killed on 7 August. Born in Italy, he had joined the Regiment in 1896 and retired as a Captain in 1911. He was recalled at the outbreak of war and sailed for Gallipoli on 28 June [IV F 17]. The **Putland** brothers, **George Arthur Temple** and **Wesley James Ethersey,** both Privates in the 1st Battalion AIF, lie close together: Wesley, killed on 18 May, is in IV A

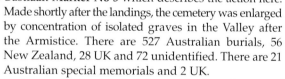

Shrapnel Valley CWGC Cemetery

47 and George, age 20, killed on 19th May, is in IV A 43. **Major Hugh Quinn** of the 15th Battalion AIF, age 27, Mentioned in Despatches, gave his name to 'Quinn's Post' (the wall of the cemetery of that name is visible at the top of the Valley). He was killed there on 29 May [III C 21]. Two RMLI officers of the Portsmouth Battalion, killed in the action near Quinn's Post, are buried here: **Major Harold Gage Bewes Armstrong,** age 37, killed on 5 May and **Lieutenant R. W. H. M. Empson**, killed on 1 May.

Beyond the cemetery is **Shrapnel Valley,** up which Simpson (qv) plied with Murphy.

Extra Visit to Plugge's Plateau CWGC Cemetery (Map A9) OP
Round trip: 1,140 metres. Approximate time: 45 minutes.

From the rear of Shrapnel Valley Cemetery take the small, very rough and difficult path, signed 570m, which becomes steeper and steeper until you reach the plateau.

Make sure you have all the recommended requisites if you are attempting the climb. Just after rounding the bend at the top of the steep climb there is a well-preserved sangar. The cemetery, 'a small triangular top with all its sides very steep' as the Official Australian History describes it, was named after Colonel Arthur Plugge (pronounced 'Pluggy'). The Turks called it Khain Tepe - Treacherous Hill. Plugge commanded the Auckland Battalion whose HQ was set up here on the day of the landings when a path was beaten from the beach to the plateau, which is the northern end of what became known as MacLagan's Ridge (named after 3rd Australian Brigade Commander, Lieutenant-Colonel Sinclair-MacLagan). Lieutenant Hedley Vicars Howe, a member of Bean's Historical Mission (qv) had, as a private in Major (later Brigadier-General) E.A. Drake-Brockman's 11th (Western Australian) Battalion, been one of the first ashore on

Plugge's Plateau CWGC Cemetery

View from Plugge's Plateau over Walker's Ridge and Rhododendron Spur to North Beach showing Canterbury CWGC Cemetery and the CWGC complex

Extra Visit continued

25 April. Landing on the point of Ari Burnu, his platoon threw off their packs and climbed up the facing scrubby ridge to the summit of what later became known as Plugge's Plateau. There they found a few Turks who fired as they ran off, killing Captain William Richard Annear, the first Australian officer to be killed in the campaign. [He is commemorated on Panel 33 of the Lone Pine Memorial.] On the evening of 25 April Lieutenant Rossiter brought up two guns and set up a battery here. They were later joined by Major Sykes's 2nd NZ Field Battery. Platforms were hewn in the steep sides of the plateau and huge water tanks capable of holding 50,000 gallons were hauled up to them by parties of as many as 110 men with drag-ropes. Water was then pumped up from the beach through pipes from the water-boats from Imbros. During the storm of 8 October the pipeline was torn away and the water boats were driven ashore. Reserves of water fell to 24,000 gallons by 11 October. Two lighters were sunk to form a breakwater for the water barges and new pipes were connected to restore the water supply to the Plateau. When the Evacuation was planned on 12 December, Plugge's Plateau was to form part of the Inner Line of defence and a 'keep', stocked with ammunition, food and water was set up here for the 275 men who were to man this Defence.

The view from the plateau is incredible - to the north the Sphinx, North Beach and Suvla Bay, to the east Rest Valley and Monash Valley, to the south Lone Pine and Gaba Tepe, to the west Ariburnu and Anzac Cove.

Because of its inaccessibility this tiny cemetery - the smallest in the Peninsula - has few visitors: the 12 Australians and 8 New Zealanders, the majority of whom were killed on the day of the landing, are seldom seen. They are **Private Frank Batt,** 10th Battalion AIF, age 36, killed on 25 April; **Private George Bell,** 11th Battalion AIF, age 28, killed on 25 April (born in Scotland); **Serjeant William Richard Bowden,** NZ Field Artillery, age 25, killed 17 May (born in Cardiff); **Private Thomas George Carroll,** 11th Battalion AIF, killed 25 April; **Lance Corporal Arthur Clarke,** Otago Regiment, NZEF, age 31, killed on 25 April; **Private Thomas Joseph Courtney,** 9th Battalion AIF, age 19, killed 2 May; **Private George Thomas Dale,** 5th Battalion AIF, age 21, killed 25 April; **Private Wolverton Edgar,** 11th Battalion AIF, killed on 25 April; **Gunner George Merry Gundry,** 2nd Battery NZ Field Artillery, age 25, died of wounds 30 May (born in Gosport); **Private Thomas Kean,** 7th Battalion AIF, killed 25 April; **Gunner John Edward Le Masurier,** 3rd Brigade Ammunition Column Australian Field Artillery, killed 29 May; **Serjeant John Naghten,** 4th Battalion AIF, killed 30 April; **Corporal John O'Donnell,** 3rd Battalion Auckland Regiment, NZEF, age 21, killed 25 April; **Private Thomas Rennet,** Otago Regiment NZEF, age 30, killed 25 April; Private **Reginald James Rossiter, 6th** Battalion AIF, age 22, killed 25 April; **Private Sydney Smith,** 6th Battalion AIF, killed on 25 April; **Private Allen Patrick Yeatman,** 9th Battalion AIF, age 37, killed 25 April and 4 unidentified New Zealand graves.

Return to Shrapnel Valley Cemetery.

Return to the main road, cross it and walk up the slope to the left to

* Turkish Monolith, Queensland Point (Hell Spit)/Anzac Cove Name Marker/Ross Bastiaan Marker No. 2/12.7 kilometres/5 minutes/Map A4,7,8

The inscription on this monolith, designed by Ahmet Gulgonen, describes how at dawn on 25 April 1915, a platoon of 8th Company, 27th Infantry Regiment, faced the first wave of 1,500 ANZACs who landed here. Their resistance caused many casualties among the ANZACs, who were forced to shelter under the steep foothills of the beach. There is an excellent view over Beach CWGC Cemetery from the left edge of the memorial area.

Nearby is the small stone which explains how on 17 April 1985, the Turkish Government decided to name the cove, formerly known as Ari Burnu, Anzac Cove, in memory of the men of the Australian and New Zealand Army Corps who landed here on 25 April 1915, and in recognition of the importance of the event in world history. Next to it is **Ross Bastiaan Marker No. 2** for Anzac Cove.

Continue around Anzac Cove to another monolith on the left.

* Turkish Monolith, Ari Burnu (Anzac Cove)/13.2 kilometres/20 minutes/Map A10

Ari Burnu means Bee Point in Turkish.

Unveiled on Anzac Day 1985 by Senator Arthur Gietzelt, the Australian Minister for Veterans' Affairs, the monument bears the moving words that Kemal Ataturk addressed to Allied pilgrims in 1934:

> Those heroes that shed their blood and lost their lives
> You are now lying in the soil of a friendly country.
> Therefore rest in peace.
> There is no difference between the Johnnies and the Mehmets to us
> Where they lie side by side
> Here in this country of ours.
> You, the mothers,
> Who sent their sons from far-away countries
> Wipe away your tears.
> Your sons are now lying in our bosom
> And are in peace.
> After having lost their lives on this land
> They have become our sons as well.

These words demonstrate Ataturk's magnanimous attitude towards his former enemies that parallels President Lincoln's treatment of the Southern States after the Civil War and have the same emotional power as Lincoln's Address at the dedication of the Gettysburg National Cemetery.

Plaques were unveiled at the same time in Canberra and Albany in Australia and in Wellington, New Zealand, to honour Ataturk and to commemorate the departure points of the ANZACs in 1914.

Behind the monolith is

Anzac Cove Name Marker and Ross Bastiaan Marker No. 2 with 'The Beach' beyond

Atarturk's memorable message on the Ari Burnu Monolith

Ari Burnu CWGC Cemetery with the Sphinx behind

Ari Burnu CWGC Cemetery/Ross Bastiaan Marker No 1/15 minutes/WC/Map A11,12

The cemetery is named after the Cape which marks the northern end of Anzac Cove and was made during the campaign on land overlooked by Turkish outposts and thus unsafe for other purposes. It contained 151 Australians (82 of them of the Light Horse), 35 New Zealanders, 27 UK (including sailors of the RND and from the Fleet), 1 Maltese Labour Corps and 37 unidentified.

There are 3 Australian and 2 New Zealand special memorials. In 1926/27 eleven graves from the Kilid Bahr Anglo-French Cemetery, (which originally contained 5 UK soldiers and 1 sailor, 4 Australians and 4 Indians) and 3 from the Gallipoli Consular Cemetery were brought here.

The Light Horse burials are mostly from the 8th Battalion's charge at the Nek of 7 August. They are in Row A, nearest the sea. In Rows E and F are the graves of the 10th Battalion from the same attack. They include the two **Chipper brothers, Lance Corporal Lindsay Lewis Stirling,** age 28 [E 19] and **Trooper Ross Richard Vivian,** age 31 [E15] and **2nd Lieutenant Alexander Phipps Turnbull,** age 27, a Rhodes scholar and solicitor who had just been commissioned [E 16]. **Private William Clarence,** age 29, of the 26th Battalion AIF, killed on 28 November, served as G.D. Ford [G 4]. Three Indian Drivers of 22nd Mule Corps, attd 3rd Cavalry Brigade - brought here after the war from Kilid Bahr Cemetery - **Alla Ditta and Imam Din,** died 20 November 1918, and **Husain Khan,** died 26 November 1918, have special memorials just below the Cross. **Guiseppe Camilleri** of the Maltese Labour Corps, age 27, killed on 7 December 1915, is in J 4. From June 1915 the British employed Greek and Maltese Labourers at Helles for unloading ships and constructing harbour works, but the work later fell on the garrison at Anzac. When they first reached Mudros, many of the Maltese refused to face the danger on the Peninsula, but 200 under their officer Captain Stivala volunteered to continue, as did about the same number of Egyptians. In September 1915 over 200 Maltese and 200 Egyptians were sent to Anzac. As winter set in, however, the Egyptians were unable to work in the cold and the over-age or unfit British labourers were allotted camps with the Maltese on the northern, exposed side of Ari Burnu, subject to Turkish machine-gun fire. The British, Egyptian and Maltese Labour Corps were withdrawn in December before the main Evacuation.

Outside the cemetery is **Ross Bastiaan Marker No 1.** Note that each Bastiaan marker summarises the following one in the bottom right hand corner.

Continue along the road. You are now entering the area of

*North Beach

This is often seen on contemporary maps as 'Ocean Beach'.
Immediately after the landings, the task of caring for the wounded and evacuating the serious cases was a priority. At Anzac it was at first the responsibility of the chief medical officer, Colonel Howse of the 1st Australian Division, who was superseded by Colonel Manders (qv), the chief MO of the NZ and A Division. The regimental surgeons followed the battalions as they went forward and quickly

established aid posts. Here on North Beach 3rd Field Ambulance set up a dressing station. It was not until August when the seaward foothills were cleared of the enemy that North Beach could be used as a port. Then a rudimentary pier was run out from the centre of the beach which was out of sight of Turkish artillery observers at Gaba Tepe. The steamer *Milo* was sunk to form a breakwater. North Beach then became the site of the main depot of reserve stores for the winter. The slopes above the beach became the HQ offices of General Godley's NZ and A and 13th Divisions and were a hive of activity, with bivouacs, ordnance, transport and staff personnel. Here were sited No 1 Australian Stationary Hospital, CCS No 13 and the YMCA tent. During the Evacuation of 11/12 December many men and guns were embarked from here. The road which runs round Anzac Cove (along which you have just driven) and continues along North Beach and towards the Suvla Flats, was made by New Zealand Engineers in preparation for the Suvla Landings in August. The laborious work had to be done at night as the entire area was under enemy observation and within rifle fire range. Men who were 'resting' crept out with their picks and shovels, each trying to work as silently as possible. To reinforce the sand, large stones had to be collected to make the foundations. On top of these was a layer of clay, brought down from the hillside by the Indian Mule Transport Service and a final top dressing of sand over which sea-water was poured to help it set.

They also constructed a communication trench to transport men and supplies from Anzac to the Outposts and the foot of the deres or gullies up which the troops reached the Plateau. In July this too was deepened - to well above the height of a man - and widened - sometimes to a width of 5 feet so that men could pass each other and laden mules could easily negotiate it. The work was carried out by No 4 Defence Section, including men of the Australian 4th Brigade, the NZ Mounted Rifles, the Australian Light Horse and, most conspicuously, the Maori Contingent from No 1 Post, known to the Turks as Chatal Tepe - Fork Hill. In places, where the sap was vulnerable to enfilade fire, overhead protection was built with precious timber and sandbags. It became known as The Big Sap.

Dominating the beach is the craggy rock called The Sphinx, known to the Turks as Yuksek Tepe - High Hill. To the troops who trained at Gizeh in the shadow of the Pyramids this dramatic outcrop reminded them of the ancient Egyptian monument, hence its name. It was clearly visible from the landing craft at dawn on 25 April - a conspicuous landmark, adding to the mystery of why the landing was made on the wrong beach. Beyond it is Walker's Ridge (qv), known to the Turks as Sercha Tepesi - Sparrow Hill - leading up to Walker's Ridge Cemetery, with The Nek to its left.
Continue along the road to the cemetery on the right.

* Canterbury CWGC Cemetery/14.2 kilometres/10 minutes/Map A13

This small cemetery was made after the Armistice. It contains the graves of 26 New Zealanders, 20 of them of the New Zealand (Canterbury) Mounted Rifles. Five are unidentified. Above the cemetery is Walker's Ridge and there are good views of Chunuk Bair and the Nek.

Off the shore opposite the cemetery are the remains of the Paddle Steamer

Marsden used as a tug during the campaign and grounded during the Evacuation. *Continue to the complex on the right.*

* CWGC Base/ Cottages/14.5 kilometres/Map A

This is a private area and may not be entered without permission - the same applies to the beach opposite. As well as a bungalow for guests (which may be rented to serious students of, or pilgrims to, the Peninsula if no Commission officials are staying here: contact the CWGC at Canakkale - see below), the area includes the Commission's base depot, workshops, nurseries and gardeners' cottages, all pleasantly landscaped. They were constructed in 1952. Behind the cottages are remnants of 'The Big Sap' (qv), leading to Outpost No. 1, now a hillock to the north of the complex. On a small mound surmounted by fir trees to the east of the cottages once stood one of the Turkish memorials erected after the Evacuation. On it the current (1999) Area Superintendent, Mr John Price, has planted an acorn from an oak planted in Ankara by Mustafa Kemal. Also within the grounds, but unfortunately not visitable, is a standard CWGC headstone to 'Bill', a horse who had survived the campaign and stayed on to work for the Commission until he died in 1923.

The great forest fire of 1994 swept fiercely towards the depot and the cottages, and the gardeners' families, complete with their furniture, fled to safety in a truck driven by Mrs Eileen Price. John Price and his staff stayed to protect their buildings and equipment, the gardeners working with extreme energy and bravery until they were forced into the sea. By some miracle the fire just skirted the buildings. *Continue to the small building on the right.*

* Fisherman's Hut/14.7 kilometres/Map A

The stone hut which exists today is on the site of the most seaward of two huts which stood on a sandy knoll there in 1915. The hut further inland was called **Shepherd's Hut** by the troops. On 25 April four boatloads carrying 140 men, mostly of the 7th Battalion AIF (temporarily commanded by Major A. Jackson), disembarked on the beach here and were shot to pieces by the Turks in the trenches on the knoll. Only Jackson, Captain Layh (badly shot through the leg and hip), Lieutenant Scanlan and thirth-five men remained after the hail of machine-gun and rifle fire. They crouched in a deserted trench which had probably been dug in the Balkan Wars and which is marked on contemporary maps as such. Major Jackson reached 3rd Field Ambulance which had landed safely along the beach to the south and sent stretcher bearers to remove the seriously wounded. Layh, though wounded, and Scanlan, held the position for the remainder of the day until they realised that the Turks were threatening to cut them off by driving towards the sea between them and Walker's Ridge. Layh withdrew his group, now numbering eighteen, to the beach where they were pinned down by a Turkish machine gun. They gradually managed to creep along the beach and eventually reached the dressing station. They were then sent up the line as reinforcements for 3rd Brigade. The next day watchers in the warships lying off shore saw two stretcher bearers making their way across the beach here to one of the three landing craft which still lay on the shore. They picked

Canterbury CWGC Cemetery with Walker's Ridge behind

CWGC Guest Bungalow

Headstone of 'Bill', the
Commission horse

Fisherman's Hut

up a man and, as fire broke out, started to run. They were both killed. Then a burial party went out and they too were fired upon, only two men carrying a stretcher managed to return along the shore. These were only two of many attempts to reach these wounded men. One stretcher party had ventured out because Lance-Corporal Noel Ross, son of the Official New Zealand War Correspondent, had noticed a man moving in one of the boats. He led the party along the beach under a hail of Turkish bullets until they found the wounded man who had crawled out of the boat and had been shot in both knees and managed to bring him in. It is thought that nine wounded men were brought in from the landing boats through such acts of unrewarded heroism.

Some 270 metres to the south of Fisherman's Hut was the area which would become **No 1 Outpost,** a 45-metre-high knoll, also occupied by the Turks. The 12th Battalion AIF, commanded by 56-year-old Colonel Clarke, landed on the beach below the position and Clarke sent Lieutenant Rafferty with a platoon of the 12th and Lieutenant Strickland with a platoon of the 11th along the beach to subdue the opposition. Rafferty saw the four landing boats of Jackson's group heading towards Fisherman's Hut and attempted to cross the intervening field to assist their landing. His group was caught in a hail of fire and twenty men were hit. Rafferty, Skinner and six men reached a rise from which they could see the landing boats of 7th Battalion and men lying on the beach in front of them. Not one of them moved. Private Stubbings volunteered to go and investigate, only to discover that all the men were dead or mortally wounded, except four who were sheltering behind the boats and were able to tell him what had happened. Stubbings ran back to report to Rafferty. They then saw a party of Australians advancing towards them and, assured that there were now Australian troops to the left of the landing, Rafferty got on with his original allotted task - of escorting the Indian Mountain Battery. He had probably seen Layh and Scanlon's small party and was unaware that they were part of the group he had set out to rescue. Colonel Clarke was later killed near the Nek, book and pencil in hand as he wrote a message to Colonel MacLagan (qv). He is buried in Beach Cemetery CWGC. His batman, waiting to take the message, was killed by another bullet.

The hill to the north of Fisherman's Hut was known as **Maori Hill.**

Continue to the cemetery on the right.

* No 2 Outpost CWGC Cemetery/15.1 kilometres/10 minutes/Map A14

As No 1 Outpost was south of Fisherman's Hut, so No 2 (known to the Turks as Mahmus Sirta - Spur Ridge) was to the north. Between them, just to the south of the cemetery, ran the Sazli Beit Dere. On 30 April the Posts were made by the Nelson Company of the Canterbury Infantry Battalion who started the cemetery. No 2 Post was at the northern extremity of the line. 'Soldiers came from far and near to draw the precious water' [*The New Zealanders at Gallipoli* by Major Fred Waite]. 16th Casualty Clearing Station (and there are 7 burials of Field Ambulance men in the cemetery) and the NZ Dental Corps clinic were established near it. There were very few dental facilities in the British and Anzac Armies and when the problem of broken teeth from hard tack biscuits reached alarming proportions, the ranks had to be scoured for qualified dentists. By the end of July 600 men from the

1st Australian Division alone had to be evacuated with dental trouble. Instruments were primitive and men would only resort to the dentist in *extremis*.

Four isolated graves were brought into the cemetery after the Armistice. It now contains 32 New Zealand burials, 7 Australian and 3 UK, with 62 unidentified burials. There are 2 New Zealand and 29 Australian special memorials, including 23 of the 7th Battalion, whose story is told above. The date on their headstones is '25 April/2 May 1915' as their bodies had to lie where they fell until the New Zealanders established the Outposts and 'Late one night a party of mounteds [the Otago Mounted Rifles] went down and buried the remains of forty Australian infantryman who had been killed at the April landing.' Also buried here is **Trooper William McKenzie** of the Otago Mounted Rifles NZEF, age 34, killed on 31 May, who had served as a young Sergeant in the S. African campaign.

No 3 Outpost - known to the Turks as Haliden Rizar Tepesi (Hills) - was established on the high ground above Fisherman's Hut. It was captured and held for two days in May by the NZMR but was abandoned to the Turks. It then became known as 'Old No 3 Post' and 'No 3 Post' was re-established just to the north of No 2 Outpost. It was retaken in the August advance, the Battle of Sari Bair.

No 2 Outpost was one of the jumping-off points for this battle.

Continue to the cemetery on the right.

* New Zealand No 2 Outpost CWGC Cemetery/15.2 kilometres/5 minutes/Map A15

The cemetery virtually consists of one long grave made in September by the Nelson Company of the NZ Canterbury Battalion. In it are buried only two named UK soldiers and 150 unidentified men. There are 13 New Zealand, 10 UK and 8 Australian special memorials, among whom is **Colonel Neville Manders**, DDMS (Anzac) Army Medical Service, age 55. Manders, who had been born in Marlborough, was Chief Medical Officer on the Staff of General Godley (qv), and responsible for collecting wounded on the shore from the moment of the Landings. Despite an appalling lack of decisiveness and communication in the plans for dealing with the wounded, which left Manders without precise instructions on the day and most hospital ships too far away to receive the unexpectedly huge number of casualties, he quickly set up a dressing and clearing station at the end of The Beach. His energetic and younger colleague, Colonel Howse of Bridges' staff, aware of the urgency to clear the beach, was commandeering every available transport to ferry men to the inadequate hospital ships. The result was that the conditions on those ships were foul and horrendous – overcrowding meant that badly wounded men lay all over the decks, the surgeons were totally overwhelmed and many men died who could have been saved had conditions been better. The problem arose all over again during the Battle of Sari Bair at the beginning of August. A pier was constructed during the night of 6 August (see below) and the wounded were brought down to it in large numbers. Tragically no boats arrived to transport them and they lay, in full view of the enemy as day broke, at the mouth of the Chailak Dere (meaning Creviced Valley). Colonel Manders appealed to the

navy for barges and a few craft arrived. But more wounded were arriving and enemy fire continued. Desperate attempts were made to clear the wounded. An NZ Dental Officer, Captain Finn, and 31-year-old Lieutenant-Commander Greenshields of HMS *Venerable* eventually used pulling-boats to evacuate them. Greenshields was killed (he is commemorated on the Portsmouth Naval Memorial, Panel 7) and then Colonel Manders, who had ordered his ambulance to hold all the men it could, was eventually killed on the 9th by a stray bullet [Sp Mem 20]. By then there were over 2,000 men lying out in the heat of the sun. The congestion was not relieved until the 11th.
Continue to the cemetery on the left.

Embarkation Pier CWGC Cemetery/15.4 kilometres/10 minutes/Map A16

The cemetery is situated to the south of the mouth of the Chailak Dere, between the sea and the site of New No 3 Post. The pier after which it was named (see above) only lasted for two days and no traces of it remain today. It was to the north of the mouth of the Dere. Buried in the cemetery are 23 New Zealanders, 7 Australians and 662 unidentified men. There are special memorials to 118 Australians, 93 from the UK (many of them of the 6th Leinsters who fell in the Battle of Sari Bair) and 51 New Zealanders.

Among them are **Private Howard Lewis Ingram**, age 49, of the Auckland Regiment, NZEF, killed on 7 August. He had served in the Sudan and in S Africa [Sp Mem B 76]. Several men buried here served under other names: **Serjt. Ernest Henry Melmott Cohen** served as 'Drummond' [Sp Mem B 53]; **Private George William 'Mee'** served as Mead [Sp Mem C58]; **Serjt. Leopold Clarence Pratt** served as 'Sefton' [Sp Mem D 28]. The **Rev. Andrew Gillison**, age 47, Chaplain to the Forces, 4th Class, attd. 14th Battalion Aust. Inf., Mentioned in Despatches, died of wounds on 22 August [Sp Mem B 62]. On 21 August a fire was started by a shell which burst among the 13th and 14th Battalions AIF and the Hampshires on Hill 60 (qv) which ignited the clothing of the dead and wounded and exploded their bombs and rifle ammunition. Anyone moving from the inferno was shot by the Turks. Chaplain Gillison, with Captain Loughran, the MO of the 14th, and Corporal Robert Reginald Pittendrigh (also a clergyman before the war) and some stretcher bearers, dragged away other wounded in the area who were in danger from the fire. The next day, as Gillison was reading the burial service over some of these dead, he heard groaning in the scrub. Despite having been warned not to move in daylight in this area he went forward and found a wounded Hampshire. He, Pittendrigh and another man of the 13th Battalion crawled out to the man. Gillison and Pittendrigh were hit by a sniper. Gillison died later that day. Corporal Pittendrigh died on the 29th in a hospital ship. He is commemorated on the Lone Pine Memorial [Panel 36]. Two brothers Pittendrigh - Corporal Norman Thomas [Panel 13] and Private Edmund [Panel 62] are also on the Lone Pine Memorial. The entire CWGC worldwide register shows only three Pittendrighs and it seems likely that all three were related.

Trooper William Albert Baker, 9th Australian Light Horse, age 35, killed on 28 November, has the original personal inscription, 'Brother Bill a-sniping fell. We

NZ No 2 Outpost CWGC Cemetery with No 2 Outpost behind

Headstone in Embarkation Pier

Embarkation Pier CWGC Cemetery

miss him still. We ever will.' [I A 12].

Just beyond the cemetery on the left is the

* CWGC End of Anzac Battlefield Area Sign/15.5 kilometres/Map A

The sign and white stone pyramid mark the boundary of the Anzac Battlefield area.

* End of Itinerary Two

Return to Eceabat
*OR Return to fork with **Upper Route***
*OR Continue to **Itinerary Four.***

ITINERARY THREE

SARI BAIR RIDGE

* **Itinerary Three** starts either in Eceabat or at the fork with the Lower Route. It heads up to the Sari Bair Ridge and follows the cemeteries and memorials along its summit. It ends at Chunuk Bair. Refer throughout to Holts' Map 4 (A).
* **The Route:** Eceabat; Gaba Tepe; Fork with Lower Route; Statue of Turkish Soldier/Wounded Allied Soldier; Turkish Monolith, Kanlisirt Kitabesi; Lone Pine CWGC Cemetery and Australian Memorial; Ross Bastiaan Marker No 5; Johnston's Jolly CWGC Cemetery; Bunker Entrance; Courtney's and Steel's Post CWGC Cemetery; Ross Bastiaan Marker No 6; Captain Mehmet Tomb; Quinn's Post CWGC Cemetery; Ross Bastiaan Marker No 7; Turkish 57th Infantry Regiment Memorial Park; Sergeant Mehmet Tomb; Ross Bastiaan Marker No 8; The Nek CWGC Cemetery; Walker's Ridge CWGC Cemetery; Baby 700 CWGC Cemetery; Mesudiye Gun; Turkish Director of Forestry's Statue; Mehmetcik Park Aniti (Chunuk Bair Complex of Memorials) - Turkish Monoliths, Tomb of Unknown Turkish Soldier, New Zealand Memorial, Ataturk Statue, Ross Bastiaan Marker No 9, Ustegmen Nazif Cakmak Memorial, New Zealand Memorial Wall, Chunuk Bair CWGC Cemetery.
* **Extra Visits** are suggested to: Shell Green CWGC Cemetery; 4th Battalion Parade Ground CWGC Cemetery; Tombs of Lieutenant-Colonels Manastir and Avni; The Farm CWGC Cemetery.
* **Planned duration,** without stops for refreshment or Extra Visits: 4 hours 45 minutes.
* **Total distance:** 27.7 Kilometres.

* *Eceabat/0 kilometres/RWC/Map*

Take the road to Gaba Tepe as per Itinerary Two, then take the right fork to the Upper Route, signed Kemalyeri etc. Continue climbing up the steep narrow but metalled road to the Sari Bair Ridge.

This road was made by the Turks after the Evacuation, following one of the goatherds' tracks which were the only paths here during the campaign. It was constructed over the maze of trenches which still then existed, crossing them with bridges of pine trunks.

Caution - today, when wet, the edges of the road can be muddy and slippery.

Continue to the statue on the right, surrounded by a flower garden.

* Turkish Soldier Carrying Wounded Enemy Captain Memorial, Mehemetcige Derin Sayi Aniti/11.4 kilometres/5 minutes/Map A19

The bronze statue of a Turkish soldier carrying a wounded Australian symbolises the chivalry and compassion shown by both sides during the campaign. It depicts a true incident, witnessed by Lieutenant R. G. Casey (A.D.C. to Colonel C. B. B. White of 1st Australian Division) on 25 April 1915, when a Turk carried a wounded Allied Captain to his own trenches. (Casey went on to win the DSO and the MC, and, as Lord Casey, to become Governor General of Australia.)

Stand just below the figure and look down the hill. Directly over the Gaba Tepe Museum area, which is in the middle distance, is the hump of Achi Baba on the skyline.

Immediately after on the right is the green **CWGC sign** reminding visitors that they are entering 'a resting place for soldiers.'
Continue to the memorial on the right.

* Turkish Monolith, Kanlisirt Kitabesi/12.6 kilometres/5 minutes/ Map A20

Meaning 'Bloody Ridge', the location was christened by Turkish soldiers who sustained heavy casualties here in May 1915. The inscription reads, 'In order to help the British 9th Army Corps landing at Anafarta district (Suvla Bay) on 6-7 August 1915, the Anzac force attacked the Turkish 19th and 16th Divisions, who were defending the Ariburnu front, to hold them here. The units of the 16th Division, in spite of their losses of 1520 martyrs and 4750 wounded during the extremely violent fights, heroically defended Kanlisirt.'
Continue to the cemetery on the left and drive into the car park.

* Lone Pine Memorial and Lone Pine CWGC Cemetery/Ross Bastiaan Marker No. 5/13.1 kilometres/30 minutes/Map A22,21,23/OP

Lone Pine, the southernmost cemetery on the upper route, derived its name from a single tree that existed on the battlefield and the popular song of the period, *The Trail of the Lonesome Pine*. The original tree was soon destroyed, but seeds were taken from a pine in the vicinity after the war and propagated in Australia. One of the resultant saplings was planted as near the original site as could be ascertained. The cemetery is 120 metres above sea level at the top of Victoria Gully and on 25 April the area was actually reached and passed by elements of 9th Australian Battalion about 0800 hours and then by other units. By nightfall it was in no-man's-land. The following day it was re-occupied by 4th Battalion, who again had to give it up that night. Its strategic importance, dominating Gaba Tepe to the south and the ravines leading up to it from that part of the coast, was evident and in May, June and July it became a Turkish strongpoint, part of Kanlisirt. The Australians tunnelled mines towards it from the end of May to the beginning of August. On the afternoon of 6 August, after bombardments from land and sea, the 1st Australian Brigade stormed the trenches [see *Historical Summary*]. By 10 August the Turkish counter-attacks had failed and the position was consolidated. It was held by 1st Australian Division until 12 September and by 2nd Division until the Evacuation.

The Cemetery stands on the plateau, over Turkish tunnels. The original small battle cemetery of 46 graves, and the scattered graves brought in from the surrounding battlefield after the Armistice, form the eastern plot. To the west of the cemetery are the plots of graves removed from the Brown's Dip Cemeteries. (Brown's Dip was named after Major (later Brigadier-General) Alfred Bessell-Brown, Commander of the 8th Battery, AIF. Bessell-Brown had commanded the 37th Field Battery in Western Australia and had asked for volunteers. The entire parade stepped forward and became the 8th Battery, AIF.) Brown's Dip North and South cemeteries were in the depression at the head of Victoria Gully, behind the Australian trenches of April-August 1915. They were made on 7-11 August by the 5th Connaught Rangers and contained the graves of 149 Australians who were removed because of the insecurity of the site. There are 1,167 graves, of which 651 are Australian, 2 New Zealand, 15 sailors, soldiers or Marines from the UK and 499 whose unit could not be identified.

The cemetery forms the focal point of the official Anzac Commemorations of 25 April each year where a service is held in the morning, attended by hundreds of young Anzac back-packers.

Here are buried **Private Benjamin Harrison Armstrong,** 2nd Battalion AIF, age 21, killed 6/9 August, 'Native of Los Angeles, California' - one of the few Americans to fight on the Peninsula [Sp Mem C 80]. Among the UK burials is **Lieutenant-Colonel Richard Nelson Bendyshe,** RMLI, Commander of the Deal Battalion, RND, age 49, killed on 1 May [III D 6]. Also buried here, and killed in the same action, fighting around Quinn's and Courtney's - in which Lance Corporal Parker (qv) won his VC - were **Major George Fison Muller,** age 39, [II B 9] and **Lieutenant J.F. Moxham** [II B 7] also of the RMLI. **Major Richard Saker** (qv) of the 5th Battalion, AIF, age 37, was killed on '25/26' April in an action near The Daisy Patch described below [I F 8]. A particularly poignant personal inscription is on the headstone of **Driver Walter Bergin,** who has the early number '75'. Aged 21, he was the son of Thomas and Lilly Bergin of Henley Park, S Australia. On his headstone are inscribed the words, 'A mother's thoughts often wander to this sad and lonely grave' [I G 8].

The Memorial is to 3,268 Australian and 456 New Zealand soldiers who fell in the Anzac area and have no known graves and 960 Australians and 252 New Zealanders who were buried at sea. The 14-metre-high, 14-metre-square pylon is built of limestone from the local Ilgadere quarries and the names are carved on panels of Hopton Wood stone. The Australian panels are on a screen wall in front of the memorial, the New Zealand on the memorial itself. The graves of five men have since been identified and appear in the appropriate registers. The Australian Light Horse alone have 472 names of officers and men on the memorial, 181 of them from the 8th Battalion who attacked the Nek and Baby 700 (known to the

Lone Pine CWGC Cemetery
and Australian Memorial

Headstone in Lone Pine

Turks as Kulich Bair - Sword Hill) on 7 August. Among them is **Lieutenant-Colonel Alexander Henry White,** Commander of the 8th Light Horse Regiment, age 33 [Panel 5]; the **Harper** brothers **Gresley,** age 31, and **Alfred,** age 25, were both troopers in the 10th Light Horse. Gresley Harper was a barrister and Alfred who 'was last seen running forward like a schoolboy in a foot-race' [Bean], was a farmer. They were killed on 7 August [Panel 10], as was **Captain Vernon Frederick Piesse,** also of the 10th Light Horse, age 26, [Panel 9]. He had been sent away on a hospital ship on the 2nd 'but contrived to get back from hospital on the eve of the fight. Piesse succeeded in rejoining during the night of August 6th. 'I'd never have been able to stand up again if I hadn't', he said.' [Bean.] Captain W.R. Annear (qv), age 40, reputed to be the first Australian officer killed on the Peninsula [Bean], is commemorated on Panel 33. **Private James Martin** of the 21st Battalion, AIF, who was only 14 when he enlisted on 12 April 1915, was probably **the youngest soldier to fight on Gallipoli.** He survived being torpedoed on the *Southland* off Mudros on 2 September, landed on Gallipoli on 8 September, immediately took part in the fighting at Courtney's and died at sea of 'sickness' on 25 October [Panel 65]. **Lieutenant Penistan James Patterson,** 12th Battalion, age 20, was killed on Baby 700 on 25 April [Panel 34], as was **Major Charles George Gordon,** 2nd Battalion, age 45, 'native of Kingstown, Ireland', [Panel 16] and **Lieutenant William John Rigby,** 9th Battalion, age 23, [Panel 30]. **Lieutenant Mordant Leslie Reid** (qv) of the 11th Battalion was killed on Battleship Hill on 25 April [Panel 33]. **Major Francis Duncan Irvine** (qv), Brigade-Major of 1st Aust Inf Brigade, was killed on 27 April [Panel 12]. **Major Samuel Alexander Grant** (qv) of the Auckland Regiment, age 36, who died of wounds on HMS *Dongola* on 11 August, was mortally wounded in the assault on Chunuk Bair [Panel 72]. **2nd Lieutenant Norman James Greig** (qv) of the 7th Battalion, Mentioned in Despatches, age 24, was killed on 12 July leading a raid on a crater at German Officers' Trench [Panel 27]. **Lieutenant-Colonel Douglas Macbean Stewart** (qv) of the Canterbury Regiment, age 38, Mentioned in Despatches, was killed at Walker's Ridge on 25 April [Panel 73].

    Corporal Alexander Stewart Burton, VC, of the 7th Battalion AIF, age 21, won his VC when on 9 August the enemy made a determined counter-attack on a newly-captured trench held by Lieutenant Tubb with Corporals Burton and Dunstan (who were great friends) and a few men. They advanced up a sap and blew in a sandbag barricade, leaving only a foot of it standing, but Tubb, Burton and Dunstan repulsed the enemy and rebuilt the barricade. The enemy twice more blew it in, but on each occasion they were repulsed and the barricade rebuilt, although Lieutenant Tubb was wounded in the head and arm and Corporal Burton was killed by a bomb while most gallantly building up the parapet under a hail of bombs [Panel 28]. **Lieutenant Tubb,** who was killed on 20 September 1917, in Polygon Wood near Ypres and is buried in Lijssenthoek Cemetery, was also awarded the VC for this action, as was **Corporal (later Lieutenant) Dunstan,** who died on 3 March 1957 and is commemorated on the Australian War Memorial, Canberra. In the same action was **Corporal Frederick Wright,** age 26, Mentioned in Despatches, who had been attempting to catch bombs and throw them back when one burst in his face and killed him [Panel 28]. **Corporal Harry Webb** had his hands blown off while attempting to do the same and died of wounds at sea that day. He was awarded the DCM [Panel 28]. **Corporal Sutton Henry ('Syd') Ferrier** (qv) of the 10th Light Horse died on a hospital ship on 9 September after losing his arm when attempting to throw back a Turkish bomb which burst in his hand. The 36-year-old Ferrier, described as a 'Landowner', was reputed to have thrown 500 bombs before his fatal wound, standing beside 2nd Lieutenant Throssell on Hill 60 when the latter won the VC (qv) [Panel 9]. The Officer who led the attack of the 10th Australian Horse on 29 August, **Captain Henry Philip Fry**, age 33, is also commemorated here [Panel 9]. The son of a former Premier of New South Wales, **Private Albert Alfred Charles McGowan**, 1st Battalion, age 18, was killed whilst carrying wounded back during the fighting of 6-11 August [Panel 15]. **Lieutenant-Colonel Arthur Bauchop**, CMG, age 44, commanding the Otago Mounted Rifles, died of wounds on HMHS *Delta* on 10 August after being mortally wounded leading his men in the attack on Sari Bair. Ian Hamilton described Bauchop and Colonel W. G. Malone (qv), killed while commanding the Wellington Battalion, as 'Soldiers of great mark and, above all, fearless leaders of men' [Panel 74]. Another **VC** is **Captain Alfred Shout**, 1st (NSW) Battalion, age 33, who had already won the MC for 'gallantry at Gaba Tepe' on 27 April. At Lone Pine on the morning of 9 August, with a very small party, he charged down trenches strongly occupied by the enemy and personally threw four bombs among them, killing eight and routing the remainder. That afternoon he captured a further length of trench under similar conditions, and continued personally to bomb the enemy at close range under very heavy fire until he lost his right hand and left eye as one of his bombs exploded in his hands. Although conscious after his wounds (he is reported to have drunk tea and sent messages to his wife) he died three days later on the Hospital Ship *Euralia*. Bean describes him as 'fighting with a splendid gaiety. [He] lit three bombs at once as a prelude to making the final dash.' It was the third of these that burst in his hand [Panel 12].

There were three surviving **VCs** of Lone Pine. **Private John Hamilton** of the 3rd Battalion, who, on 9 August during a heavy bomb attack by the enemy on the newly captured position, with utter disregard for personal safety, exposed himself to heavy enemy fire on the parados in order to secure a better fire position against the enemy's bomb throwers. His daring had an immediate effect. The defence was encouraged and the enemy driven off with heavy loss. Hamilton went on to serve on the Somme and was commissioned in 1918. He survived the War without a wound and served again throughout WW2. He died on 27 February 1961, the last surviving Lone Pine VC. **2nd Lieutenant** (later Lieutenant-Colonel) **William John Symons**, 7th Battalion, was in command of a section of newly-captured trenches on 8/9 August and repelled several counter-attacks with great coolness. An enemy attack on an isolated sap early in the morning resulted in six officers becoming casualties and a part of the sap being lost, but 2nd Lieutenant Symons retook it, shooting two Turks. The sap was then attacked from three sides and this officer managed, in the face of heavy fire, to build a barricade. On the enemy setting fire to the head cover, he extinguished it and rebuilt the barricade. His coolness and determination finally compelled the enemy to withdraw. After the War he moved to England and served with the Home Guard in WW2. He died on 24 June 1948 in impoverished circumstances and in 1967 his widow was forced to sell his medals for £800. His VC was purchased by the RSL and is now in the Australian War Memorial at Canberra. **Private** (later Lieutenant) **Leonard Keysor** of the 1st Battalion on 7 August was in a trench which was being heavily bombed by the enemy. He picked up two live bombs and threw them back at the enemy at great risk to himself and continued throwing bombs until wounded. On 8 August at the same place he successfully bombed the enemy out of a position where they had gained temporary mastery over his own trench, again being wounded. He refused to go to hospital and, volunteering to throw bombs for another company which had lost its bomb throwers, continued bombing until the situation was relieved. Keysor's sustained gallantry over a period of fifty hours was described as 'one of the most spectacular individual feats of the war'. He went on to serve on the Somme and was commissioned on 13 January 1917. Born in Ramsgate, he returned to England after the War, taking part in a film which depicted his bomb-throwing exploits called *For Valour*. He died on 12 October 1951, aged sixty-five.

[The descriptions of the above VC deeds are taken from their citations in the *London Gazette*.]

Before the entrance is **Ross Bastiaan Marker No. 5:** Lone Pine/Kanlisirt.

Extra Visit to Shell Green CWGC Cemetery/Ross Bastiaan Marker No 4 (Map A24) Round trip: 1 kilometre. Approximate time: 45 minutes (by foot).

From the car park area outside the cemetery follow the sign pointing to the 'Rough Track' to Shell Green. Local taxis occasionally drive down, but the track is very uneven and muddy and slippery when wet. Walking is advised.

The track is the upper end of Artillery Road (qv) which starts at The Beach. The cemetery is built on what was a sloping cotton field on the seaward side of Bolton's Ridge. It was captured and passed by the 8th Australian Infantry Battalion on the morning of 25 April but remained, throughout the campaign, close to the Turkish line and was subject to frequent shelling from the Olive Grove and Gaba Tepe. It was used from May to December, principally by the Australian Light Horse and the 9th and 11th Infantry Battalions. Originally it was two cemeteries, a short distance apart, but after the Armistice they were joined and enlarged by the concentration of 64 graves from the surrounding battlefields and small burial grounds. Of the 398 war graves all are of the AIF, save **Gunner William Turnbull** of A Battery, Royal Field Artillery, age 27, died 22 October [II F 5]. Eleven graves are unidentified. Three men served under different names; **Trooper M. Jones**, who served as Taylor [I G 12], **Trooper Horace McMahon**, who served as Carey [I B 27] and **Private William Williams** who served as Hayes. It also includes 20 non-World War graves of sailors and soldiers who died in 1922/23 and were moved here from Kelia Liman, near Eceabat. Here is buried the uncle of Alan Moorehead, author of the classical account, *Gallipoli* – **Private Frank Moorehead**, 8th Battalion, age 24, killed

The way down to Shell Green CWGC Cemetery

between 25-28 April [Artillery Road Plot 19]. The real name of Private **Anthony Springhouse**, 2nd Battalion, age 21, was Sprinkhuysen. His parents lived in Amsterdam [II C 7]. **Lieutenant-Colonel Hubert Jennings Imrie Harris,** who commanded the 5th Light Horse, age 44, was shot through the jugular and died almost instantly on 31 July during the attack on Twin Trenches. A ridge on the sea side of Bolton's was named after him. **Major John Edwin** of the 8th Battalion, AIF, age 45, killed on 25 April, has the inscription, 'Mate o' Mine'. He was killed by a shell as he started leading his company forward on Bolton's Ridge [Artillery Road Plot 6].

In front of the cemetery is a flat grassed area, scene of the only recorded cricket match in the Anzac sector, with Major G.M. Onslow fielding at cover point. It was held on 17 December as part of the plan to deceive the Turks about the impending Evacuation. Here is **Ross Bastiaan Marker No 4.**

Return to the main road.

Continue along the road.

The dip you are passing through was known as **Owen's Gully**, named for Lieutenant-Colonel R.H. Owen. He was one of three officers recommended by Captain Sherborn, the chief clerk of New South Wales, to Colonel H. N. MacLaurin (qv) (commanding the Australian 1st Division) to command the infantry battalions. He named Lieutenant-Colonel Braund (qv), who commanded the 2nd Battalion, who was killed on 4 May, Lieutenant-Colonel A. J. Onslow Thompson (qv), who commanded the 4th Battalion, who was killed on 26 April, and Owen, who commanded the 3rd Battalion and who survived the War. Lieutenant-Colonel L. Dobbin had already been nominated to command the 1st Battalion and he also survived the War.

To the left of the road, at the head of the gully, was the 90metre square, flat as a tennis court, known as 'The Daisy Patch', on the south side of which was a protuberance known as 'The Pimple' (not to be confused with the feature of the same name on the Kirectepe Ridge). In the darkness of the night of 25 April isolated trenches had been dug on the reverse slope at Brown's Dip by Major R. Saker's men of the 5th Battalion. General Bridges, seeing that they constituted a dip of 180 metres in the line, muttered, 'They're no damn good,' as he made an inspection tour (during which he terrified his staff by insisting on standing upright to look around him) to see if the front lines of Colonels M'Cay (Commander of 2nd Infantry Brigade, later Lieutenant-General the Hon Sir J.W. M'Cay,) and MacLagan (Commander of 3rd Brigade, later Major-General Sinclair-MacLagan) had actually joined. Without issuing a firm order, he gave the impression that the line should be straightened and Major Duncan Glasfurd (of the Argyll & Sutherland Highlanders, who had been largely responsible for the training of the Australian 1st Division at Mena Camp) collected a number of men from the offending trench and led them forward to the Daisy Patch, where he ordered them to dig in. Saker then received an order to advance his line to the Daisy Patch and then swing to the left. Already twice wounded, he led his men forward. Then 'after thirty-six hours of ceaseless and most devoted work...he swayed and fell dead' [Bean]. Without their leader, the men continued their move to the left towards Johnston's Jolly, but had no notion of their objective or aim. Noticing the movement, other parts of the line joined in. To the south, in the 4th Battalion sector, a messenger burst in with an 'Order for a general advance.' This led to one of the most archetypically 'Australian' actions of the campaign – indisciplined and foolhardy but sublimely brave. Major Macnaghten shouted to Colonel Onslow Thompson, 'I'll take the right, Colonel, if you'll take the left.' Without precise orders, these fearless and highly motivated officers led their men blindly on towards Lone Pine. As they crossed the Daisy Patch 'a furious fire was opened upon them. Men fell thickly.' The realisation that they were blundering up no-man's-land hit them. Onslow Thompson established his HQ in Owen's Gully. Machine guns swept Johnston's Jolly, disorder reigned as officers and men were slaughtered, and a general retirement erupted. Glasfurd attempted to rally the men near the Wheatfield (below Lone Pine) and led them back to the Daisy Patch. Ahead of them isolated groups were still attempting to advance. Eventually, his firing line having gone and no instructions still received, Onslow Thompson decided to return to the Australian lines with his surviving men. At this moment the Turks opened fire and the Colonel was killed instantly. His body was carried towards the trenches by Lieutenant Massie, who was eventually forced to abandon it, where it lay until found by 3rd Battalion on 11 May. He is buried in 4th Battalion Parade Ground Cemetery.

N.B. There is also a Daisy Patch near Krithia.

Continue to the cemetery on the right.

Immediately before the cemetery on the right is the entrance to underground defensive positions. In the ground to the left of the road are traces of Australian trenches which were damaged in the fire of 1994. The cemetery is on the site of Turkish trenches and in the gullies behind it the Turks buried many of their dead in the Armistice of 24 May (qv).

* Johnston's Jolly CWGC Cemetery/13.4 kilometres/10 minutes/Map A25

The cemetery is built on the area called by the Turks Kirmezi Sirt (Red Ridge) on the northern section of 400 Plateau (Lone Pine being the southern section). Its name derives from Colonel (later Major-General) G. J. Johnston, CB, CMG, VD, commanding 2nd Australian Division Artillery, who placed field guns opposite the position to 'jolly up the Turks'. Johnston was a furniture manufacturer in Melbourne before the War and in 1918 went on to become Military Administrator of German New Guinea. This position was reached by the 2nd Australian Infantry Brigade on 25 April and lost on the 26th. It was never again taken during the campaign.

The cemetery was made after the Armistice by the concentration of graves from the battlefield. It contains 2 Australians, 1 New Zealand and 141 unidentified. Only one grave is firmly identified - that of Lance Corporal Herbert Norman May of the 15th Battalion [E 3]. The other named graves, mainly of 4th and 7th AIF who fell in the capture of Lone Pine, are commemorated by 36 special memorials.

The inscription on the stone wall of the entrance mis-spells the cemetery as 'Johnson's' Jolly.

THE ARMISTICE OF 20-24 MAY

On 18 May there was an unusual lull in the Turkish firing followed at 1700 hours by a fierce artillery bombardment. News filtered through to the Australian staff that large numbers of Turkish reinforcements were being sent over from the Asian side and that reinforcements were also marching north from the Helles area towards Anzac. This was confirmed by Lieutenant G. L. Thomson of the RNAS who, flying over the Peninsula, saw that 'two of the valleys east of the Anzac line were packed with Turkish troops, densely crowded upon the sheltered slopes' [Bean.] Birdwood ordered his men to stand to arms at 0300 hours on 19 May, but at 1145 on the 18th Turkish rifle fire broke out the length of the Anzac line. Five minutes after the stand-to a line of Turkish bayonets appeared quietly down Wire Gully, just above Johnston's Jolly, and attacked, wave upon wave, all along the line. In many places they had to cross large expanses of exposed ground and they were mown down, line after succeeding line, as the British would be on the Somme on 1 July 1916. Soon the ANZACs learned to wait for a whole Turkish company to appear following their officer and then they wiped out the entire group, picking off the scuttling survivors described by Moorehead as 'terrified rabbits in search of cover.' It became a frenzy of carnage by the ANZACs, unaccustomed to such easy targets, but the Turkish officers had been ordered to press on to the sea and continued to do so, driving their terrified men, many without weapons or helmets, until there were no more left to advance. Mustafa Kemal, in command of the 19th Division, was the only divisional commander to make any headway. By midday, of the 42,000 Turks who went into the attack, 10,000 had fallen, 5,000 of whom were lying dead or gravely wounded in the hot sun in no-man's-land. Essad Pasha, the Turkish General in command of the central and northern portions of the Peninsula, had no alternative but to break off the attack. Unbelievably, the ANZACs had lost only 160 killed and 468 wounded. In many cases the Australians and New Zealanders had seen their enemy face to face in this terrible slaughter. A new feeling of respect, even of friendliness, for their brave opponents crept into the ANZAC psyche and a new spirit of chivalry was born. But their officers were contemplating a counter-stroke to exploit the situation. They left it too late to mount a strong, co-ordinated attack and the small isolated attempts that ensued – such as the attack by 100 Wellington Mounted Rifles at the Nek – met with murderous fire as the men emerged from their trenches. The enemy wounded lying between the opposing trenches were becoming a problem. 'No sound came from that dreadful space,' wrote Bean, 'but here and there some wounded or dying man, silently lying without help or any hope of it under the sun which glared from a cloudless sky, turned painfully from one side to the other or slowly raised an arm towards heaven.' The ANZACs, in the new mood of comradeship that was the aftermath of their killing, felt a strong desire to help these poor creatures. In addition, the dead presented a severe threat of infection and the stench of them became overpowering.

The idea of an Armistice is generally attributed to Captain the Hon. Aubrey Herbert, who was presently attached to General Godley's staff. Birdwood had been contemplating such an act and Herbert got his permission to take the suggestion to Sir Ian Hamilton, then aboard HMT *Arcadian*. Hamilton agreed, 'provided Birdie clearly understands that no Corps Commander can fix up an armistice off his own bat and provided it is clear we do not ask for the armistice but grant it to them - the suppliants,' as he recorded in his diary. But events took their own momentum and on 22 May Hamilton somewhat peevishly wrote, 'News in to say that yesterday, whilst Herbert was here to take orders about an armistice, some sort of a informal parley actually took place. Both sides suddenly got panic stricken, thinking the others were treacherous, and fire was opened, some stretcher bearers being killed. Nothing else was to be expected when things are done in this casual and unauthorized way. I felt very much annoyed, but Aubrey Herbert was still on board ... and [I] told him Walker seemed to have taken too much upon himself parleying with the Turks and that Birdwood must now make this clear to everyone for future guidance. Although Aubrey Herbert is excessively unorthodox he quite sees that confabs with enemies must be carried out according to Cocker [meaning to abide by the rules, after an arithmetic book and its methods written by Edward Cocker 1631-1677].' Hamilton may well have been aware of Sir John French's equally ambivalent attitude to the Christmas Truce of 1914 on the Western Front.

Johnston's Jolly CWGC
Cemetery

Entrance to underground
defensive position,
Johnston's Jolly

Generals have to recognise that when men become too friendly with the enemy they no longer have the stomach to kill them.

What had actually occurred at Anzac was that Colonel Owen (qv), learning from captured Turks that Australian wounded lay in Wire Gully, maintained that 'We should not be British if we did not attempt to get those men in', and hoisted a Red Cross flag to indicate a truce. It was shot at, but a Turkish officer shortly ran to apologise and an informal armistice then took place. General Walker, concerned that advantage might be taken of the situation, strode across no-man's-land and chatted to Turkish officers in French until he saw Turkish soldiers taking rifles from the dead. He closed the proceedings and insisted on a formal parley in an hour's time. But nervous shooting broke out which developed into a full-scale barrage (a process known as 'wind-up') and nothing happened until the next day when negotiations commenced for an armistice on 24 May, Liman von Sanders writing directly to 'Sir John [sic] Hamilton' with his consent.

At Gaba Tepe on 22 May Aubrey Herbert met Mustafa Kemal and other Turkish officers who were blindfolded and taken to Birdwood's headquarters. Herbert was in turn blindfolded and taken into the Turkish lines as a hostage and, after a hair-raising trip on horseback, spent a pleasant day eating cheese and drinking coffee before being returned. The whole proceedings had a surreal and somewhat farcical nature, as is well described by Moorehead, especially when a Digger, unaware of the solemn conference that was taking part in Birdwood's tent, popped his head round the flap and demanded, 'Have any of you bastards got my kettle?' This story was also told by Compton Mackenzie (qv) who used the word 'muckers' instead of 'bastards', probably nearer the truth with the substitution of one letter.

As arranged, Herbert and his party duly met the Turkish contingent on The Beach at 6.30 on the 24th and they climbed up the hill through the Poppy Field, the overwhelming odour of rotting corpses hitting them as they reached the plateau and were confronted by about 4,000 Turkish dead. Although there was nervousness on both sides, the terrible work was soon underway, supervised by Herbert, and much fraternisation took place. The extraordinary Aubrey Herbert - an ex-Member of Parliament, poet, scholar, and Turkophile, energetic and intelligent, eccentric to the nth degree - had for some time been a figure of considerable curiosity, if not suspicion, since being sent by Hamilton to the ANZAC front line. He came complete with servants, horses, mules, Greek and Levantine interpreters, conducted his own parleys with the Turks in their front-line trenches (he spoke fluent Turkish) and often drew Turkish fire or bombs. Now, watched by an amused Compton Mackenzie who had come to observe from the *Arcadian* with Jack Churchill, Herbert bustled around, 'loose-gaited, his neck out-thrust and swinging from side to side as he went, peering up into people's faces to see whether they were the enemy or not, so that, if they were, he could offer them cigarettes and exchange a few courtesies with them in their own language'.

A line was pegged out down the centre of no-man's-land by fifty Turks with Red Crescent armlets and 50 ANZACs with Red Cross armlets - the Turkish burial parties working on one side of the line, the ANZACs on the other. Until 1630 hours they laboured at the terrible task of interring the already rotting bodies, the chaplains searching for identity discs and repeatedly reading the burial service. Most of the Turkish dead were buried in three old communication trenches which led from Quinn's to the Turkish lines and in Wire Gully. A Turkish Captain said to Herbert, 'At this spectacle even the most gentle must feel savage and the most savage must weep.' Although both sides profited by doing some surreptitious surveys and the odd improvement of trenches, the armistice passed without undue incident. Herbert bade an amicable farewell to his Turkish acquaintances and at 1645 hours a Turkish sniper's bullet heralded the resumption of hostilities. But things were never the same again. Instances of fraternisation, acts of humanity, the exchange of rations, a degree of mutual respect, trust and tolerance became more frequent in this grotesque and dangerous colony.

Continue to the sign to the left to 4th Battalion Parade Ground Cemetery (13.6kms).

Extra Visit to 4th Battalion Parade Ground CWGC Cemetery (Map A26) Round trip: 400 metres. Approximate time: 30 minutes.

Follow the sign which indicates a steep path. It is indeed steep and rocky and can be slippery when wet, so caution is advised.

The cemetery, set in such an isolated position, and, in the springtime when the iris are in bloom, is absolutely lovely and well merits the effort of the climb. It was named for the 4th Battalion AIF, drawn from New South Wales. From the end of April to the beginning of June the battalion buried its dead here beside what was Bridges Road, which led from Wire Gully to Anzac Cove, and was named after Major-General Bridges. It was enlarged after the Armistice by the concentration of 31 graves from 3rd Battalion Parade Ground Cemetery. This was a little way to the south on the opposite side of the valley, which Bean described as 'probably the only place where choral singing was heard at Anzac during the campaign. The good Dean [Chaplain Talbot of Sydney] held his services there, and my brother [Captain J. W. Bean, the battalion medical officer], always a missionary in a good cause, and with an enthusiasm for music, sent to Cairo for some hymns and anthems and supported his friend by trying to train a number of his Diggers to sing them.' In the August Offensive the 3rd Battalion lost 21 of its 23 officers and two-thirds of its men and Captain Bean was wounded. The cemetery also contained 13 soldiers from 22nd

Battalion Parade Ground Cemetery and 32 graves from the surrounding battlefields. It now contains the graves of 107 Australians, 3 RMLIs from the UK and 6 men whose unit is unknown.

The Battalion's commanding officer, **Lieutenant-Colonel Astley Onslow Thompson** (qv), Mentioned in Despatches, age 50, is in A11. **Colonel Henry Normand MacLaurin**, Commander of 1st Australian Infantry Brigade, Mentioned in Despatches, age 37, was killed by a sniper on the hill which bore his name (just below Steel's Post) on 27 April. The son of the Chancellor of Sydney University, MacLaurin was described by Bean as 'a man of lofty ideals, direct, determined, with a certain inherited Scottish dourness rather unusual in a young Australian, but an educated man of action of the finest type that the Australian Universities could produce.' Once on the Peninsula, MacLaurin proved himself a fine leader.

MacLaurin's brigade-major, **Major F.D. Irvine (qv)**, was killed ten minutes before his commander. On 27 April he collected 200 'stray men' and himself climbed to Steel's to observe the situation. Exposed to Turkish snipers, he was shouted at by fellow officers but replied, 'It's my business to be sniped at.' 'The next moment, at 3 p.m., he was shot from behind' [Bean]. Irvine is commemorated on the Lone Pine Memorial.

Several men buried here served under different names: **Driver William Henry Hume** of the 16th Battalion, age 36, killed on 10 May, 'a native of Manchester', served as Court [B 8]; **Private William Jon Dearlove**, 4th Battalion, age 22, killed on 19 May, served as Edwards [D 18]; **Private Walter Gell**, 3rd Battalion, age 26, killed 20 May, served as Harding [A 1].

Return to the main road.

Continue to the cemetery on the left.

* Courtney's and Steel's Post CWGC Cemetery/Ross Bastiaan Marker No. 6/13.7 kilometres/10 minutes/Map A27,28

Courtney's was named after Lieutenant-Colonel Richard E. Courtney, age 44, who commanded 14th Battalion, the reserve of the Army Corps, and brought them here on 27 April. Bean describes it as a 'steep scrubby recess in the gully side'. The position had been reached on the 25th, as was Steel's, named after Major Thomas Steel of the battalion, but which was known at the time as Steele's Post. Bean called it 'a still steeper niche, of which the top was a sheer landslide of gravel where a man could scarcely climb on hands and knees'. The ground falls away from the two posts into Monash Valley, so-named when Colonel Monash set up his 4th Infantry Brigade HQ at the head of it on 27 April. It is at the top of Shrapnel Valley. The slopes which led up to the posts became a shanty town of bivouacs and dugouts, erected on a series of terraces. By the end of the second day there was a mound with crosses inscribed, 'Here lie buried twenty-nine soldiers of the King'. Two of them - an Australian of the 14th Battalion and a New Zealand sapper - were found,

4th Battalion Parade Ground CWGC Cemetery with view over Monash Gully towards Quinn's Post

Courtney's and Steel's Post CWGC Cemetery with Quinn's Post and the Turkish 57th Regiment complex behind

just below Courtney's, with their arms clasped round each other's waists .
   When approaching from Johnston's Jolly, Steel's Post was actually below
Courtney's. To the right of the road - which is on what was no-man's-land -
opposite Steel's and MacLaurin's Hill, was German Officers' Ridge, so-called
because two German officers had been spotted there early in May. The Turks called
the area Merkez Tepe - Central Hill. On May 19 the Turkish 5th Division attacked
up the hill with heavy losses. It was an area of vigorous Turkish mining activity,
especially after the disastrous 19 May attack. This was matched by extensive
Australian mining when tunnels were pushed out under the Turkish front line (a
fact that the Turks learned about from their 'agents in Egypt' [Zeki Bey]). Several
large explosions caused severe damage to Turkish tunnels and shook a number of
their trenches. A Turkish machine gun that had caused the Australians much
trouble had to be moved to firmer ground lower down the hill.
   German Officers' Trench was a covered trench, which was a succession of rifle
pits, opposite Steel's Post, a section commanded by Zeki Bey of the 57th Regiment
when he returned after his hospitalisation from his wound in April.
   Zeki spoke with great admiration to Bean of a 'fine looking, handsome young
man' who had been killed in one of the mine craters at the trench. Bean identified
him as Lieutenant Norman James Greig, of the 7th Battalion, AIF, who volunteered
on 12 July to lead the attack on the crater. At 0815, with eleven other volunteers, he
rushed the crater. Three men were instantly killed and Greig was heard calling for
reinforcements. Half a dozen men of the 6th Battalion responded, but charged in
the wrong direction - towards the trench - and were shot. Shortly afterwards all of
Greig's remaining men returned and he was last seen, bleeding from the head,
holding back the Turks while his men escaped. Zeki described how he told his men
not to kill the young officer as he wanted to take him, but his men said, 'He will
not allow himself to be taken'. Greig was then hit by a bomb, both his legs broken.
Zeki had him buried in the valley behind the lines 'with more ceremony and care
than the Turks usually devoted to their dead opponents' [Bean]. Lieutenant Greig
is commemorated on the Lone Pine Memorial.
   The cemetery, which was built over an extensive tunnel system, contains the
graves of 6 identified Australians, 1 identified Marine of the RND, **Private J. W.
Crafts** of the Portsmouth Battalion, killed on 27 May [E 15] and 54 Australians, 2
Marines, 1 sailor of the RND and 1 New Zealander. Many of the Australian dead
are of the 14th Battalion, AIF. The Marine Brigade (comprising Portsmouth and
Chatham Battalions) were landed at Anzac and moved into Quinn's and
Courtney's on 28 April to cover the approach to the gully from the east and with
the intention of relieving the 1st and 3rd Australian Brigades. They remained in
the trenches here until 2 May. To the ANZACs the struggle to hang on to the
ground reached on the ridge on the first day was desperate and unrelenting. Men
'wandered in a half-sleep, like tired children,' and collapsed with exhaustion with
their much-needed rations uneaten in their hands, uniforms disintegrated. Their
casualties were horrendous. When they heard that British Marines were landing
they had expected much from this famous British unit, but the unsuspecting raw
recruits seemed 'strangely young and slender to represent the seasoned regular

Marines'. The next day they did indeed waver but were reinforced on the 29th by the Deal Battalion, General Mercer's 1st Brigade and Staff, Nelson Battalion of the RND and elements of the 3rd Australian Infantry Brigade. By 30 April the Australian 1st Division had lost 5,000 men, only one of whom was a prisoner, and on that day Mustafa Kemal extended his trenches and brought up five fresh battalions for a great counter-attack designed to push the invader back into the sea. The situation in the areas held by the Marines was desperate and Lieutenant R. W. H. M . Empson sent an urgent message to Anzac Cove calling for medical and other aid. It was passed on to Portsmouth Battalion's medical team, commanded by Surgeon Basil Playne, which had settled on The Beach on 28 April. A medical volunteer was called for and Lance-Corporal Walter Parker, who had already shown consistent bravery in commanding the battalion's stretcher bearers, immediately offered to go. He joined the relief party under Sergeant M.W. Minter. Under darkness they reached Empson's post (some 45 metres only from the Turkish lines) where a hail of bullets greeted them, hitting one of the group. Parker stayed with the wounded man and so got separated from the main party in Empson's trench. As day broke he saw the bodies of many Australians between his position and Empson's post and was ordered at gun-point by an Australian officer to turn back. But he jumped over the parapet and sprinted over 350 metres of scrub raked by rifle and machine-gun fire to Empson's now cut-off trench to the cheers of the watching Marines, the only one of the original party of ten to reach it. Ignoring his own painful wounds, Parker immediately set about tending the wounded in the trench. At dawn the following day the Turks mounted a fierce attack and Lieutenant Empson was killed. [He is buried in Shrapnel Valley Cemetery.] The position was clung on to throughout the hot day by Lieutenant A. B. F. Alcock, but his men were reduced to about forty unwounded who were down to their last fifteen rounds of ammunition. After defending the position for four nights and three days, the exhausted band was forced to withdraw, under murderous Turkish fire. Parker assisted the wounded to escape but was again wounded himself in the groin and right thigh, in addition to his already injured chest and shin, and had to crawl the last few yards to safety.

After a two-year consideration of the case, **Lance-Corporal Parker** was eventually awarded the VC for his successive acts of gallantry, the first RND VC of the War and the first at Anzac. [Parker survived, a very frail man from his many wounds, until 28 November 1936.] Lieutenant Alcock was awarded the DSO for his heroic stand and Mentioned in Despatches, as were Lieutenant-Colonel Luard, Major A. M. Clark, Major H. G .B. Armstrong (killed on 6 May and also buried in Shrapnel Valley Cemetery), Captain D. J. Gowney (who also got the DSC) and Lieutenant R. W. R. Sanders, all of the Portsmouth Battalion. Surgeon Playne was awarded the DSO. Thus, after a shaky start, the Marines earned their spurs in this area around Courtney's, Pope's (qv) and Quinn's, which thereafter was known as 'Dead Man's Ridge' because of their heavy casualties there when the clay slopes were 'stained with British blood' [Waite].

When Bean visited this area in February 1919 'the bones and tattered uniforms of men were scattered everywhere'. A member of his Historical Mission, Lambert (qv) described the area as 'a perfect rabbit warren, and too ghastly for me to people with the image of fighting'.

By the entrance is **Ross Bastiaan Marker No. 6** - Courtney's & Steel's Posts. *Continue along the road.*

Extra Visit to Tombs of Lieutenant-Colonels (Yarbay) Manastir and Avni (Map A29) Round trip: 1.2 kilometres. Approximate time: 20 minutes

Take the small road to the right signed to Yarbay Huyesin Avni. Descend into Mule Valley (known by the Turks as Kesik Dere - Broken Valley) then up to Mortar Ridge to the area known as the Olive Grove.

In the centre of the white-railed cemetery is the marble tomb which once bore a photograph of the Colonel. It is inscribed, Hero, 57th Infantry Regiment Commander Yarbay Ali Oglu Huseyin Manastir, Martyr. 31 July 1881 - 13 August 1915. Pray for his soul. In the right-hand bottom corner is the tomb of Yarbay Huseyin Avni and to the top left is a memorial board to the 57th Infantry Regiment which sustained fearful losses on 25 April 1915.

Return to the main road.

Continue to the tomb on the right.

* Tomb of Captain Mehmet (Yuzbasi Mehmet Sehitligi)/14.01 kilometres/5 minutes/Map A30

Captain Mehmet's tomb is bordered by a stone wall. The Cypress trees which once surrounded it were destroyed in the 1994 fire.

Opposite is.

* Quinn's Post CWGC Cemetery/ Ross Bastiaan Marker No. 7/10 minutes/MapA31,32/OP

In May Quinn's was the apex of the Anzac position and the furthest inland, about half a mile from the sea, due east of Anzac Cove. It was established on the afternoon of 25 April by a New Zealand machine-gun crew and was taken over the following day by 4th Battalion, AIF. On the 29th Captain Hugh Quinn of the 15th Battalion was sent to it with 225 officers and men. The position was held throughout May, despite fierce attacks on the 10th and the 29th, when at 0320 hours a Turkish mine exploded and was followed by a wave of about twenty Turks into the trenches. No 3 Subsection was blown in and the men in No 4 were cut off from 1 and 2. Quinn led his men in a counter-attack in short rushes until they reached No 3 and a small party of Turks were trapped in a section of trench. Showers of bombs indicated the presence of other Turks and Quinn rallied his men for another counter-attack. With bayonet and bomb they hurled themselves into the ranks of the enemy, which finally broke and fled. But Quinn, an officer much loved by his

Tombs of Lieutenant-Colonels Manastir and Avni with Lone Pine on the horizon

men, was killed. He is buried in Shrapnel Valley Cemetery. In early June the New Zealand Infantry took over the position, followed by the 17th Australian Light Horse in July and the 17th Battalion in September. Throughout these months the post was continually engaged in hand-to-hand fighting with the Turkish post opposite, who named the area Bomba Sirt (Bomb Ridge). Compton Mackenzie visited Quinn's on the day of the Whit Monday (24 May) truce and described walking over trenches whose parapets were made up of the dead. 'The smell of death floated over the ridge above and settled down upon us, tangible, it seemed, and clammy as the membrane of a bat's wing,' he wrote. 'Nothing could cleanse [it] from the nostrils for a fortnight afterwards. There was no herb so aromatic but it reeked of carrion, not thyme, nor lavender, nor even rosemary.'

The cemetery was made after the Armistice by the concentration of 225 unidentified graves buried in rows E to I and 73 graves were moved from Pope's Hill Cemetery (located at the foot of Pope's Hill, a razor-backed hill to the northeast of Quinn's named after Lieutenant-Colonel Harold Pope, the white-haired commander of 16th Battalion, AIF, who reached the position on 25 April), 70 of them Australian, 3 New Zealanders, plus 6 graves found later, into the section called Pope's Hill Plot. There are special memorials to 100 Australians, 3 New Zealanders and one British Marine, **Private Alfred William Clark,** Portsmouth Battalion, RND, age 24, killed on 11 May [Sp Mem 37].

The burials reflect the many units who were posted here. Among them is **Lieutenant Frances Leofric Armstrong,** 15th Battalion, Mentioned in Despatches, age 34, a Boer War Veteran, killed on 10 May at the Post as he tried to climb out of his trench to see if any wounded remained in no-man's-land after a withdrawal by

Turkish Infantryman Statue, 57th Inf Regt area

Turkish Veteran, Huseyin Kacmac, with his grand-daughter

Symbolic Cemetery and Memorial, Turkish 57th Inf Regt area

Plaque to Captain L.J. Walters and Lieutenant Mustafa Asim Bey

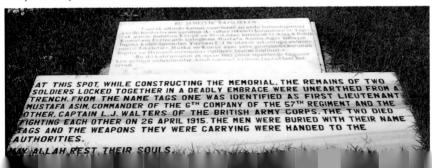

BU SEHITLIK YAPILIRKEN

AT THIS SPOT, WHILE CONSTRUCTING THE MEMORIAL, THE REMAINS OF TWO SOLDIERS LOCKED TOGETHER IN A DEADLY EMBRACE WERE UNEARTHED FROM A TRENCH. FROM THE NAME TAGS ONE WAS IDENTIFIED AS FIRST LIEUTENANT MUSTAFA ASIM, COMMANDER OF THE 6TH COMPANY OF THE 57TH REGIMENT AND THE OTHER, CAPTAIN L.J. WALTERS OF THE BRITISH ARMY CORPS. THE TWO DIED FIGHTING EACH OTHER ON 26 APRIL 1915. THE MEN WERE BURIED WITH THEIR NAME TAGS AND THE WEAPONS THEY WERE CARRYING WERE HANDED TO THE AUTHORITIES.
MAY ALLAH REST THEIR SOULS.

his digging party [Sp Mem 29], the **Sherwood brothers, Troopers Frederick,** age 29, and **Harold,** age 25, of the 1st Light Horse [C 6 and C 5].

There are superb views from the back of the cemetery over Pope's Hill and The Nek to the north and Monash Valley to the south. Immediately to the north of the cemetery is a small gully which became known as 'The Bloody Angle' where, after fighting for a desperate week from 25 April, men became delirious and hollow-eyed from exhaustion and lack of water.

To the right of the entrance is **Ross Bastiaan Marker No. 7:** Bombasirti/Quinn's Post.

Continue to the complex of Turkish memorials on each side of the road.

* Turkish 57th Infantry Regiment Memorial Park, 57 Alay Sehitligi ve Aniti/14.4 kilometres/20 minutes/Map A33,34,35,36

Under their commander, Colonel Huseyin Avni Bey, the Turkish 57th Infantry Regiment bore the brunt of the Australian landing assault of 25 April 1915, and here Lieutenant-Colonel Mustafa Kemal, commanding the 19th Infantry Division, first showed his outstanding leadership qualities. This important memorial area was constructed in 1992 to honour the soldiers who lost their lives that day and the commander who went on to establish the new Turkish Republic.

The 57th Regiment was also heavily engaged in the Turkish counter-attack of 19 May and fought with great determination. Six new junior officers were assigned to the 3rd Battalion which opposed Pope's Hill (qv) the day before. At the end of the 19th five of them lay dead on their own parapet, killed as they jumped out to set an example to their troops. In all Zeki Bey estimated that 10,000 Turks were killed or wounded in the attack, reducing the defenders to three divisions and that by 4 August the 57th had spent forty-five continuous days in the line at German Officers' Ridge (qv).

To the left is a large car park, at the top of which is a

Large Turkish Soldier Statue, Turk Askerine Saygi Aniti ('Respect to the Turkish Soldier'). This statue of an infantryman was sculpted by Tankut Oktem and erected in 1992. Across the road is **Statue of Turkish Veteran and Child.** This depicts Huseyin Kacmaz, who died on 10 September 1994, at the age of 108, the oldest Turkish veteran, with his grand-daughter.

Behind and to the right is

Outdoor Mosque and fountain

Straight ahead is a

Bas Relief Panel of Kemal Ataturk and the 57th Regiment charging on 25 April

To the left is a

Symbolic Cemetery with plaques bearing the names of martyrs of the 57th Regiment and, incorporated in its north wall, a tall Memorial

In front of the cemetery, to the left and right of the entrance are

Memorial Tablets, to which English translations on marble tablets were added in 1998.

The cemetery complex, built on the area known as **'The Chessboard'** because of the way the trenches criss-crossed over it, at the southern ends of Sword Spur (Kilicbayiri) and Mortar Ridge (Edirne Sirti), was designed by architect Nejat Dincel. It is built mainly of Kevser stone. It was officially opened on 12 December 1992 by the Turkish Minister of Culture. During its building the remains of two soldiers were found lying side by side with their pistols and flasks. They were identified by their name tags as Captain L.J. Walters ('Woiters' in the Turkish version), of the 'British Army Corps', and 1st Lieutenant Mustafa Asim Bey, commander of 6 Company, 57th Infantry Regiment. They were buried together at the top of the cemetery under a plaque. According to the Peace Park Catalogue (qv), the ceremony was held 'in the presence of both their relatives', invited by the Turkish Minister of Culture. No trace, however, can be found in CWGC records of Captain L. J. Walters. There are 50 burials/commemorations under the name 'Walters' for 1915. Only two of these are officers and both died on the Western Front. However, there is a Lieutenant Leslie John *Waters*, 15th AIF, killed on 27 April, who is buried in Quinn's Post [A 23].

As well as quotations from Ataturk, there are marble plaques with quotations from General Birdwood and other distinguished Australians.

Continue to the brown and yellow cemetery signs to the left and follow the path to

* The Nek Memorial Area: Sergeant Mehmet Tomb/Ross Bastiaan Marker No 8/The Nek CWGC Cemetery/ Walker's Ridge CWGC Cemetery/14.9 kilometres/30 minutes/Map A37,38,39,40

Continue to the Turkish cemetery

Sergeant Mehmet Tomb

The white obelisk is set in a walled grassy area. It commemorates the Sergeant and his squad of twenty-five soldiers who fought here to the death after the landings. Mehmet's last words, according to Bean, were, 'I die happily for my country, and you, my comrade, will avenge me.' The cemetery is on the spot where the Australian charge of 7 August was halted. When they had run out of ammunition, the determined Turkish defenders used stones and their bare fists in their attempt to halt the attack. They named the site Courage Hill (Cesaret Tepe). After the Allied Evacuation of December 1915 three monuments were erected: one at Lone Pine, one on North Beach and the third, here, the only one to survive. The base is original, the obelisk was added later, replacing the four shells on top of the monument. It was built next to the semi-circular trench dug by men of Captain J. P. Lalor's 12th Battalion on the morning of 25 April and to which Private Howe's party later climbed from the Nek.

To the left of the tomb enclosure is

Ross Bastiaan Marker No 8.

This marks the site of the Australian Light Horse's attack of 7 August 1915 [see *Historical Summary*]. The charge can be pictured by imagining a trench in the same place and orientation as the east wall of the Nek cemetery and from which line after line of men emerge to charge side by side towards area of Marker No 8. It was this action that formed the core of the 1981 film *Gallipoli*.

Sergeant Mehmet Tomb

Further on is

The Nek CWGC Cemetery/OP.
'The Nek' was actually a track leading along the narrow spur from Russell's Top (to the south-west) to Baby 700 (to the north-east). The position was reached, but not held, on 25 April and never retaken.

The cemetery was made after the Armistice on what had been no-man's-land. It stands on a ridge with Pope's Hill to the south-west and Malone's Gully to the north-west. The latter was a dry water course named for Lieutenant-Colonel William G. Malone (qv) who commanded the NZ Wellington Battalion. It contains 4 identified New Zealanders of the NZ Otago Regiment, 1 Australian and 316 unknown burials, the majority of them in all probability of the 3rd Light Horse, killed on 7 August. There are 5 Australian special memorials. In February 1919 Lieutenant Hughes of the GRU buried more than 300 of these men whom he found lying together in a strip the size of three tennis courts.

From the back of the cemetery there are excellent views to the north over Itineraries 2 and 4 across Malone's Gully, the CWGC base, Outpost No. 1 and traces of the Big Sap, Suvla Bay and the Salt Lake.

Walk along the dirt track, to the left of which are recreated trenches, to
Walker's Ridge CWGC Cemetery/OP
Walker's Ridge, so-called because it was the command post of Brigadier-General (later Lieutenant-General) Sir H. B. Walker, KCMG, DSO, commander of the New Zealand Infantry Brigade, on 25 April, was a spur that stretched almost from the coast near Fisherman's Hut (qv) to Russell's Top (called Yukset Sirt by the Turks). On the 27th the ridge was held by the New Zealanders and on 30 June by the 8th and 9th Australian Light Horse.

The cemetery was started during the occupation and consists of two plots, with an 18-metre gap between them, through which ran a trench started by Colonel Braund (qv) on 25 April and held throughout the campaign. It contains 40 New Zealanders (29 of whom are of the Auckland or Wellington Mounted Rifles), 12 Australians, 1 Royal Marine (**Private G. Drummond** of Deal Battalion, killed on 8 May [II B 3]), and 12 unidentified burials. There are 18 Australian special memorials and 8 New Zealand. **Major David Grant** (qv) of the Canterbury Regiment NZEF, age 41, was killed on Baby 700 on 25 April [Sp Mem 10]. The son of Lieutenant-General Cornwallis Oswald Maude, **2nd Lieutenant Cornwallis**

Walker's Ridge CWGC Cemetery

Headstone on Walker's Ridge

View from Walker's Ridge to Ari Burnu and North Beach

Charles Wyndham Maude of the 9th Australian Horse, age 39, 'a native of Cheltenham, England', was killed on 13 August [II B 2].

To the left of the cemetery is a superb view over Walker's Ridge to the Sphinx and North Beach.

Return to the main road and continue to the cemetery sign to the right. Walk up the gravel path.

* Baby 700 CWGC Cemetery/ 15.4 kilometres/10 minutes/Map A41

Baby 700 was the name given to the 180-metre-high hill which connected Russell's Top with Battleship Hill (known to the Turks as Dus Tepe - Sword Hill - and originally called 'Big 700' as it was considerably higher than 'Baby 700') because it was marked on maps as 700 feet above sea level. The Turks called the area Kilicbayire, meaning Sword Spur. It was the objective of 3rd Australian Brigade and was occupied early in the morning of 25 April by parties of the 11th and 12th Battalions. They were later joined by elements of the Auckland Infantry Battalion and half the Canterbury Battalion under Lieutenant-Colonel D. McB. Stewart, but in the afternoon they were driven from the hill when a formidable Turkish force moved against Baby 700. Colonel Stewart was killed [he is commemorated on the Lone Pine Memorial] and men started to run back calling, 'Get to beggary! The Turks are coming on - thousands of 'em'. The advancing Turks were led by Zeki Bey (qv) who was wounded in the arm. The Turks paid dearly for their charge, one battalion of the 27th Regiment losing all its company commanders (three out of four being killed) and most of its junior officers.

Although it was the objective of several other attacks, notably in May and August, it was never again reached. A gravel path leads to the cemetery which was made in 1919 when the bodies of men who had reached this advanced position on 25 April were found. Some of the bodies were in graves dug by the Turks during the Armistice of 24 May (qv). There are 23 Australians, 10 New Zealanders, 1 seaman of the RNR, 449 unidentified men and 10 Australian special memorials. An analysis of the battalions and the dates of death of the identified burials clearly chart when and by whom attempts to take this hill were made. Twenty-two men were killed on 25 April. They are of the 1st, 2nd, 9th, 10th, 11th, 12th and 16th Battalions, AIF, and of the Auckland and Canterbury NZ Battalions. **Stoker G. Watson** of HMS *Queen* was killed on 30 April [D 1]. On 2 May fourteen men were killed from the 1st, 2nd and 11th Battalions, AIF. Between 7-10 August six men were killed from the 10th Australian Light Horse, and the Auckland, Otago and Wellington NZ Battalions.

Captain Joseph Peter Lalor of the 12th Battalion, age 30, killed on 25 April [Sp Mem 4] was one of the most colourful characters to fight on the Peninsula. The grandson of Peter Lalor, the leader of the only armed revolt in Australian history, at the Eureka Stockade on the Victorian goldfield, he enlisted as a boy in the British Navy, deserted and joined the French Foreign Legion. He fought through the South American Revolution and was finally appointed to the Australian permanent forces as an aide-de-camp. Against all regulations he carried with him a family sword, its bright hilt wrapped in khaki cloth on that fateful 25 April. While digging the horseshoe trench at the Nek, Lalor observed Baby 700's unoccupied slopes, barring the way to the range beyond – the objective. He and Major S.B. Robertson of the 9th Battalion instigated an advance on the hill. Lalor remained in support at the Nek and sent Lieutenant I. S. Margetts ahead. By 0900 hours Margetts led his men right over Baby 700 and they lay down in the scrub, there being no other Australians in sight, with bullets pinging around them. By 0915 Margetts saw Turks aproaching from Battleship Hill and machine-gun fire rained upon them, losses were heavy and he was soon forced to withdraw. Lieutenant-Colonel Sinclair MacLagan, commanding 3rd Brigade, had set up his headquarters on the high shoulder of MacLaurin's Hill, where he could see every movement on Baby 700, which he perceived to be the key position on the pitifully thin line. He determined to send all possible reinforcements to retake this vital hill. **Major Blair Inskip Swannell** of the 1st Battalion, age 39, killed on 25 April, was an English rugby international who had settled in Australia [Sp Mem 10]. Delayed by dumping packs on their way uphill, Swannell's company was the last of the 1st Battalion. They were diverted towards Baby 700, where reinforcements were so urgently needed. With the party were Lieutenants Shout (later Captain A. J. Shout VC (qv)) and Street (later Brigadier the Hon G. A. Street (qv)). By 11 o' clock they made their way over the Nek and joined the remnants of Lalor's line. They charged the Turks and swept over Baby 700. There they came under heavy fire. Swannell had had a premonition of his death on the *Minnewaska* before landing: 'he realised that he would play this game as he had played Rugby football - with his whole heart' [Bean]. Kneeling up to show his men how to take better aim at the Turks he was shot dead. On the right of the line his second-in-command, Major Kindon, with Major Gordon of the 2nd Battalion on the left, continued 'doubling up the long summit of Baby 700 to its right'. Eventually Kindon's remaining party was pinned down by fire from each flank. Kindon lay 'steadily puffing an old pipe'. Some time after noon reinforcements from the Waikato Company of the NZ Auckland Battalion arrived to find Kindon with only four or five men - all the others had been killed or wounded, and Kindon refused to leave them. At about 2.30 two New Zealand machine guns arrived about 65 metres to his rear and Kindon finally drew back to them from the precarious position to which he had tenaciously been clinging and went to report the situation to Lieutenant-Colonel MacLagan. The line was now held by the New Zealanders, commanded by Major D. Grant of the Canterbury Battalion, who was soon killed. He is buried in Walker's Ridge Cemetery.

On the left of Baby 700 the line was exposed to Turkish fire whenever they moved. Major S. B. Robertson of the 9th Battalion, already wounded three times, raised himself to look forward and was shot. 'Carry on, Rigby,' he said to Lieutenant W. J. Rigby, the junior officer beside him, and died. He is buried in Beach Cemetery. Rigby carried on until he too was killed. He is commemorated on the Lone Pine Memorial. A withdrawal was then made to Malone's Gully (see Holts' Map 4). There Major Gordon of the 2nd Battalion, 'a fine, tall, square-shouldered man and without fear', was speaking to his men when he fell shot through the head [Bean]. He too is commemorated on the Lone Pine Memorial. His company then attached itself to the remnants of Swannell's company.

Meanwhile Margetts, despite his bewilderment at his first experience of battle being so infernal, and completely without instructions, had hung on to the forward slope with a fast diminishing band until he was the most senior officer in sight; nearly all had been killed or wounded. Eventually another, more senior, officer told him to gather all his men – by then numbering only ten – and assault the hill once more. Running out of ammunition, Margetts ran down the hill looking for Lalor. He found Lieutenant Patterson, who, seeing that Margetts was 'done up', set off with 30 men to reinforce the position. He was never seen again and is commemorated on the Lone Pine Memorial. Margetts then found Lalor, who gave the shattered Lieutenant a swig of whisky and told him to lie down. But reinforcements were again called for and Lalor ordered Margetts to take his men. Then, realising just how exhausted the young man was, decided, 'No. I'll go'. Margetts objected, but, at about 1515 hours, Lalor took off with his men towards Baby 700 while the tired Lieutenant, 'his puttees trailing in the mud', made his way to Glasfurd's HQ to beg for more reinforcements. Meanwhile Lalor, his precious sword lost in the rush, had met up with Captain Morshead (later Major-General L. J. Morshead) of the 2nd Battalion and agitatedly begged him to join on his left. Resolving to charge with this newly supplemented line, Lalor stood up and cried, 'Now then, 12th Battalion,' and was immediately killed by a Turkish bullet.

Finally, after sweeping over the bullet-torn summit of Baby 700 five times, being beaten back, pushing forward again, often pinned down under the scorching sun, the exhausted, nerve-wracked remnants were driven back down the hill by a concerted Turkish attack at about 1600 hours, there being then no more reserves to send and no supporting artillery.

The terrifying, confusing and totally exhausting experiences of the dogged young Lieutenant Margetts through this long and dreadful day are a microcosm of the macrocosm of the saga of Anzac on 25 April 1915. Having somehow got through the next two days of equally bitter struggle, Margetts was found by a friend on the 27th 'standing, one hand with his revolver resting on the parapet, his head on his arm, asleep' [Bean]. A schoomaster from Hobart before the War, he survived the hell that was Gallipoli, only to be killed on 23 July 1916, age 24 and then a Captain, in France. He is commemorated on the Villers Bretonneux Memorial to the Missing with over 10,000 of his countrymen.

Continue to the sign to the right to Mesudiye Topu. Walk up the dirt track.

* *Mesudiye Gun/15.5 kilometres/5 minutes/Map A42*

The gun is from the Turkish cruiser *Mesudiye*, torpedoed off Sari Sighlar Bay by the submarine *B11* (qv) on 13 December 1914. Her guns were salvaged by the Turks and used in the defence of the Straits. This one was placed here after the Evacuation.

Return to main road and continue, passing on the right the signs to 10 Alay Cephesi (10th Turkish Infantry Regiment area) (16kms).

From this position, along a dirt track, the Scrubby Knoll Monolith (qv) can be seen in the distance.

Mesudiye Gun with Baby 700 CWGC
Cemetery behind

Director of Forestry Memorial Statue

Continue climbing up the road over
Battleship Hill
This is marked on Allied maps as 'Big 700' (as opposed to 'Baby 700' - 700 being the height in feet), the hill is actually 210 metres above sea level. It was christened Battleship Hill by Lieutenant W. R. Hodgson because of the constant bombardment from Royal Navy battleships falling on it on 27 April. He marked it, and also Scrubby Knoll and Gun Ridge, on an artillery map. The next day he was seriously wounded but survived to be promoted to Captain.

Early on 25 April 32-year-old Captain Eric W. Tulluch (a Melbourne brewer before the war) of the 11th Battalion crossed the Nek and pushed on over the right-hand shoulder of Baby 700 with 60 men, determined to make his designated rendez-vous with other elements of the 11th on Big 700. At the highest point of their climb, which they reached by 0900 hours, they were in view of their goal, the shining waters of the Straits, and had made one of the furthest advances of the day. They met their first opposing shots on the shoulder of the second hill, when about ten men were hit. Silencing the Turks with answering fire, they pushed on until they again met heavy fire. Nevertheless they carried on, took cover when forced to, and reached the south-east shoulder of Big 700. On the skyline at Chunuk Bair they saw a Turkish officer who was obviously in command of the battle and who seemed oblivious to the bullets they sprayed around him. Could it have been Kemal Ataturk? Tulluch's party fought on for half an hour until fire from the left became heavier and closer. Lieutenant Mordaunt Reid ('a born leader' according to Bean), controlling the fire from the right, was badly hit in the thigh. A man helped him crawl back to safety, then Reid disappeared, never to be seen again. He is commemorated on the Lone Pine Memorial. Then, when it became obvious that the enemy was enfilading his left flank and that he was pinned down from the front, Tulluch gave the order to withdraw. This was done in a controlled fashion to Baby 700 and the Nek in time to join the bitter struggle that was taking place there.
Continue to the statue on the right.

* Turkish Director of Forestry's Statue/16.4 kilometres/5 minutes/Map A43

The statue commemorates Talat Goktepe, Canakkale Region Director of the Ministry of Forestry, who died in an heroic but unsuccessful attempt to extinguish the disastrous fire of 25 July 1994. Behind him are symbolic trees and he holds out his hand to try to stop the flames licking upwards.
Continue to the small stone tablet to the left.

* Mehmetcik Park Aniti/16.9 kilometres/45 Minutes for entire Chunuk Bair complex/Map A44,45,47,48,49,50,51,52/WC/OP

This marks the area of the Chunuk Bair (Conkbayiri) Complex of Memorials To the right of the road are public toilets.
Immediately afterwards, up some stone steps to the left are

* Turkish Monoliths, Chunuk Bair

The five stone monoliths were designed by Ahmet Gulgonen, winner of a national competition in 1970, and represent a hand turned upward to God. They were dedicated to the soldiers, 'Mehmetcik', (literally little Mehmets, the affectionate Turkish name for 'Johnny Turk') who lost their lives fighting here. Each has an inscription in Turkish, repeated on a plaque in English, which tells a story:

1. After learning of the enemy landing at Ariburnu on 25 April 1915, Staff Officer Lieutenant-Colonel Mustafa Kemal (Ataturk), Commander of the 19th Infantry Division, on his own initiative dispatched the 57th Regiment to this sector. At this time, a small number of soldiers, whose ammunition was finished, were guarding the shore. They made a bayonet charge and gained enough time to successfully prevent the enemy reaching Chunuk Bair.

2. On the morning of 25 April 1915, Mustafa Kemal (Ataturk) gave this order to the 57th Regiment, just before the regiment's attack on the enemy approaching the Conk Slope: 'I do not order you to attack, I order you to die. In the time which passes until we die, other troops can take our places and other commanders can master the situation.' This order angered the Mehmetciks, who continuously and relentlessly attacked the enemy under the continuous and heavy fire of the naval artillery and forced the enemy back to Cesaret Tepe (the Nek).

3. Again, enemy forces in the Ariburnu sector, which were strengthened by reinforcements, began to attack Chunuk Bair on 6 August 1915. At the end of the bloody battles, which continued uninterrupted, day and night, both sides suffered heavy casualties. Turkish soldiers stopped the enemy 25 metres from the line of hills around Chunuk Bair on the evening of 9 August 1915.

4. The Turkish counter-attack, due to the narrowness of the land between the trenches of the two sides, began as a bayonet charge on the morning of 10 August 1915. During the battles of Chunuk Bair, which became hellish under the thick fire of the enemy's naval artillery, Colonel Mustafa Kemal, Commander of the Anafarta Group, did not leave the observation point even for a minute. His life was saved by his watch in his breast pocket which was shattered by a piece of shrapnel. And so, at the end of this attack, the enemy was thrown back as far as Aghyl Dere .

5. The continuous attacks of the enemy forces, aimed to capture Chunuk Bair, the most important area and the peak of the Gallipoli Peninsula, and divide the Turkish forces into two and so conquer the Dardanelles, was unsuccessful due to the courageous defence operation and zeal of the heroic Turkish soldiers. During the battles fought in this sector, the Turkish Army suffered 9,200 casualties and the enemy 12,000.

Continue to a T-junction, turn left signed Conkbayiri and stop in the car park. (17.1kms). To the left is

* Tomb of Unknown Turkish Soldier

The remains of this unknown soldier were discovered in 1985.

Extra Visit to The Farm CWGC Cemetery (Map A46). Round trip: 1,080 metres. Approximate time: 30 minutes.

From beside the tomb walk down the dirt track signed ahead as a steep path of 540 metres. A further sign points to the right.

Here the path becomes narrower, rougher and steeper until it reaches the plateau on which the cemetery is built. The return journey is quite strenuous and stout shoes are essential, a stick an asset. To be among the relatively few visitors to see this isolated cemetery, the scene of such desperate but ultimately futile heroism, makes the effort well worth while.

In the following account, 'left' and 'right' are as viewed from the coast which is where the attack on the Sari Bair Ridge started.

The Farm was a stone hut on a small sloping field, the site of the present cemetery, known to the Turks as Aghyl (sheepfold). Below it were two rises known as The Apex and The Pinnacle. The Farm was on the route of the forces attacking Chunuk Bair up Rhododendron Ridge (also known as a Spur - named for the beautiful flowering shrubs which still cover it) on 7 and 8 August in the attempted diversion from the Suvla Landings known as the Battle of Sari Bair. General Godley (qv) planned a two-column attack ('right' and 'left'), each assaulting column having a 'covering force' to clear the path for the assaulting force.

The left-hand column, led by General Sir H. V. Cox commanding the 29th Indian Brigade comprised his own Brigade, the 4th Australian Infantry

View of the Farm from Chunuk Bair

The Farm CWGC Cemetery

Extra Visit continued

Brigade, the Indian Mountain Battery and 2nd Field Company NZ Engineers. Their covering force, commanded by Brigadier-General J. H. Travers, comprised the 4th South Wales Borderers, the 5th Wiltshires and half of 72nd Field Company, RE, all of Kitchener's New Army 13th (Western) Division. They were to capture Kocacimentepe (Hill 971, meaning Hill of the Great Pasture), the highest point on the crest. Their route up the Aghyl Dere (Sheepfold Valley) from the north-west had been partly reconnoitred by Major Overton (qv) who led the assault but was later killed. He is buried in 7th Field Ambulance Cemetery. Elements of the Gurkhas and Sikhs were to push out to the Abdul Rahman Spur via Azmak Dere.

The right-hand column was to advance up Rhododendron Spur (also reconnoitred by Major Overton) to take Chunuk Bair. At 0100 hours on the morning of the 7th the NZ Infantry Brigade, commanded by Brigadier-General F. E. Johnston, with No. 1 Field Company NZ Engineers and the 26th Indian Mountain Battery, supported by artillery fire from five vessels stationed off Gaba Tepe and four vessels stationed to the north, gathered at the foot of the valley for the assault. The covering force of the right column, commanded by Brigadier-General A. R. Russell, consisted of the NZ Mounted Rifles Brigade, the Otago Mounted Rifles, a Maori contingent and a troop of NZ Engineers.

Extra Visit continued

In this right-hand column the Canterburys were to ascend via Sazli Beit, the Otagos, Aucklands and Wellingtons up the Chailak Dere. They had already fought their way from Nos 2, 3 and Old No 3 Posts (qv), over Bauchop's Hill (qv) to their left (where Lieutenant-Colonel Bauchop (qv) was killed; he is commemorated on the Lone Pine Memorial) and the Table Top to the right to clear the gullies and deres for their final assault on Chunuk Bair. The night was dark and the country rough, resulting in a certain amount of delay and confusion. At dawn a small group under Major Frank Statham ('a dauntless-spirited soldier and a born leader' [Waite]) reached the lower slopes of Rhododendron Spur [Holts' Map 4] where they were astonished to see the valley filled with demoralised Turks streaming back towards Battleship Hill. Others, led Major S. A. Grant, a newly-arrived officer, crying, 'Come along, lads,' pressed on to be met by withering fire. Grant was mortally wounded. (He is commemorated on the Lone Pine Memorial.) Command and control were fragmented but the men were heartened by news that they were to be joined by the famous Gurkhas on their left.

They reached the Pinnacle but the eagerly awaited Gurkhas had swerved right and left and the Canterburys, waiting for support to come up, lost 7 officers and about 100 men. Watching from below, Brigadier-General Johnston realised that it would not now be possible to reach Chunuk Bair in force during daylight.

The Turks barring the way of the New Zealanders and the Gurkhas to their left had been hurriedly despatched by Mustafa Kemal from his headquarters behind Battleship Hill. They were the 1/14th Battalion, his only reserves, and they held on until reinforced by the Turkish 9th and 4th Divisions, which had raced exhaustedly up from Helles.

Hopes of the left column reaching Hill 971 that day had also now vanished. Cox called on reserves of the 39th Brigade under Brigadier-General W. de S. Cayley to help him take Chunuk Bair before more Turkish reinforcements arrived. All four of his battalions took off in the wrong direction, the 7th Gloucesters ending by joining up with the New Zealanders. The day finished with units lost or scattered, and men exhausted by hill climbing and desperate for water. On the ridge overlooking the Farm were the Gurkhas and Sikhs. The Canterbury gunners had hauled their guns to the Apex, in front of which were the Aucklands.

A dawn assault on Chunuk Bair was planned for the next day, 8 August, and the disarrayed force was reorganised into three columns, the right under Johnston, the centre and left under Cox. The latter were to work their way towards Kocacimentepe, but Turkish reserves had now arrived and the 4th Australians fell back to the former line. In the centre 39th Brigade pushed on past The Farm but heavy Turkish fire halted them on the slopes overlooking it. The first line of the right-hand column - the Wellingtons and the Gloucesters

Extra Visit continued

under Lieutenant-Colonel Malone - left their trenches on the Rhododendron Spur on what the New Zealanders would regard as their blackest day. In the second line were the 8th Welch, in the third the Maoris and the Auckland Mounted Rifles. A forward contingent of the Wellingtons pushed over the crest with the main body dug in behind and some Gloucestors to their left. Then a leaden curtain of machine-gun fire met them. The crews of all the machine guns the New Zealanders had pushed up the hill were killed or wounded, save one Maori machine gun which fought on with a few officerless men. At daylight a fierce Turkish bayonet charge followed an intense shrapnel and bombing attack which left only a few wounded men alive, a Turkish sergeant saving the wounded from being bayoneted. They were taken to a German dressing station behind Hill Q.

Meanwhile at the Apex the Welch, led by 'young, athletic and spirited officers', emerged into a hail of fire from Battleship Hill as daylight revealed them to the Turks. They were shot down and scattered in the Aghyl and Sazli Deres.

The Gloucesters had at an early stage lost every officer, company sergeant-major and quartermaster sergeant but nevertheless hung on at the extreme flanks of the Wellington line. Malone moved his HQ to a sheltered position at the top of Rhododendron Spur but artillery and sniper fire effectively cut him off. He ordered and led frequent short attacks suffering heavy losses, particularly among the inexperienced men of the New Army. Few of the Gloucesters, under Major Stevens of the 8th Welch, survived. Malone then sent for his reserves and at 11 o' clock the Auckland Mounted Rifles started a slow and difficult climb to the Pinnacle and thence to the firing line. The Maoris veered into the Aghyl Dere and on to The Farm. The situation became increasingly desperate as more and more Turks poured in: the 24th Regiment of 8th Division joining the 64th and 25th Regiments of the 9th Turkish Division who had attacked during the morning. Finally Malone, impetuous and gallant, was killed by a shell which burst near his headquarters. He is commemorated on the Chunuk Bair NZ Memorial.

When darkness fell supplies and some reinforcements reached the worn out but determined remnants, but around midnight, with a shout of 'Allah! Allah!', the Turks rushed their precarious positions and the remnants of the Wellingtons (only 70 out of the 760 who had reached the crest that morning), the Gloucesters and the Welch were withdrawn. 'Throughout the day not one had dreamed of leaving his post. Their uniforms were torn, their knees broken. They had had no water since the morning; they could talk only in whispers; their eyes were sunken; their knees trembled; some broke down and cried like children. But they had gained and held a foothold for their force on the summit of Sari Bair' [Bean].

Yet another plan had to be made for the 9th. Birdwood and Godley

Extra Visit continued

simplified it to concentrate on the area between Chunuk Bair and Hill Q to the left, where Major Allanson and the Gurkhas were clinging on, completely out of touch. The main assault, up the Chailak Dere, was entrusted to General Baldwin commanding the untried 6th E Lancs, 5th Wilts, 10th Hants and 6th RIR. To their south the Otagos and the Wellington Mounted Rifles commanded by Colonel Meldrum - the right column - were attacked before they could assemble for their assault. Major Statham and his brother, Corporal C. H. F. Statham, were killed side by side by a shell at about 0500 hours. (They are commemorated on the Chunuk Bair Memorial, Panel 14.) Meldrum and his officers rallied their men, but soon Major Elmslie (commemorated on the Chunuk Bair NZ Memorial, Panel 4) who died with the words, 'I'm afraid I can't help you much further, boys, but you're doing well - keep on [Bean'] and the adjutant, Captain Kelsall, (commemorated on the Chunuk Bair Memorial, Panel 4) were also killed.

Of Cox's left column the 10th Gurkhas and 9th Warwicks already near The Farm (where the Maoris still were) made no progress, but further north the 6th Gurkhas and the South Lancs, led by Major Allanson of the Gurkhas, reached a portion of the summit and drove back a body of Turks, but as Baldwin's central column was nowhere to be seen, and heavy HE shells burst among them, a retreat was ordered. Lieutenant J. W. J. Le Marchand urged the Gurkhas to stay and die in the trench, but Allanson persuaded him it would be folly, and they ran down the hill. Every officer of the Gurkhas was hit and Le Marchand was killed. (He is commemorated on the Helles Memorial.)

During the night march to their start line Baldwin's column lost their way and his attack went in hours late and was pitifully ineffectual. The East Lancs (whose commanding officer, Colonel Cole-Hamilton, was mortally wounded and is buried in 7th Field Ambulance Cemetery) and the 6th RIR then reached The Farm which became a meeting point for the 10th Gurkhas, the 5th Wiltshires and the Maoris. The Irish were ordered to advance, and were seemingly killed to a man, their bodies found 25 yards from the crest in 1919. The 10th Hants reached a gap between the Pinnacle and The Farm but no further progress was made. The third day's attack had failed with more appalling losses and the wounded again made their hazardous and painful way down the stricken gullies - (see No 2 Outpost above). On the fourth day, 10 August, Godley had to formulate yet another plan to hurl scarce and precious men into the killing ground just below the crest.

During the night all the New Zealand units - or what remained of them - were withdrawn. By this time the Otagos had lost 17 officers and 309 men, the Wellington Mounted Rifles mustered only 73 out of 183, the Aucklands had lost 12 officers and 308 men. Of the 4,549 who went in on 6 August only 1,871 remained. Now the New Army battalions took the punishment: the Loyal North Lancs, the 6th Leinsters and the 10th Hants, followed later by the 5th

Extra Visit continued

Wilts. Between 0300 and 0330 hours the Turkish attack began with bombing, followed by shelling as day broke and waves of Turkish Infantry came pouring over the crest in the greatest enemy attack ever launched in Gallipoli. The British were swamped until the Allied warships ranged on the attackers, as did the 10 machine guns of the NZ brigade on the Apex, breaking up the murderous waves. But the persistent Turks reached the Pinnacle and were close to the Apex. The depleted British huddled round The Farm. General Baldwin himself had been killed shortly after daybreak (he is commemorated on the Helles Memorial), as were so many officers that day. At 7.45 Birdwood sent in his last reserves, the Connaught Rangers, who had been burying the dead near Lone Pine. But by nightfall the line was withdrawn to the foot of the ridge, The Farm left vacant. The Turks once more held all the significant heights on the Peninsula. The 10th Hants had lost 22 officers and 508 men, the 6th RIR 19 officers and 361 men, the 5th Connaughts 8 officers and 105 men, the 6th Leinsters 11 officers and 250 men and Brigade Headquarters 5 officers and 16 men. Of these, and their ANZAC brothers-in-arms, 652 are buried here at The Farm. Under Special Memorials lie **Lance Corporal Alan Boddington,** age 25, of the 10th Hants [1]; **Major E. W. Boyd-Moss,** DSO [2], **Major Charles Woodward Crofton,** age 50 [3], **2nd Lieutenant Leonard Ernest Hiscock,** age 19 [5], and **Lieutenant-Colonel Mervyn Henry Nunn,** age 50 [7], all of the 9th Worcesters, **Private H. Davies** of the 8th Welsh [4] and Private **William George Lowther,** age 29, of the Aucklands [6].
Return to the Chunuk Bair car park.

* New Zealand National Memorial, Chunuk Bair

The tapering stone pylon, designed by the NZ architect S. Hurst Seager, stands 20.5 metres high. Before the fire of 1994 New Zealand manuka trees stood in the surrounding shrubs. It was erected 'In honour of the soldiers of the New Zealand Expeditionary Force. 8th August 1915. From the uttermost ends of the earth'. It is 50 metres north of the left flank of the Turkish trench taken by the forward elements of the Wellingtons on 8 August.

* Ataturk Statue/Cannon Balls Turkish Memorial

Near the 10-metre-high bronze statue of Mustafa Kemal are four large concrete cannon balls which mark the spot where he was hit. 'A large piece of shrapnel hit me exactly on my heart,' wrote Kemal later. 'I was shaken. I put my hand over my heart but there was no blood. Nobody saw this event except Lieutenant-Colonel Servet Bey. With my finger I signalled him to keep silent. Because if it was known it would cause a panic throughout the battlefield. My watch in my pocket over my heart has been completely destroyed. That day I fought more eagerly, leading the units until nightfall. But this shrapnel left a deep bruise under the skin over my heart which lasted for months.' That night Ataturk gave his damaged watch to Liman von Sanders as a souvenir who in return gave Kemal his gold watch. Marble tablets with English translations of the inscriptions were added to the base of the statue in 1998.

In front of the memorial and statue are

* *Ross Bastiaan Marker No 9/ Bas Relief Map Showing Positions of Bastiaan Markers*

* *Ustegmen Nazif Cakmak Memorial*

This obelisk memorial is to 1st Lieutenant Nazif Cakmak, brother of Marshal Fevzi Cakmak (qv), who fell here as he jumped into the enemy trenches leading a bayonet charge on 26 July 1915.

Beyond the memorial and statue are **reconstructed trenches,** including the trench occupied by the forward contingent of the Wellingtons on 8 August, a **Battle Observation Post** and the most superb views over Suvla.

To the right of the Ataturk Statue is

* *New Zealand Memorial Wall*

The wall records, on panels of Hopton Wood stone, the names of 852 officers and men of the NZEF who 'lost their lives in the heroic assault on the heights of Sari Bair, 6th-10th August, 1915, in the capture of Chunuk Bair, and in subsequent battles and operations from August and December, 1915, and who are not definitely recorded as buried in this or adjoining cemeteries'. Four men have subsequently been identified and are recorded elsewhere. There are 83 Auckland Mounted Rifles, 15 Canterbury Mounted Rifles, 57 Wellington Mounted Rifles, 32 Otago Mounted Rifles, 10 NZ Field Artillery, 92 Auckland Infantry Regiment, 92 Canterbury Infantry Regiment, 134 Otago Infantry Regiment, 310 Wellington Infantry Regiment and 19 of the Maori Contingent.

On the wall are commemorated **Lieutenant-Colonel William Malone** (qv), age 53, CO of the Wellington Battalion, Twice Mentioned in Despatches, killed 8 August [Panel 17]; **Major James McGregor Elmslie** (qv) of the Wellington Mounted Rifles, Mentioned in Despatches, age 38, and who had served in the S.African campaign, killed on 9 August [Panel 4] and **Captain Victor Albert Kellsall** (qv), age 44, his Adjutant, (killed on the same day but recorded as killed on the 9th) [Panel 4]; there are several **brothers: Corlett - Private Alfred Harpham,** age 24, and **Private Franklin,** age 22, both of the Wellington Regiment and killed 'side by side' on 8 August [Panel 19], **McKinnon - Trooper John,** age 24, and **Private Kenneth,** age 20, both of the Auckland Mounted Rifles and killed on 8 August [Panels 22 and 10], **Mellor - Private Arthur Foster,** age 30, and **Lance-Corporal Clement,** age 21, both of the Wellington Regiment and killed on 8 August [Panels 22 and 18], **Murphy - Troopers Michael and Richard** of the Wellington Mounted Rifles, both killed on 9 August [Panel 5], **Statham - Major Frank**

Hadfield and Corporal Clive Heathcote Falk, (qv), both of the Otago Regiment, killed together on 8/9 August [Panel 14], Stokes - Privates James Fawcett, age 25, and Sydney Herbert, age 26, both of the Wellington Regiment and killed on 8 August [Panel 23]. The father of Private Arthur Jules Hayden Bourgeois of the Wellington Regiment, age 31, and who was killed on 8 August [Panel 19], was 'a Veteran of the Franco-Prussian and Crimea Wars' while the father (Major F. Coore Mein) of Private George Frederick Coore (Eric) Mein of the Canterbury Regiment, age 34, killed on 7 August [Panel 13], of the KSLI served in the S. African Campaign, the Samoan Expedition of 1914-15, and 'again volunteered for service in 1915 and proceeded to the Dardanelles, with 4th Reinforcements'. The 53-year old Private William Campbell of the Canterbury Regiment, killed on 7 August [Panel 12], served in the S. African Campaign, as did Trooper Ernest Long of the Wellington Mounted Rifles, age 36, killed on 9 August [Panel 5]. Private Owen Gaffney of the Canterbury Regiment, killed on 7 August, served as 'Queenan', his parents' name being 'Queenan Gaffney' [Panel 13]; Trooper William Hawkins of the Auckland Mounted Rifles, age 32, killed on 8 August, served as 'Grant, D. [Panel 2]; Private Frederick Larsen of the Wellington Regiment, age 29, killed on 9 August, served as 'Lawson' [Panel 21]. Private Thomas Kelly of the Canterbury Regiment, age 42, killed on 10 August, served in the Indian Frontier and in the S. African Campaign with the Gordon Highlanders [Panel 13]. Private John Robert Dunn, age 26, of the Wellington Regiment, killed on 8 August, had been sentenced to death on 18 July for sleeping at his post at Quinn's, but the conviction was not carried out on 'medical grounds' as he had not been relieved at the due time [Cupper].

Below the memorial is

* Chunuk Bair CWGC Cemetery

The Cemetery was made after the Armistice on the site where the Turks buried the Allied dead of 6-8 August. In it are 622 unidentified soldiers (2 being New Zealanders) and Trooper William Gill, age 34, [5] and Trooper John Allan Newton, age 24, [4] of the Wellington Mounted Rifles; Trooper Harry Wilfred Paulsen, age 21 [9] and Lance Corporal John Henry Winston, age 29, [6] of the Auckland Mounted Rifles [9]; Serjeant David Robert Breingan Lascelles, age 25, [1], Private Basil Ernest Mercer, age 19, [3] and Private Martin Andrew Persson, age 17, [2] of the Wellington Regiment; Private Richard Enoder Tonkin, age 22, of the Otagos [12] and Havildar Punahang Limbu of the 10th Gurkhas [7].

Lying on the forward slope of Chunuk Bair, these are the only Allied men who rest overlooking the unattainable prize of the Narrows, clearly visible beyond the cemetery.

Despite the numerous acts of supreme heroism and gallantry which occurred during those terrible four days of struggles to take Chunuk Bair, only one VC was awarded - probably because all those who would have made recommendations for the award were themselves killed. It was won by Corporal Cyril Royston Guyton Bassett, New Zealand's first VC of WW1 and her only one at Gallipoli. He had

New Zealand National Memorial and Ataturk Statue, Chunuk Bair

Father
grandfather
great-grandfather

SERGT. MAJOR G. F. A. SARGEANT.
Otago Infantry Battalion,
Wounded.
Evacuated to England. Died of his wounds
back home in New Zealand.

WE WILL REMEMBER YOU

Private Tribute on New Zealand Memorial

The New Zealand Memorial Wall in a rare snow scene, March 1998 Courtesy of John Price

Lieutenant Nazif Cakmak Memorial

Gurkha Headstone, Chunuk Bair
CWGC Cemetery

Preserved trenches, Chunuk Bair

Tomb of Unknown Turkish Soldier

landed at Anzac on 25 April in command of a Signals section and was recommended for an award in May for carrying telephone wire across ground swept by fire between Walker's Ridge and Pope's Hill. On 8 August Bassett was placed in command of a party of signallers by Brigadier Johnston (qv) who were to climb up the exposed slope of Rhododendron Spur with a telephone wire, stepping over the bodies of the New Zealanders and Gurkhas killed there the previous day and dodging machine-gun and rifle fire. About three-quarters of the way up, a squadron of Mounted Rifles commandeered his phone but HQ sent up another line which also was lost. Bassett sent down for another line and started to make repairs to the tangled wires. He continued this work throughout the 8th and into the 9th. That night they laid a new wire to the Wiltshires and brought in one of their men who had been lying wounded for a day and a night. Then Bassett and his small team continued their suicidal job of continually repairing broken lines in the open, under fire and often during Turkish attacks. Miraculously Bassett survived unscathed, despite several near misses from bullets - an escape which he attributed to his short stature so that 'the bullets passed over me' [Snelling]. Bassett's citation gives the date 7 August for his act of gallantry, whereas in reality it was for repeated acts on the 8th-10th. After being evacuated for nine months to England when taken seriously ill, he went on to serve on the Western front. He was commissioned in September 1917, twice wounded and recommended for the MC. During WW2 he served in the NZ National Military Reserve and ended his service career as a Lieutenant-Colonel in December 1943, age 51. He died on 9 January 1983, the last-surviving Gallipoli VC.

Return to your car and take the road between the Memorial Wall and the cemetery signed Kemalyeri (Scrubby Knoll) and Kocacimentepe/Hill 971.

The road is on the eastern slope of Hill Q, the scene of Major Cecil Allanson's foray with the 1/6th Gurkhas on 9 August. Gurkha bodies were found here in 1919.

Continue to the parking space by the hut on Hill 971.

* Kocacimentepe, Hill 971/Ross Bastiaan Marker No. 10/19.3 kilometres/ 10 minutes/MapA53/OP

At the summit of the highest point on the Sari Bair Ridge there is an observation platform, giving breathtaking views of the surrounding battlefields. In the area are helicopter landing pads, recreated trenches and **Ross Bastiaan Marker No. 10.**

Stand in the far left-hand corner of the platform and face forward. The Ataturk Statue, standing immediately in front of the New Zealand Memorial, is at 12 o' clock. At 1 o' clock on a clear day the island of Imbros may be seen on the horizon. At 2 o' clock is Nibrunesi Point and beyond it the island of Samothrace. To its right are, in sequence, Lala Baba Hill, Suvla Bay and the Salt Lake with the Kirectepe Ridge behind them. Beyond the Ridge, perhaps just visible in part, is the Gulf of Saros. To the right of the Salt Lake are Chocolate Hill (now covered in green vegetation) and Green Hill. Scimitar Hill with its three white monoliths is at 3 o' clock. At 4 o' clock is Kucukanafarta and at 5 o' clock Buyukanafarta. The hut is behind you at 6 o' clock and at 9 o' clock is Canakkale over the Straits. At 11 o' clock is the protuberance of Achi Baba and to its right Camburnu Point. To the left of the Ataturk Statue are the five monoliths at Chunuk Bair.

Here the fire of 1994 was accidentally started by a farmer's child heating up his lunch. It then swept down the Sari Bair Ridge with frightening vigour.

N.B. Alternatively Kocacimentepe may be reached from the Extra Visit to the Camtekke Turkish Cemetery at the end of Itinerary Four (see below) along a spectacular route.

Turn round and return to Chunuk Bair (21.5kms). Drive past the car park to the junction and turn left signed Kemalyeri. Continue to the wooden sign with yellow lettering on the left.

Watercourse (Suyatagi) Memorial/21.7 kilometres/Map A54

This small memorial records the fact that Mustafa Kemal spent the night of 9-10 August here. At daylight he climbed to the crest of Chunuk Bair to launch his successful counter-attack.

Continue along the crest of Suyatagi, which becomes Gun Ridge, to

*Kemalyeri (Kemal's Place)/Scrubby Knoll Monolith/23.6 kilometres/10 minutes/Map A55

This is the monolith which can be seen from the 10th Alay Cephesi sign, just past the Mesudiye Gun (see above). You are now standing at the northern highpoint of 'Third Ridge' (Gun Ridge, so-named because many Turkish guns fired from behind its crest), some 6kms from the Straits, the final objective of the Australian 11th Brigade on 25 April. The hill was called 'Scrubby Knoll' by the Allies because of the dense vegetation that grew on it.

Look towards the Aegean and identify Lone Pine Memorial. To its left is the Kanlisirt Monolith. Visible in sequence to the right of Lone Pine are Johnston's Jolly, Courtney's and Steel's, Quinn's, the 57th Turkish Regiment Memorial, Baby 700 and Chunuk Bair. The valley to the right came to be known as Legge Valley, named for Lieutenant-General J. G. Legge, (who somewhat controversially - he had no battle experience and Colonel M'Cay of 2 Brigade was expecting the job - was appointed in June to command the Australian 1st Division on the death of General Bridges). Beyond it is Pine Ridge, a spur of 'Second Ridge', which leads up to the Sari Bair Ridge and Chunuk Bair.

Here, on the evening of 25 April 1915, Mustafa Kemal established his headquarters, where he stayed until appointed to command the Anafartalar Group of the Turkish 5th Army. The monolith memorial is inscribed with the fifth paragraph of Kemal's Order of the Day for 3 May 1915: 'All soldiers fighting here with me must realise that to carry out completely the honourable duty entrusted to us there must not be one step towards the rear. Let me remind you all that your desire to rest does not merely mean that you are being deprived of your rest but may lead to the whole nation being so deprived until eternity.'

There are many claimants for 'first ashore' and 'furthest advance' on that incredible day. The latter accolade is normally awarded to the small party led by Lieutenant N. M. Loutit of the 10th Battalion. Immediately on landing the group clambered up to Plugge's Plateau, driving the bewildered Turks in front of them. On reaching the 400 Plateau they were joined by Major Brand, the Brigade-Major. When they saw the Turks rushing to man their battery at Lone Pine, Brand told Loutit to press on. He led his men through Owen's Gully (Map 4), through an abandoned Turkish camp (where Loutit had to drag his men away from scavenging), searching for more Turkish guns, which, in fact, he missed (they were in a depression known as 'The Cup' beyond the summit of Lone Pine). He was then joined by Lieutenant J. L. Haig of the 10th with a few men of the 9th. They worked their way down into Legge Valley. Seeing what he took to be his objective, Third Ridge, ahead of him, Loutit, with Haig and their party of thirty-two men, climbed the ridge, only to discover that it was just a spur, called by the Turks Adana Bair, and that the main ridge lay 350 metres away, covered with Turks. Leaving Haig with the main party and taking two men, Loutit headed for the Scrubby Knoll. Reaching the summit, they were able to see the shining water of the Straits. No other Australians could be seen on Third Ridge. They were, however, being raked by rifle and machine-gun fire and withdrew with their wounded towards Haig. There they were pinned down. Loutit sent a messenger to a party on Lone Pine under Captain Ryder, who crossed the Valley with his men to support Loutit. It was now between 0800 and 0900 hours and the Turks had begun to work their way round the flank of the isolated group whose position became untenable. They withdrew to the end of the 400 Plateau, the Turks in hot pursuit and finally dug in near Johnston's Jolly (known to the Turks as Kirmezi Sirt - Crimson Slope). They were acknowledged to have reached the farthest point inland until Bean, in the Preface to the Third Edition of his *Official History*, felt that 'there were the strongest grounds for belief' that two scouts of the 10th - Private Arthur Seaforth Blackburn (who as a 2nd Lieutenant won the VC at Pozières in 1916 and went on to become a Brigadier in WW2, serving as G.O.C., AMF, Java) and Lance-Corporal Philip de Quetteville Robin, age 30, who was killed on 28 April and is commemorated on the Lone Pine Memorial [Panel 32], crossed Third Ridge at a plateau north of Scrubby Knoll before being driven back by the advancing Turks.

On the slopes of Third Ridge Lieutenant Hughes (qv) pitched camp with his section of the GRU in the winter of 1918/1919. Bean chose to camp with his Historical Mission (qv) in Legge Valley.

Return to Eceabat via Chunuk Bair - the way you have come, OR (if the ground is dry) continue down Gun Ridge along the dirt track to the left of the monolith, keep right at the junction and continue along a wide path lined with pines until you emerge to the left of the Gaba Tepe Information Centre (27.7kms).

* End of Itinerary Three

ITINERARY FOUR

SUVLA

Itinerary Four starts at Eceabat (or from the end of Itinerary Two), continues northwards to the area of the Suvla Bay Landings, follows the Kirectepe Ridge to the villages of Kucukanafarta and Buyukanafarta, and returns to Eceabat.
Refer throughout to Holts' Map 3 (S).
* **The Route:** Eceabat/Anzac Battlefield Demarcation Marker; 7th Field Ambulance CWGC Cemetery; Green Hill CWGC Cemetery; Hill 10 CWGC Cemetery; Suvla Point - Little West Beach, Kangaroo Beach and East Beach, Turkish Memorial; Azmak CWGC Cemetery; Scimitar Hill Turkish Memorials; Krupp Naval Gun Battery, Kucukanafarta; Turkish Cemetery, Buyukanafarta.
* **Extra Visits** are suggested to: Nibrunesi Point and Lala Baba CWGC Cemetery; Walk Along Kirectepe Ridge; Turkish Gendarme Cemetery and Memorials, Kirectepe Ridge; Camtekke Turkish Cemetery.
* **Planned duration,** without stops for refreshment or extra visits: **3 hours 20 minutes.**
* **Total distance: 55.9 kilometres**

* Eceabat/0 kilometres/RWC/Map P

Take the Gaba Tepe road to the fork of the Upper and Lower Routes. Take the Lower Route to the Anzac Battlefield Demarcation Marker beyond Embarkation Pier CWGC Cemetery. **Set to zero again here.**
Continue to the sign to the right to a cemetery set back from the road. Walk up the track.

Sign to 7th Field Ambulance CWGC Cemetery in Taylor's Gap

* 7th Field Ambulance CWGC Cemetery/0.7 kilometres/10 minutes/Map A17

The cemetery is under the shelter of Walden's Knob or Point, a triangular hill on the north-west tip of Bauchop's Hill. Legend has it that it was named for a daring sniper who did much reconnoitring on the Suvla Flats as a machine-gunner with the Maoris and who was killed on the Apex. Two Australian Private Waldens are listed in CWGC records: Private H. N. Walden, 11th Battalion AIF, killed on 1 August and buried in Shell Green CWGC Cemetery [II G 41] and Private J. B .H. Walden 18th Battalion AIF, killed on 22 August and commemorated on the Lone Pine memorial [Panel 63]. The cemetery lies north of the old Aghyl Dere in Taylor's Gap, or Hollow (named after Captain G. N. Taylor of the Canterbury Mounted Rifles). It gets its name from 7th Australian Field Ambulance, which landed on the Peninsula in September, but of the 433 graves in it, 353 were brought in after the Armistice from earlier cemeteries which were mostly named for those who used them: Bedford Ridge, West Ham Gully, Walden's Point, Essex, Aghyl Dere, Eastern Mounted Brigade, Suffolk, Hampshire Lane Nos 1 and 2, Australia Valley, 1/6th Essex, 1/8th Hants, Norfolk, Junction and 1/4th Northants. It is believed that the great majority belonged to the 54th East Anglian Division. The register records 288 UK, 68 Australian, 20 New Zealand, 2 Indian and 276 unidentified burials. There are 158 UK, 47 Australian and 2 Indian special memorials. They are burials from the Battle of Sari Bair of 7-10 August, the capture of Hill 60 in late August and the period from September to December.

Buried here is **Major Percy John Overton** (qv) of the Canterbury Mounted Rifles who at dawn on 7 August was leading the Indian Brigade up the southern fork of the Aghyl Dere towards The Farm when he was killed. Overton had also served as a scout in S. Africa. He was buried where he fell, under a tree [A 5]. Another of his scouts, **Trooper Malcolm McInnes,** was killed on 7 August. Also buried here is **Lieutenant-Colonel Arthur Richard Cole-Hamilton** of the 6th East Lancs, age 56, killed in the attack on Chunuk Bair on 10 August [Sp Mem B 5]. **Lieutenant-Colonel Sir William Lennox Napier, Bart,** age 47, of the 4th SWB, was commanding the 7th RWF as an Acting Major when he was killed on 13 August [Sp Mem A105]. **2nd Lieutenant Owen Sherwood Phillips,** also of the 4th SWB, age 23, was killed on 21 August. He was a 'Scholar of Keble College, Oxford, and Captain of Boats, 1913-4' [IV A 14]. **Farrier QMS Frank Stanley Kennaugh** of the 1st Welsh Horse, age 47, killed on 30 October, 'had 23 years service with the 13th Hussars' [Sp Mem A 33]. **Private Cecil George Searles** of the 19th Battalion Australian Infantry, age 19, served as 'Barratt' [IV D 8].

Continue to a track to a Turkish monolith set back off the road to the right. Park.

* Damakcilik Bayiri Turkish Monolith/1.4 kilometres/10 minutes/Map A18

The memorial is on a small knoll some 50 metres from the road. The inscription reads, 'Colonel Mustafa Kemal, commander of the Anafarta Group, gave his order to the 7th Division to attack towards Damakcilik slope on 9 August 1915, and so prevented the collaboration of the Anzac Corps with the British 9th Army Corps and stopped a probable danger in the direction of Cimentepe (Hill 971)'.

Continue to a sign to the right to Hill 60 Cemetery (2.7kms) and proceed to the cemetery, some 600 metres up a rough track, which can be extremely difficult to negotiate if wet.

* Hill 60 CWGC Cemetery/ New Zealand Memorial/3.3 kilometres/20 minutes/Map S1,2/OP

The cemetery is just to the south-west of the summit of Hill 60 (its height in metres above sea level) first called Kaiajik Aghyl – Sheepfold of the Little Rock – by the Turks, who in August named it Bomba Tepe – Bomb Hill) built over the trenches of the August actions around the hill, the remnants of which can still be seen beside the cemetery today. It is the end of the range of hills which runs south-eastward to Hill 100 between the Kaiajik Dere and the Asma Dere (a tributary of the Azmak Dere). At the beginning of August it was in Turkish hands and, with its superb view over the Azmak Dere Plain, commanded the shoreward communications between the Allied forces at Anzac and Suvla. It was also important because of the two good wells in the vicinity.

In the Sari Bair attack of 7 August the NZ Scout, Major Overton (qv), mistakenly sent the 13th and 15th Australian Battalions of Monash's 4th Brigade up the Kaiajik Dere by Hill 60, not – as they believed – up a foothill of the Abdel Rahman Bair, a fact which was not confirmed until the Australian Historical Mission (qv) uncovered new evidence in 1919. The mistake led to the men coming under murderous machine-gun fire from Regiment Hill (Alay Tepe) as they crossed the site of the present cemetery and the brigade was forced to retire with terrible casualties on 'one of those "black days" which most deeply affect the spirits of soldiers' [Bean].

On 21 August an attack was mounted on Hill 60 by the 5th Connaught Rangers and 10th Hampshires of the 29th (New Army) Brigade - both at half strength - the Canterbury and Otago Mounted Rifles - also very weak - and the 13th and 14th Battalions AIF. Bean describes the Hill 60 spur thus: 'If a man rested his right forearm on a table the hand flat and palm downwards, the projection of the elbow would represent Hill 100, the forearm the "Flat Hill", and the hand itself Hill 60.... Along the summit, from Hill 60 to the "wrist", ran several lines of Turkish trenches, the foremost almost fringing the slope. At the "wrist" this trench receded round the indentation - a little grassy gully - and then bent forward again to encircle the lower slopes of the knoll. It was this re-entrant which was to be attacked by the 4th Australian Brigade, while the Mounted Rifles assaulted Hill 60 itself lower down, and the Connaught Rangers Kabak Kuyu, which would be on the flat near the point of the "thumb".' The Turks were crowning the summit with a redoubt consisting of several rings of trenches, some not yet completed. At the last minute the hour for the Anzac attack was delayed by 30 minutes, but unfortunately the British attack had already started. Because of the confusion caused by the partial delay, the bombardment did not materialise. Opposition was heavy. Although

Turkish Monolith, Damakcilik
Bayiri

Hill 60 CWGC Cemetery, with the
New Zealand Memorial in the
centre

some progress was made by the left-hand New Zealand column, losses were high and no ground was captured.

On the right the battle-weary Australians, weighed down with 50 lbs of ammunition and equipment, were met by a torrent of fire. Nevertheless they rushed over the first spur until they had either reached the farther slope of the Kaiajik Dere or had been killed or wounded and forty men of their first line under Major Ford were only 70 yards from the Turkish trenches. The second line under Major Dare then crossed the Dere and waited for elements of the third line under Major Herring, with some of the Hampshires, to reach the same spot. But a shell fell in the midst of the Hampshires and only one man reached Dare's party who were now cut off and they made a protective parapet with sandbags. Then a fire, started by the shell which had burst among the Hampshires, reached the dead and wounded who lay on the ledges of the hill, igniting their clothing. Those who attempted to move were shot by the Turks. Into the smokescreen raised by this scene from Dante's Inferno Captain Loughran, the medical officer of the 14th, Chaplain Gillison and Corporal Pittendrigh (qv), also a minister, came with stretcher bearers to drag the wounded from the flames. The attack died out. With a tenuous foothold on Hill 60, it was deemed vital to find reserves to take the enemy's long communication trench before daylight broke. Some strong, but inexperienced, battalions of the 5th Australian Brigade had newly arrived 'like a fresh breeze from the Australian bush. "Great big cheery fellows, whom it did your heart good to see"' [Bean]. The untried 18th Battalion fixed bayonets and charged in two lines until they were attacked on the left by bombs and by machine-gun fire. They formed a barricade with sandbags from which they made several attempts to advance. One attack was 'finely led by some of their officers, among them was Lieutenant Wilfred Emmott Addison, who, with dying and wounded around him and machine-gun bullets tearing up the ground where he stood, steadied and waved forward the remnant of his platoon until he himself fell pierced with several bullets.' Age 28, he is commemorated on the Lone Pine Memorial [Panel 59]. The attempt to complete the capture of Hill 60 with a raw battalion, without reconnaissance, eventually ended in failure. Nevertheless, by their enthusiasm and bravery the 18th - who marched out 750 strong of whom they lost 11 officers and 372 men - succeeded in gaining and holding a section of enemy trench.

On 27-29 August further attacks were made by the 13th, 14th, 15th, 17th and 18th Australian Battalions, the NZ Mounted Rifles, the 5th Connaught Rangers and the 9th and 10th Australian Light Horse. By this time the bodies of attackers and defenders lay thick around the hillside, mingled together after the fighting at close quarters in trenches shared by both sides, putrefying in the hot sun, adding to the horror of these last attempts to take the hill. The objective of the 10th Light Horse, led by Captain Phil Fry, was to seize a 150-yard stretch of trench on the summit, attacking with 'bombs' over open ground. First a Turkish machine-gun emplacement had to be put out, then two waves would rush the trench. All went according to plan, and a barricade was constructed in a bend in the trench. Then the Turks began to advance up the trench. They were repulsed by 2nd Lieutenant 'Jim' Throssell (who had only been on the Peninsula for three weeks and had miraculously survived the murderous attack on the Nek on 7 August) and his small party with bombs, returning some of the long-fused Turkish ones which landed in their section of the trench. When the Turks succeeded in destroying the barricade, Throssell's group retreated to another, half-completed barricade and there held off repeated attacks. Captain Fry was killed (he is commemorated on the Lone Pine Memorial), leaving Throssell in command of the operation. He continued bombing until 0400 when an insistent attack forced him twice to cede 5 yards, then erect a sandbag barricade, during which period Throssell received bullets in the shoulder and neck. Finally the Turks clambered out of their trenches and rushed at the dwindling, and now almost surrounded, Australian force who responded with frenetic rifle fire and cheers. Their noise seemed to deceive the Turks into believing they were more numerous than anticipated and when a New Zealand machine gun was rushed up the Turks were eventually beaten back and the trench was held. Throssell was then forced to go to a dressing station and was evacuated on the Hospital Ship *Devonnah*, suffering not only from his wounds but from deafness incurred by the noise of the bombs which he had thrown all night. He recuperated in Wandsworth Hospital, where he contracted meningitis, and there heard from his brother, Ric, who had also been wounded on the Peninsula, that he had been awarded the Victoria Cross. Throughout his inspired action Throssell had been supported by, and was geneous in his praise of, Corporal McNee and Troopers Henderson and Renton, who all were awarded the DCM. The seriously injured Corporal Syd Ferrier, who lost an arm but who continued to throw bombs (thought to total about 500), was evacuated with Throssell but died on board the hospital ship. He is commemorated on the Lone Pine Memorial. The tragic post-war story of Throssell, this popular hero who committed suicide on 19 November 1933, is movingly recounted in Stephen Snelling's *VCs of the First World War. Gallipoli.*

Many of the men from these diverse units lie in the cemetery here, among the 41 Australian, 20 UK, 28 New Zealand and 699 unidentified burials. There are also 16 Australian, 16 New Zealand and 2 UK special memorials in this unusual circular-shaped plot. Buried here is **Lieutenant-Colonel Carew Reynell** of the 9th Light Horse, Mentioned in Despatches, age 32, killed on 28 August [Sp Mem 4]. He was from Reynella, S. Australia. His body was found in the open with those of **Captain Alfred John Jaffray** of the same regiment [Sp Mem 27] and **Chaplain Grant** (see below) near an unfinished trench they were attempting to recapture which was found to be almost full of Turkish dead. Captain Philip Ignatius Callary, age 29, was also killed in the same action. He is commemorated on the Lone Pine Memorial [Panel 8].

The New Zealand Memorial stands in the centre of the cemetery. It is a 6.7-metre-high obelisk on an 8.5-metre-square stone platform and records the names of 182 New Zealanders who 'fell in the Actions of Hill 60, August 1915, and in September 1915, and who have no known grave'. Many of these names relate to the unidentified graves in the cemetery. There are 27 Auckland Mounted Rifles, 65 Canterbury Mounted Rifles, 31 Otago Mounted Rifles, 48 Wellington Mounted Rifles, 9 Maoris and 2 New Zealand Engineers. Others are recorded on the Lone

Pine Memorial. Among the men commemorated here are the **brothers Brittan - Lance-Corporal Henry,** age 27, and **Trooper Edward,** age 24, of the Canterbury Mounted Rifles, killed on 28 August [Panel 5], and **Chaplain the Reverend William Grant** (see above), attd. Wellington Mounted Rifles, age 56 [Panel 8]. On 28 August Grant went out with another Chaplain from behind the low barricade that had been constructed to reach a wounded man of the Mounted Rifles in 'Trench 2'. They dressed the wounds of several of the wounded Turks who lay in the trench and then, turning a bend in the trench, still searching for the wounded New Zealander, Grant was shot.

Return to the main road and take the left fork signed Mestantepe/Jandarma Sehitligi/Green Hill/Azmak Cemeteries.

Extra Visit to Nibrunesi Point and Lala Baba CWGC Cemetery (Map S3) Round trip: 9.4 kilometres. Approximate time: 45 minutes.

After 30 metres, take the left fork signed with a wooden CWGC sign to Lala Baba CWGC Cemetery.

A four-wheel-drive vehicle is more or less essential for this visit. The going can be virtually impossible for a normal car, especially if it has been raining. The alternative is to go on foot, taking adequate refreshments. You may encounter sheep dogs fiercely protecting their flocks, so don't forget the dog biscuits.

Continue along the track, crossing the Soguilu Dere which, though running swiftly, has a good firm base. Continue past Lala Baba Hill to the cemetery on the left.

Stand with your back to the entrance of the cemetery and take the forward direction as 12 o'clock. In that direction across the water of Suvla Bay is Suvla Point and stretching clockwise behind it on the horizon is the Kirectepe Ridge. At 3 o'clock is Lala Baba Hill and at 9 o'clock Nibrunesi Point.

The Turkish observation post on Lala Baba had been raided several times before the Suvla landings. On 20 April the Navy landed a small party at Nibrunesi Point and destroyed a telephone wire and on 28 April a low-flying Allied seaplane noticed a great deal of activity at Nibrunesi Point, and, fearing that a gun (which would have commanded the Anzac beachhead) was being brought into place, a tremendous naval bombardment was brought down on Lala Baba. Then on 2 May a party of fifty New Zealanders led by Captain C. W. Cribb of the Canterbury Battalion and two other officers landed here from the destroyer *Colne*. They surprised the sleeping Turks and killed several, capturing 15. They also blew up several huts, destroyed a telephone wire and embarked before midday without further opposition.

To the left of Nibrunesi Point, looking out to sea, is the 1,600 metre stretch of 'C' and 'B' Landing Beaches. On 'B' Beach at 2130 hours on 6 August the destroyers carrying 32nd and 33rd Brigades and 11th Division HQ lined up for the disembarkation. Seven lighters grounded on the undefended beach and by

Extra Visit continued

1000 hours four battalions had landed with only one casualty (a naval rating shot from the shore). On the right were the 7th S Staffs and the 9th Sherwood Foresters. They quickly completed their task of entrenching a line from the coast to the edge of the Salt Lake to protect the right flank of the landings. On the left were the 6th Yorkshires and the 9th W Yorkshires, both under Colonel J. O'B. Minogue.

The assault on the 146-metres-high Lala Baba was the first made by any unit of the New Army in the Great War. It was the immediate object of two companies of the 6th Yorkshires under Major Archibald Roberts. A third company under Major W.B. Shannon headed for Nibrunesi Point. Instructed to use bayonets only until daybreak, the two leading companies moved forward until they 'came under a hot fire, and officers and men fell thickly; but the line trudged on till the top of the hill was won.' Though most of the Turks holding the position scattered in front of the assault troops, some lay in trenches until they had passed, then sprang up to shoot them in the back. Major Roberts, age 47, was mortally wounded and is buried in Pieta Military Cemetery, Malta [A. 11. 5]. He and all but two of his junior subalterns had fallen in the attack. Following behind with his party, Colonel E. B. Chapman was also killed. He is buried in Azmak Cemetery [Sp Mem 5]. The inexperienced and leaderless men now 'flung themselves down and waited' [*Official History*]. Major Shannon, having put out of action two Turkish posts near Nibrunesi Point, headed for Lala Baba to join the main attack, only to discover he was the only senior

Headstone of Brig-Gen Kenna, VC, in Lala Baba

Lala Baba CWGC Cemetery

Extra Visit continued

officer left. Leaving one of the remaining subalterns in charge at Lala Baba, Shannon then occupied a trench near the spit and sent a message to Brigade HQ to report the capture of the hill. Although the messenger was unfortunately killed and his message not received, the 9th Yorkshires eventually arrived to support the depleted 6th. So far all had gone according to plan, other than the 6th Yorkshires' heavy losses, and the way to the all-important Hill 10 was clear. Now, however, according to the *Official History*, 'the high-water mark of success had already been reached and the tide was on the turn.'

Both the Yorkshire battalions should now have pushed on to Hill 10 to assist 34th Brigade, but, aware of confusion ahead, and in the darkness, Colonel Minogue commanding the battalions decided not to move. By daybreak of 7 August other battalions of the 32nd and 33rd Brigade were now in the vicinity of Lala Baba, making a total of six battalions, together with eight mountain guns and a battery of 18-pounders. Some battalions to the south of the hill had not yet been in action. Precious advantage was being lost in this area because of uncertainty and inactivity. Eventually four companies were sent on from Lala Baba with imprecise instructions. Major Shannon, commanding the right-hand company, was badly wounded and the attack petered out.

The cemetery, which is built on 'Little Lala Baba' Hill, contains 200 UK graves, 53 un-named graves and 16 Special Memorials. Among them is 53-year-old **Brigadier-General Paul Aloysius Kenna**, VC, DSO, ADC 21st Lancers. His VC was won in 1898 in the Battle of Omdurman. Kenna was given temporary command of the 5,000-strong dismounted Yeomanry of the 2nd Mounted Division on 18 August and in the confusing attack on Hill 112 near Scimitar Hill of 21 August he was ordered by General Marshall to recall the Yeomanry and march them back to Lala Baba. He was mortally wounded by a shell on 29 August and died the following day [II A1]. **Lieutenant the Hon. K. R. Dundas,** RNVR of the Anson Battalion, RND, age 33, son of the 6th Viscount Melville, was killed on 'C' Beach on 7 August by a German bomb [III B 9]. Dundas had been a District Commissioner in British East Africa before the war and was a fluent German speaker. **Private Alfred Edwards East,** 2nd/10th Middlesex, age 20, 'Died of exposure' on 1 December 1915 [III A 9]. **Private Thomas Parkinson** of the 9th W Yorks was only 16 when he was killed on 7 August [II D 4]. Private G. Rushworth of the 1st Fife and Forfar Yeomanry, age 28, killed on 3 November, was an artist with the *Dundee Courier* [I D 1]. **Private Joseph Vaghi** of the 3rd Scottish Horse, age 18, killed on 7 October, was a 'Native of Milano, Italy' [I A 3].

Return to the main road.

Continue, crossing the Azmak Dere, with a water pumping station on the left (4.6kms).

After a few metres to the right of the road is the area of Hetman Chair (from Cayir, meaning field or meadow). In 1915 it was seamed with irrigation ditches and there were several important wells here, one of which, Dervish Alu Kuyu (Dervish Ali's Well), was the second objective of 34th Brigade's 21 August attack on Scimitar Hill. The first objective of 11th (Northern) Division (which included 32nd, 33rd and 34th Brigades) was the Turkish front line trench and communication trench which led from the Azmak Dere to Hetman Chair and beyond. The preliminary bombardment (which began at 1430 hours) failed to shake the garrison in the Turkish forward trench and heavy losses were incurred by the 6th Yorks and 6th York & Lancs. The 8th West Riding and 9th W Yorks were hurried forward but they were driven back to the southern slopes of Green Hill. Then (soon after 1500 hours) the 33rd Brigade, headed by the 9th Sherwood Foresters, moved from Lala Baba around the Salt Lake in open formation. The Sherwoods attempted to storm the Turkish trench at the northern end of Hetman Chair. During the attack, which was repulsed, their commanding officer, 53-year-old Lieutenant-Colonel Lionel Bosanquet, was killed (he is commemorated on the Helles Memorial [Panel 150]), as was their second-in-command, Major John Blackburne, buried in Green Hill Cemetery. On the left, two companies of the 6th Border Regiment were caught by heavy fire from the communication trench and fell back 'in some confusion', their commanding officer, Lieutenant-Colonel G. F. Broadrick, being killed. (He is commemorated on the Helles Memorial). By 1700 hours the attack on the Turkish work at Hetman Chair had failed.

Continue along the road.
Immediately to the left of the road is **Chocolate Hill,** so named from the dried or burnt scrub which covered it in August 1915, but now covered in green vegetation. It adjoins **Green Hill** (which remained green because it had not been burnt) to the right of the road and both are 52 metres above sea level. On 21 August 22 machine guns, manned by sailors, had been rushed to Chocolate Hill to cover the attack on Scimitar Hill (which is over to your right beyond Green Hill). The attack was observed by the war correspondents Ellis Ashmead-Bartlett and Henry Nevinson who had walked across the Salt Lake to a viewpoint on Chocolate Hill. 'To attempt further frontal attacks on Scimitar Hill and W Hill appeared to me sheer madness. The Turks had two divisions entrenched up to their necks...They had also concentrated a powerful artillery to support their infantry,' he commented with accurate fatalism. Private Atkinson took part in the action and recorded in his diary, '...go across the salt lake in twos, feet sink in 1 foot every step, nearly exhausted but cannot stop as we sink in further...Chocolate Hill in view... arrive under hell of fire. 87th Brigade attacking...our spot just like hospital, all troops (Yeomanry) coming across open ground hit by shrapnel, chaps lying wounded in bushes, get burnt as all bushes get set alight, some crawl to our shelter... some crawling out and dying there, others getting hit... not a bit of shelter for a fly'.

The 29th Division was to attack with 87th Brigade to the north and 86th Brigade to the south of the hills. On the right (southern) flank the Munsters advanced into patches of scrub in front of Green Hill that had been set alight by shell fire. They continued through the smoke but were caught by murderous enfilade fire from the

Turkish machine gun at Hetman Chair and the advance petered out. To the north the 1st R Inniskillings were to make straight for Scimitar Hill. They dashed forward with great elan and captured the crest. Then their line was raked by shrapnel and machine-gun fire and the line broke, the troops pouring back down the hill. The 1st Border Regiment then swept forward but by 1700 hours the attack died away. 'The western slopes of the hill were strewn with dead, and very few of the attacking officers were left' [*Official History*]. It was then the turn of the Yeomanry to try and take Scimitar Hill. To the north was the 2nd (S Midland) Brigade under Brigadier-General Lord Longford; to the south the 4th (London) Brigade under Brigadier-General A. H. M. Taylor was to capture Hill 112. Orders were scanty and confused, exacerbated by the haze of the scrub fire, failing daylight, wounded men streaming back and overwhelming fire from their right flank. Ashmead-Bartlett felt that here the 2nd SWB were 'employed like the old Guard at Waterloo, to make a final effort to break through the enemy's front. [They failed]. This was really beating a willing horse to death. The division was only at half its peace strength.' All the officers and all four company sergeant-majors of the SWB were hit. No further progress was made but a line was held half-way up the hill. In the north Lord Longford's troops managed to reach the crest, but the leading detachment was surrounded and overwhelmed. Longford and his Brigade-Major were missing. Once darkness fell further attempts were made to storm the crest until 'there was a loud shout of "retire" from the left and the whole line swept back.' Soon after nightfall an attempt was made by Brigadier Kenna (qv) to clear the Turks from Hetman Chair with the 3rd Notts & Derby Brigade. The commanding officer of the Sherwood Rangers, Lieutenant-Colonel Sir John Milbanke, VC, was briefed but could only tell his officers, 'We are to take a redoubt, but I don't know where it is and don't think anyone else knows either.' Nevertheless the column went ahead and Milbanke was killed at its head. Born in 1872, John Peniston Milbanke, age 42, won his VC at Colenso on 5 January 1900. He had been at Harrow with Winston Churchill and they had remained friends ever since. He is commemorated on the Helles Memorial [Panel 16]. Other friends of Churchill to be killed this fatal month on what he dubbed 'this dark battlefield of fog and flame' were Brigadier-General Kenna (qv), whom he had seen winning his VC at Omdurman with the 21st Lancers, and Brigadier-General Lord Longford (qv).

Continue to the cemetery on the right.

* *Green Hill CWGC Cemetery/6 kilometres/10 minutes/Map S4*

The cemetery was made after the Armistice by the concentration of isolated graves from the August battlefields and from other small cemeteries (called York, 40th Brigade, Nos. 1 and 2, Green Hill Nos. 1 and 2, Chocolate Hill, Inniskilling, Salt Lake and Scimitar Hill (which contained 520 mostly unidentified graves). In the shape of a cross, it contains 773 UK burials (many of them from the Yeomanry), 2 Newfoundland, 1 Indian and 2,196 unidentified. There are 117 UK special memorials. Buried here is **Brigadier-General Thomas Longford (qv)**, 5th Earl, K.P., M.V.O., commanding 2nd (South Midland) Mounted Brigade, aged 50, [Sp

Green Hill CWGC Cemetery

Headstone of Lt Nowell Oxland in Green Hill

Mem E 3] killed on 21 August. **Lieutenant Nowell Oxland,** 6th Battalion the Border Regiment, killed 9 August 1915, age 24 [I C 7], was a close friend of W. N. Hodgson (who would be killed on the Somme on 1 July). Fellow poets, they were at Durham School and Christ Church, Oxford together. When Hodgson saw his friend's name in a newspaper casualty list he was badly shaken and wrote a poem (unpublished) *In Memory of Nowell Oxland.* In May 1915, when he and Oxland were both serving their country, Hodgson considered their commitment and their likely fate as he looked back to the scene of their school days:

Durham
...We are men of little measure,
Yet we hope by freely giving,
So in dying as in living,
To attain thy gracious pleasure
That our gift may lie for always in thy everlasting treasure...

Also buried here is **Private Harry Salter** of the 6th E Lancs, age 24, executed on 11 December 1915 for desertion, having had a previous conviction for absence [I G 26].

Continue to the junction and go straight on, signed Jandarma Sehitligi.

The height ahead of you, that stretches across the skyline, is the Kirectepe Ridge.

Drive around the Salt Lake, crossing the Azmak Dere North (9.1kms). Bear left at the sign to B Kemikli (9.7kms). Drive up to the cemetery on the left.

Hill 10 CWGC Cemetery

* Hill 10 CWGC Cemetery/10.2 kilometres/15 minutes/Map S5

Hill 10 is a low isolated mound, described as 'a mere pimple', to the north side of the Salt Lake. It was the original objective of three companies of 34th Brigade on 7 August but when they were landed in the wrong place they failed to find it. The hill was held by a Turkish battery and 100 men and shortly after the landings the gorse which covered the mound was set ablaze. It was eventually located at about 0430 hours and was taken by the 9th Lancashire Fusiliers and the 11th Manchesters. There, with his men exhausted and the enemy having retired, Brigadier-General Sitwell (34th Brigade commander, who was himself 'looking old and haggard' and was 'already worn out with worry and physical exhaustion') decided to dig in. There he stayed, despite pleas from Colonel Malcolm, General Hammersley's senior staff officer, and from Brigadier-General Hill (who had tramped all the way from Lala Baba) to press on to Chocolate and 'W' Hills.

The cemetery was made after the Armistice by concentration of isolated graves and small cemeteries (88th and 89th Dressing Stations, Kangaroo Beach, 'B' Beach, 26th CCS and Park Lane) on a site where three 1915 graves already lay. Edged by colourful Judas trees, it contains 492 UK sailors and soldiers, 8 Newfoundland, 1 Australian and 142 unidentified burials (many of whom died of wounds at the CCS overlooking Old A Beach). There are 55 UK special memorials and 1 man of the Royal Australian Naval Bridging Train.

Among the burials here are **2nd Lieutenant Edmund Yerbury Priestman** of the 6th York and Lancs, age 26 [I. H. 14]. Priestman, who volunteered in October 1914, had been a keen Scout; he was Scoutmaster of the 16th Sheffield Scouts and his letters were published in 1916 as *With a B.-P. Scout in Gallipoli*. They provide some vivid accounts of training at Belton Park, Grantham and his brief time on the Peninsula when he was able to do some 'real serious scouting work with people's lives depending on it', notably in the attack at Hetman Chair of 21 August. On the night of 18/19 November Priestman led a patrol into no-man's-land to take an isolated hillock near Jephson's Post on the Kirectepe Ridge. The Turks mounted a counter-attack and the patrol was overwhelmed, Priestman and many others being killed. They include **R.S.M. F. S. Warr** buried here [I. 1. 11]. The next night, however, the battalion recaptured the hillock and it was named 'Priestman's Post'. The headstone [V. D. 1] of **Lieutenant-Colonel Harry Marion Welstead** of the 9th Lancashire Fusiliers, age 54, records his date of death as 17 August. In fact he was killed on 7 August. He led his battalion northwards across The Cut (qv) searching for his objective, Hill 10. He established his HQ just south of The Cut, keeping six platoons in reserve. There he was slightly wounded by a Turkish sniper and two hours later was killed. Welstead had served in the S. African Campaign where he was Twice Mentioned in Despatches. He retired in 1908 but was recalled to command the 9th Lancashires in March 1915. **Lieutenant George Geoffrey Needham, MC,** Mentioned in Despatches, Lancashire Fusiliers, age 20, died on 22 August [Sp Mem 16]. His MC was won in the First Battle of Krithia on 28 April and he was mortally wounded in the Battle of Scimitar Hill. **2nd Lieutenant Leon Arthur Gaffney**, 6th Battalion Royal Munster Fusiliers, age 20, died of wounds on 12 August after a raid from Jephson's Post to clear a nearby Turkish trench.

Continue along the road towards Suvla Point.

On Suvla Bay Commander Unwin (qv) of the *River Clyde* and his faithful Midshipman Drewry (qv) were again working together during a landing on the Peninsula, Unwin being the Beach Master at Suvla. For five days they ferried men and stores from ship to shore. Drewry was struck with the contrast of the calm landings here with the bloody ones at Helles: 'It was uncanny, the troops got ashore in record time and then came batteries and mules and munitions. I could not understand it, I stood on the beach and saw guns being landed and horses, and behind us a few yards away was the dark bush, containing what? There was little firing, now and then a sharp rattle quite close and then silence. I thought of Helles and then wondered if we had landed by mistake at Lemnos or if we were ambushed and the Maxims were just going to clear the beach of living in one sweep.'

At the northern end of Suvla Bay are Kangaroo Beach, Little West Beach and West Beach harbour. The plan below shows the complicated work conducted by the Royal Engineers in this busy area. Note the tramways, pipelines, depots, magazines and other essential military offices. It was on West Beach that 32nd Field Ambulance was put ashore after sailing from Lemnos on the steamer *Partridge* that used to ply between Scotland and Ireland. Part of the 10th (Irish Division), they were wearing their full tropical kit of khaki drill uniforms and pith helmets. With them was all the paraphernalia of their trade: an operating marquee, tents and poles, surgical needles, splints, tourniquets, stretchers, an extra water bottle for the wounded and their own iron rations of bully beef, biscuits, sugar, tea and $1^1/_2$ pints of water. As the men waited for the order to go ashore, Sergeant John Hargrave, with at his side his unofficial batman, 50-year-old Fred Boler, who had been Kitchener's dispatch rider in S Africa, watched in disbelief the sight of men of 11th Divison, clearly visible with distinguishing white armbands, assemble on the shore as if on parade only to be scattered by Turkish artillery fire. It was, he wrote in his telling book *The Suvla Bay Landing*, 'heroic imbecility'.

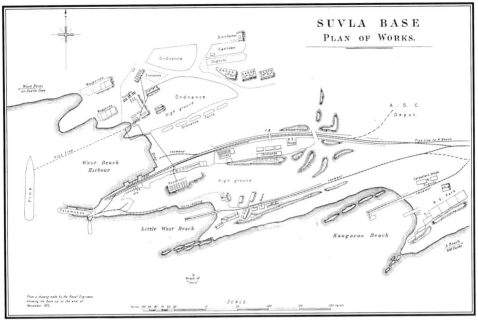

Suvla Base Plan of Works. Courtesy of HMSO

* Suvla Point/Turkish Monolith/13.3 kilometres/20 minutes/Map S6

Suvla Point was the objective of the two left-hand companies of 34th Brigade on 7 August, who were to clear the enemy post on Ghazi Baba - the hill at the Suvla Point end of the Kirectepe Ridge - then swing along the ridge 'if possible' to Point 156. When these companies were landed on the wrong beach, the 11th Manchesters were despatched to Suvla Point on a 3.5kms night march over the soft sand, with its uneven tussocks, sniped at from the dunes and bushes as they struggled on. By 0300 hours they had gained a position on the ridge 3kms east of the point, just beyond Karakol Dagh. At 1430 hours the 7th Royal Munsters landed and were despatched to support the Manchesters. After marching under the burning sun they halted when they reached the Manchesters, at which point they began to suffer casualties. The 5th R Inniskillings were sent to relieve the Manchesters who had lost 15 officers and nearly 200 men. No further advance was made along the ridge.

On the crest of the knoll overlooking Suvla Cove is one of the monoliths designed by Ahmet Gulgonen. Its inscription reads, 'The enemy forces which landed at Ariburnu on the morning of 25 April 1915, and at Port Anafarta (Suvla Bay) during the night of 6-7 August realised, after bloody battles lasting many months, that they could not overcome the Turkish defence and therefore evacuated these fronts on 20 December.'

The remains of landing piers can still be seen in the two small bays to the north of the point.

Suvla Bay, with Lala Baba to the right and the Sari Bair Ridge to the left

Suvla Point 1915. Courtesy of Australian War Memorial

Extra Visit: Walk along Kirectepe Ridge (Map S) One-way trip: Approximately 7 kilometres. Approximate time: 3 hours 30 minutes.

The complete walk along the Ridge from Suvla Point to just below the Turkish Gendarme Memorial is, taking account of the up and down, wiggling route that one has to follow, approximately 7 kilometres. It takes about 3 hours, 30 minutes to complete. A walking round trip is virtually unfeasible: the going is tough and the usual advice about sensible shoes/water/protection etc. strongly apply. Binoculars are a must. Transport should be arranged at a pick-up point at one end or the other. **Starting from Suvla Poin**t - and doing the walk in the direction of the Allied assaults,

Head for the highest ground and continue along the ridge, taking the easiest route. Sometimes this will be narrow goat/sheep tracks through scrub, shale and rock, sometimes the path widens along obvious tracks which in some places are probably supply routes made in 1915 on the

Sangar in area of Jephson's Post, Kirectepe Ridge

The 'Middle' Cairn, Kirectepe Ridge

Extra Visit continued

Gulf of Saros flank of the crest. Across the Suvla Plain are splendid views over Suvla Bay and the Salt Lake to Lala Baba and Nibrunesi Point at the extreme right and Chocolate, Green and Scimitar Hills in the centre, with the Sari Bair Ridge and Chunuk Bair beyond.

Continue along the ridge, frequently passing obvious stone fortifications and shelters/trench lines/sangars to a **cairn** of unknown, but probably ancient, origin, which is on the summit of **Karakol Dagh**. With one's back to the cairn, looking down across the plain, Hill 10 is visible at 12 o' clock.

Continue along the high ground towards another cairn. About 250 metres before the cairn is the area of **Jephson's Post**, the beginning of the centre section of the ridge known as the Hog's Back. It was named after Major John Jephson who led the 6th Munsters here on the morning of 8 August and briefly held the position. Jephson was wounded and died on 28 August. He is buried in East Mudros Cemetery. His elder brother served in Gallipoli and won the MC. There are obvious trenches and sangars around. The position was taken again during the 10th Division attack which began on Sunday 15 August. Although on the ridge, and to its west, advances were made beyond The Pimple (qv), the combination of loss of leadership (during the fighting General Mahon, the divisional commander, packed his bags and left, and General Stopford the force commander was sacked), shortage of ammunition and water and severe casualties, saw the troops back where they had started within 48 hours This is the highest part of the ridge and the trenches which can be seen running down the eastern slope are those of the final Allied lines. Standing with one's back to the cairn and looking straight down towards the plain, the four trees denoting Azmak Cemetery can be seen and beyond them the road that leads between Chocolate and Green Hills.

*Continue..*There is a third **cairn** which is on the feature known as **The Pimple** (called Shuheidlar Tepe - Martyrs' Hill - by the Turks). This lies to the right of the path which you are likely to be following and you need to keep a sharp look-out for it. That this cairn (and therefore in all probability the other two as well) existed before the Allied assault along the Ridge is confirmed by John Hargrave (qv): 'Along this rock-hackled spine rose three small prominences, the central one being marked by a cairn of stones, known to us as "The Pimple".'

Continue to the road that leads down to Azmak and then up to the Turkish Gendarme Cemetery (to which you could continue - see Extra Visit below). This is where you should arrange to meet your transport or where you should start the walk along the Ridge if going in the other direction - in which case your four-wheel-drive transport should meet you at Suvla Point.

Either walk or drive down to Azmak and pick up the main Itinerary.

Return towards Anzac Cove and Eceabat, parallel to the Kirectepe Ridge, to the sign to the turning to Hill 10. Stand with your back to the sign and face the Kirectepe Ridge.
Straight ahead is Azmak Cemetery on the foothills of the Ridge.
Continue to the sign to Azmak CWGC Cemetery. Turn left.

Extra Visit to Turkish Gendarme Cemetery and Memorial/Monolith, Hill 156, Kirectepe Ridge (Map S7,8,9) Round trip: 12 kilometres. Approximate time: 45 minutes.

At the junction signed to Azmak to the right, take the left fork and proceed uphill. The cemetery can be reached in a four-wheel-drive vehicle up a rutted, winding track, otherwise it is an arduous walking tour, with no 'comfort' stops, through flocks of sheep and goats well-protected by dogs. It is, therefore, only for the fit and the stout-hearted, who should equip themselves with suitable walking shoes, wet/hot/cold weather gear and plenty of water/refreshments. Effort is rewarded by attaining the crest of the Kirectepe (meaning Limestone Hill) Ridge, which affords some magnificent views over the Salt Lake, Suvla and the Sari Bair Ridge and the sight of a seldom-visited memorial.

Inside the cemetery wall is a tall memorial made of Turkish shells (and in the Information Centre Museum at Gaba Tepe there is a photograph of Kemal Ataturk visiting this memorial). Many of the inscriptions on the graves and the monument are in Arabic characters. The monument was originally erected after the Evacuation and commemorates soldiers of the 11th and 12th Artillery Brigades of the Turkish 4th Division. It was repaired in 1996 by the Eceabat Gendarmerie.

Fifty metres east of the cemetery is a monolith memorial, erected in 1985. It bears the inscription, 'On 6-8 August 1915 the Gallipoli and Bursa Gendarme Hero Battalions stopped the English forces, consisting of two brigades, on Karakol Dagi and Kirectepe, and defended northern Anafartalar.'

On 18 June Major Willmer, a Bavarian officer, took command of the Anafarta Detachment, which included the Gendarmerie Battalions, with the responsibility of opposing any landing between Azmak Dere and Ejelmer Bay. Willmer appreciated that his force was too small to prevent a landing at Suvla and that the most he might hope to achieve would be to delay the enemy until reinforcements could arrive - probably about 36 hours. He decided to place his force forward on three strong points - the top of the Kirectepe Ridge (one Gallipoli company on Suvla Point), on Hill 10 (one Broussa company) and on Chocolate and Green Hills (three companies of the 1/31st Regiment) - with a fall-back main position. He distributed his mountain and field guns around the high ground and constructed dummy positions and trip-wires with contact mines. On top of all that he made his troops rehearse movement into and out of their positions by night in order to deceive the British air observers. The attack on the Ridge, so well set in motion by the Manchesters on 6/7 August, was renewed by 30th Brigade at 0730 hours on 9 August supported by naval

Turkish Gendarme Cemetery, Memorial and Monolith, Hill 156

Extra Visit continued

fire.The troops were tired and thirsty (the 7th Royal Munster Fusiliers had left their water bottles behind) and the oppostion, though slight, was determined, and what little progress was made, ended at a small post near the crest of the Ridge taken by the 6th Munsters led by Major J. N. Jephson, hence its name 'Jephson's Post'. Willmer and his Gendarmes had achieved their object - they had stopped the enemy.

Return to the fork with Azmak and turn left signed to Azmak Cemetery. Pick up the main itinerary.

Continue towards Azmak Cemetery, but if wet, you may have to leave your vehicle and walk the last few metres. Stand at the left-hand side of the cemetery wall facing the ridge. There is a cairn on the crest immediately ahead, probably only visible through binoculars. It is on the high point of the Ridge where the attack of 30th Brigade came to a stop on 9 August

* Azmak CWGC Cemetery/18.4 kilometres/10 minutes/Map S10

The cemetery, one of the least-visited on the Peninsula, is on the south side of the Azmak Dere, a watered ravine which runs south-west into the north side of the Salt

Azmak CWGC Cemetery (note mis-spelling on entrance wall)

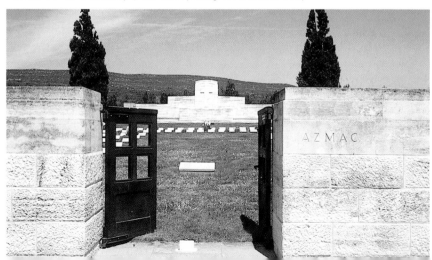

Headstone of Private Carter, 1/5th Norfolks with Lieutenant Gunes and Sergeant Dost of the Turkish Army

Lake (which should not be confused with the river of the same name which runs between Hetman Chair and Hill 60). It was made after the Armistice by the concentration of isolated graves and of small cemeteries: Dublin - made by the 1st RDF; Sulajik; 5th Norfolk - under the foothills of Tekke Tepe, where some of the 1/5th Norfolks who fell on 12 August were buried; Oxford Circus; Worcester - made by the 4th Worcesters; Kidney Hill; Irish; Azmak Nos 1,2,3,4; Jephson's Post; Essex Ravine; Hill 28; Lone Tree Gully. It is the most northern of the CWGC Cemeteries on the Peninsula and to the east lies the Kucukanafarta Ova (Plain). The 3,875 square metres covered by the cemetery contain the graves of 562 soldiers from the UK, 12 from Newfoundland and 500 whose unit could not be identified. There are special memorials to 53 soldiers from the UK and 3 from Newfoundland. There are 114 graves of officers and men of the 1st/5th Norfolks, almost all unidentified.

Rev Charles Pierrepoint Edwardes (on the right) standing in Australia Valley in 1919 overlooking the Suvla area in which the 1/5th Norfolks disappeared. IWM Q14384

The Vanished Battalion

One of the most mysterious episodes of the Gallipoli Campaign concerned 250 officers and men of the King George V's Own Sandringham Company of the 1/5th (Territorial) Battalion, the Norfolk Regiment who, apparently, disappeared without trace on 12 August 1915.

The Great War produced many so-called 'mysteries', such as the legendary Angels of Mons who supposedly rallied the weary men of the B.E.F. on the Retreat of August 1914 but who were later admitted by Arthur Machen of the *Evening News* as figments of his journalistic imagination, or 'The Lost Battalion' of the American 308th Regiment in the Meuse-Argonne in 1918 who were, in fact, neither lost nor a battalion.

The 1/5th was that WW1 phenomenon – a Pals Battalion: men from one locality who had all enlisted together. But the 1/5ths were unique in that they were a Royal Pals Battalion, drawn exclusively from the King's country estate of Sandringham in Norfolk. They were the royal household servants, gamekeepers, gardeners and farm labourers, known and loved by the Royal Family over many years.

The 5th Battalion the Norfolks was formed in October 1909, part of the new Territorial Force supported by HM King Edward VII who asked his land agent, Frank Beck, to form a company from the estate and surrounding area. Beck, a captain in the third Volunteer Battalion of the Norfolks, enthusiastically set about raising 100 close-knit men, related by family or work, who became 'E' company of the 5th Battalion. They were commanded by Lieutenant-Colonel Sir Horace George Proctor-Beauchamp CB who had seen service with the 20th Hussars in the Sudan and South Africa and who was, at first, popular with the men. His nephew, 2nd Lieutenant Montague Proctor-Beauchamp, and Beck's nephews, Albert Edward Alexander and Arthur Evelyn, also served with the battalion, as did many other brothers and closely related officers and men.

When war broke out the Territorials and Volunteer Forces were invited to enlist in the 5th Battalion the Norfolk Regiment (Territorials). 'E' Company gathered at Beck's house at Sandringham and marched away to tears and cheers from friends and families to Dereham. Whilst training at Colchester they were inspected by Sir Ian Hamilton who pronounced, 'A finer, smarter, keener looking lot of young soldiers it would be difficult to find.' They were later visited by King George V who expressed his delight at seeing them. On the eve of their departure to the front (and at this stage they had been informed they were not destined for France as they had expected, but for Gallipoli) the King sent them a telegram, 'I have known you all for many years and am confident that the same spirit of loyalty and patriotism, in which you answered the call to arms, will inspire your deeds in the face of the enemy. May God bless and protect you.'

On 29 July the battalion sailed on the *SS Aquitania* from Liverpool and arrived at Imbros on 6 August. The bulk of the battalion transferred to SS

Osmaih which was carrying 1,700 troops. She had accommodation for only 800 and the conditions were appalling. Finally she sailed for Suvla Bay on 10 August, landing at 0530 hours. The men were issued with two pints of water and ordered forward - into thorough confusion, through thick scrub, dead bodies and well-disguised Turkish snipers. Companies got lost but finally bivouacked for the cold night. The next morning, after an 0500 hours breakfast of bully beef and biscuits, the men were ordered to advance in line of platoons in double file. They crossed the rocky ground between the Kirectepe Ridge and the Salt Lake and reached the cultivated area beyond, under heavy shrapnel fire. They then came under shellfire from their own ships before spending another night. Finding water became a priority and men were sent in groups of eight to get water from a well near the enemy line, often, to their dismay, being separated from their closest mates. The following night they were given their orders: to attack the next morning on the right of the line with the Hampshires in the centre and the Suffolks on the left. The objective had been changed several times. Originally it had been planned to attack the crest of the Tekke Tepe Hills and, when that appeared unrealisable (Stopford, in particular, was against it, insisting that his Territorial Divisions were "sucked oranges"), the 'W' Hills. Even this offensive was postponed until 0400 hours on 12 August when it was to go ahead with the support of naval guns, an 18-pounder battery and two batteries of mountain guns. There was little realistic chance of success: orders were vague, the officers and men were inexperienced, the ground (which was, after a stretch of open land interspersed with dry water-courses, covered with thick prickly scrub) had not been reconnoitred and the Turkish opposing strength was unknown but it was evident that their guns on either side of the Suvla plain could enfilade any attack over it. The attack was not launched until 1645 hours and the men were in plain view of the Turks on the high ground to each side and casualties soon became heavy. Troops fell back in confusion and by nightfall only about 800 men of the 163rd Brigade could be mustered on a line in a sunken cart track. According to the *Official History*, The Isle of Wight Rifles lost 8 officers and 300 other ranks, the Norfolks 22 officers and 350 men.

And here the mystery begins. It was compounded by the C-in-C himself. In his final despatch before being relieved of command he wrote,

THE ARDENT NORFOLKS

In the course of the fight, creditable in all respects to the 163rd Brigade, there happened a mysterious thing. The 1/5th Norfolks were on the right of the line and found themselves for a moment less strongly oppposed than the rest of the brigade. Against a yielding force of the enemy Colonel Sir H. Beauchamp, a bold, self-confident officer, eagerly pressed forward, followed by the best part of the battalion. The fighting grew hotter, and the ground became more wooded and broken. At this stage many men were wounded or grew exhausted with thirst. These found their way back to camp during the night.

But the Colonel, with 16 officers and 250 men, still kept pushing on, driving the enemy before him. Among these ardent souls was part of a fine company enlisted from the King's Sandringham estates. Nothing more was ever seen or heard of any of them. They charged into the forest and were lost to sight or sound. Not one of them ever came back.'

At Beauchamp's side leading the attack was his relative, Captain Randall Cubitt (whose brothers Victor and Eustace, his cousin Randall Burroughes and brother-in-law Rolland Pelly were all in the battalion). They were both smoking and Beauchamp brandished his cane above his head exhorting, 'On the Norfolks, come on my holy boys.' Captain Frank Beck led his beloved Sandringham men, stick in hand, shouting 'Good old Sandringham'. For some reason they were the only battalion to receive the orders to veer to the right, causing a dangerous gap in the line. Major Purdy and Captain Knight saw the danger and tried to stop the charge, but Beauchamp cursed and ordered them on in 50-yard rushes, their bayonets glinting brightly in the sun, an easy target for the Turkish guns, and by now unsupported. Exhausted and parched they ran into heavy Turkish opposition, notably from well-disguised snipers, some of whom were reputed to have been sixteen-year-old girls. Casualties mounted, among them Randall Cubitt and 19-year-old 2nd Lieutenant Randall Burroughes. Beck was last seen in a seated position under a tree, probably dead. Private Carr, 14 years old, totally exhausted, was safely withdrawn to a dressing station.

Then a relieving force, mistaking them for Turks as they were so far ahead of the main line, fired on the Norfolks. Lieutenant Beauchamp was last seen going into a small farm building. Confusion built up, with the two survivors later reporting many instances of individual bravery, of men helping the wounded, of the wounded ignoring their wounds and continuing. Colonel Proctor-Beauchamp was last seen arm-in-arm with Captain Ward in a farm where he issued his last order, 'Now boys, we've got the

David Jason as Captain Frank Beck in the BBC1 film All the King's Men, *November 1999.*
Courtesy of the BBC

village. Let's hold it.' The Turks then set alight the wood near the village and encircled the remaining Norfolks, whose fate at that time was unknown. They were probably at the furthest point reached inland by the British from Suvla Bay.

The following day Major Purdy gathered the survivors on a hospital ship which sailed to Imbros and then to Malta but the extent of the tragedy did not emerge until he arrived home. At this stage the unaccounted-for men were reported as missing, not killed. It was known that the Turks held some prisoners, but they provided little information about them. An MO attached to the Welsh Division then reported treating 18 men of the 5th Norfolks with dreadful bayonet wounds who talked of their comrades having been shot at very close range by a large body of Turks who surrounded them.

The King cabled Sir Ian Hamilton, 'I am most anxious to be informed as to the fate of the men of the 1/5th Battalion Norfolk Regiment as they include the Sandringham Company and my agent Captain Frank Beck'. On 1 September Hamilton replied to the King that he had no news of the men beyond the fact that 14 Officers and about 250 men were missing, including Proctor-Beauchamp, Beck and his nephew, after attacking 'with ardour and dash'.

Soon the press were reporting on 'How the King's Servants Died at the Dardanelles', with messages of sympathy and pride from the King. The confusion continued. Men who had been reported killed suddenly turned up in hospital, others were confirmed as having been taken prisoner. One of these was Captain A. C. M. Coxon of the 1/5ths and his adventures are recounted in the book *A Prisoner in Turkey* by John Still, published by the The Bodley Head in 1920. Still, a Lieutenant in the 6th East Yorks, quoted *A Report on the Treatment of British Prisoners of War in Turkey* which stated that out of 16,583 British and Indian prisoners believed captured, 3,290 were dead and 2,222 untraced and almost certainly dead. Still believed that the true total was greater and that about 75% perished within two years of capture. The prisoners were held in camps in Ankara, Afion Kara Hissar and Constantinople. Treatment varied wildly from 'almost theatrical politeness and consideration' to starving, flogging and torment. Sanitation and medical treatment were almost non-existent and Coxon, known as 'Bill', who was training to be a doctor before he enlisted, saved many lives, though he had himself been shot in the neck. He was permitted to visit the local shops in Afion (where the only means of communication was in French) where he would enquire, 'Avez-vous ammoniated tincture of quinine?' and if the answer was 'No', would continue, 'Avez-vous aucun else that will do similaire?' Coxon survived his experiences, qualified as a doctor in 1919, practised dentistry until 1959 and lived until 1968.

Still describes his own experiences in the attack of the 6th E. Yorks of 9 August and of being taken prisoner with four other men. They were apparently condemend to death but saved by an Imam and marched back to General Liman van Sanders' HQ. From there they were moved to the Turkish G.H.Q.

where von Sanders (who knew England well) interrogated them.'Why did General Hamilton send a handful like yours to attack the great hill that commands all my position?' he asked. 'Did he think that I could be so blind as not to defend it against even a much stronger force?' Still had the impression that the Turks only took prisoners when they wished to interrogate them, otherwise they were murdered. He concluded that of 700 officers posted as missing in Gallipoli, only 17 were taken prisoner (8 at Suvla) and of 11,000 men, about 400.

Questions were asked in the House of Commons about the missing Norfolks and whether they could be confirmed as being taken prisoner. The Turkish Government still refused to supply lists but General Braithwaite confirmed that 'a number of prisoners' had been taken to Constantinople. Queen Alexandra got General Sir Dighton Probyn, VC, (Edward VII's Keeper of the Privy Purse) to ask the American Ambassador, Walter H. Page, if he could find what had happened to the Sandringham men, in particular Frank Beck, through the American Embassy in Constantinople. (Rudyard Kipling would also enlist his help in trying to find out what had happened to his son John.) In December Page replied that the Turkish Foreign Office could not trace either of the Becks.

In January 1916 Alec and Evelyn Beck were awarded the Military Cross (Alec posthumously) and Corporal Beales the DCM. By June 1916 the distraught families started to receive telegrams stating that 'in view of the lapse of time... death has now been accepted for official purposes.'

But the story was not over. At the end of 1918, when the Graves Registration teams were clearing the battlefields, the Rev. Charles Pierrepoint Edwardes (sometimes seen as 'Edwards') who had won the MC for bringing in the wounded under heavy fire after the 12 August 1915 attack, was sent on a special mission to discover what happened to the 5th Norfolks. He worked with the Graves Registration and Enquiry Unit, one of whose soldiers excavating the ground near where the missing Norfolks were last seen found a Norfolks' regimental cap badge and nearby the remains of several soldiers. Further investigation unearthed 180 bodies in a mass grave, 120 of them identified as Norfolks, the rest being 5th Suffolks, 8th Hants and Cheshires. Only two could be fully identified - Private Carter and Corporal Barnaby of the 1/5th Norfolks. Of the remains of three officers found it was thought that one was actually Colonel Sir Horace Proctor-Beauchamp because of the distinctive silver badges found by the body.

On 7 October 1919 the men were buried by the Rev Charles Edwardes in Azmak Cemetery and once again the newspapers covered the finding of the bodies. Edwardes wrote an official report which included his reasons for supposing that the bodies were those of men missing from the 12 August 1915 action. It remained secret for over 50 years. On his return he apparently decided that the truth was too much for the bereaved relatives and the Royal

Family to bear and did not disclose his gruesome findings to them.

The next development was the extraordinary case of the gold Hunter watch which was located in the hands of Turkish General Musta Bey who had been commanding the section in which the Norfolks attacked. The watch had been presented by Queen Alexandra to Sir Dighton Probyn who in turn gave it to Frank Beck. Musta Bey asked £150 for its return but settled for £10 plus safe conduct from Constantinople to Smyrna. The watch, and other of Beck's possessions, were returned to Probyn who duly inscribed it with the story and presented it to Beck's daughter on her wedding day.

But still the speculation about the Norfolks' disappearance refused to die. On the 50th Anniversary of the Landings in 1965 a New Zealand veteran, Frederick Reichardt, produced a detailed written statement, signed also by two of his wartime comrades, which described how, high on the hills above Suvla, he had seen six or eight identical, dense, light grey 'loaf of Bread' shaped clouds hovering over Hill 60, not moving at all in the stiff breeze. Beneath them was another cloud 'measuring about 800 feet in length, 220 feet in height and 200 feet in width... A British Regiment, the First Fourth Norfolks, of several hundred men' were then seen marching into the cloud and when, an hour later, it drifted up to join the smaller clouds which then moved off, there was no trace of the men. The account contained several inaccuracies - the Norfolks were nowhere near Hill 60, the battalion number is wrong and the total of missing men and the date of 21 August for the incident are incorrect. Nigel McCrery, in his detailed account of the Norfolks' action, *The Vanished Battalion*, published by Simon & Schuster in 1992, believes that the New Zealanders may well have been describing the action of the Sherwood Rangers Yeomanry against Scimitar Hill which took place in swirling mist and from which few men returned.

In 1993 a version of the story appeared in the US magazine *Flying Saucers* and it regularly crops up in similar publications which describe supposedly supernatural occurrences. The next significant revival was in the Australian *Sun-Herald* in July 1973. The Gallipoli Association then appealed to its veteran members to provide information about the incident. Gordon Parker, a Royal Engineer attached to 54th Division, reported that during a discussion about the 5th Norfolks' disappearance with Pierrepoint Edwardes the latter told him that every man he found in the mass grave had been shot in the head. This seemed to corroborate Still's theory of the Turks taking few prisoners.

In 1991 BBC2 produced a programme about the Norfolks in Gallipoli, presented by Prince Edward, entitled *All the King's Men*. During the making of it, the sister-in-law of Private Arthur Webber of the Yarmouth Company of the 5th Norfolks, who had been wounded and taken prisoner on 12 August 1915, recounted a story that Arthur told her before he died in 1969. When he was wounded, he fell to the ground helpless and heard Turkish soldiers moving among the dead and wounded, collecting the former and shooting or bayonetting the latter. Webber had a bayonet stuck in his thigh but was saved from being finished off by a German officer who insisted he should be taken prisoner. The mystery of the Norfolks' disappearance and the manner of their deaths finally appeared solved. Then on Remembrance Sunday, 14 November 1999, BBC 1 showed a major dramatised film, also entitled *All the King's Men*, based on Nigel McCrery's book, about the Vanished Battalion. It starts by showing the tightly-knit, idyllic rural life, almost Victorian in its simplicity, on the Sandringham estate. Concentrating on the three Becks, Frank (brilliantly played by David Jason) and his nephews, it shows the men leaving for Gallipoli, going into action and finally disappearing into the mist. The concern of King George V (David Troughton) and Queen Alexandra (Maggie Smith) and the eventual discovery of the mass grave by Pierrepoint Edwardes, with its implication of a massacre, are all included. But a parallel, mystical ending leaves the supernatural door open. The programme caused controversy because of the depicting of the massacre by the Turks and because there were some obvious inaccuracies (notably, as the film was shot in Spain and not in Turkey, the incongruous vegetation of prickly pears and palm trees). It must, however, be remembered that this was a *drama*, not a *documentary* and that in the heat of battle the principles of the Geneva Convention were sometimes ignored - on both sides.

The rare named men of the 1/5th Norfolks killed on 28 August are **Corporal J. A. Barnaby** (see above), age 25 [I. G. 3] and **Private W. Carter** [I. C. 7]. **Lieutenant Gerald Edmund Bradstreet** of 72nd Field Coy, RE, Twice Mentioned in Despatches, age 25, killed on 7 December, was the son of Sir Edward Bradstreet [II. E. 14]. **Lieutenant-Colonel Edward Henry Chapman,** 6th Yorks, age 40, who had served on the North-West Frontier in 1897/8 [Sp Mem 5] was killed on 7 August while assaulting Lala Baba, as was his cousin, **Captain Wilfrid Chapman,** age 35, who had served in the S. African Campaign [Sp Mem 35]. **Captain Arthur John Dillon,** 6th RDF, Mentioned in Despatches, age 29, was killed on 15 August in a bayonet charge on the Pimple [Sp Mem 50].

Return to the road and turn left (20.1kms) towards Anzac Cove. Just before Green Hill Cemetery, turn left signed Kucukanafarta.

Taking the road as your line of sight the Kirectepe high point cairn should be visible on top of the Ridge.

Continue to, on the left

Turkish Memorial, Yusufcuktepe, Scimitar Hill/24.9 kilometres/10 minutes/Map S11 /OP

The three stone monoliths are on the crest of Scimitar Hill, so-called by the Allies because from the sea the shape of the yellow gravel hill resembled a Gurkha's kukri, or an old Turkish scimitar. The Turkish name, Yusufcuktepe, means 'Dragonfly Hill', so named by Colonel Kannengiesser, deputy commander of the Turkish XVI Corps. The inscriptions on the monoliths read:

Atarturk's view from Scimitar Hill to Lala Baba over the Salt Lake

Krupp Naval Battery, Kucukanafarta

Turkish Cemetery, Buyukanafarta

1. The enemy forces who landed at Anafarta Port (Suvla Bay) on 7 August 1915, faced weak reconnaissance units and went as far as the Ismailoglu [meaning son of Ismail] and Usufcuk Hills in order to surround the Turkish forces on the Ariburnu front.
2. At the end of the first battle of Anafarta, 9-12 August 1915, Turkish forces under the command of Colonel Mustafa Kemal, commander of the Anafarta Group, defeated the enemy forces and drove them back to the line of Kirectepe and Mestantepe [Chocolate and Green Hills].
3. At the end of the second battle of Anafarta, 21-22 August 1915, which was fought by the larger forces of the two sides, the enemy's assault strength was broken on the line of Sivritepe [Sharp Hill] and Mestantepe. These battles resulted in Turkish casualties of 8,155 and enemy casualties of 19,850.

The approach routes of the Allied attempts to take this hill on 21 August are described at Hetman Chair above. Soon after midnight the truth dawned on IX Corps Headquarters that the day had been a complete failure. General Marshall ordered a withdrawal from Scimitar Hill and the bringing in of the many wounded who still lay out. Brigadier Kenna marched back to Lala Baba with the Yeomanry and stretcher parties hurried out. By dawn the old British line had been reached once more. Out of the 14,300 men of the Corps who had taken part in the attack, 5,300 were killed, wounded or missing. 'It was the largest action fought upon the Peninsula, and it was destined to be the last,' summarised Winston Churchill. The men had fought with determination and valour against an equally determined and valorous foe. One deed in particular was rewarded by the Victoria Cross. Private (later Lance-Corporal) Frederick William Owen Potts of the 1st Berks Yeomanry, although wounded in the thigh, remained for over 48 hours with another severely wounded man of his regiment who was unable to move. Finally he fixed a shovel to the equipment of his wounded comrade and using this as a sledge, dragged the man back over 600 yards to safety, under fire all the way.

The war correspondents Ashmead-Bartlett and Nevinson had been caught up in the battle. At about 5.30 Ashmead-Bartlett set up his movie camera 'to get some pictures of the wonderful panorama of the shell-fire and burning scrub'. He was immediately targetted by the Turkish gunners and was buried by a shell. He was dug out by a soldier but had lost all his equipment save his camera. Nevinson was shot in the head and was returned by horse ambulance. The following day Ashmead-Bartlett returned to Chocolate Hill. 'The battlefield presented a ghastly sight, being covered with the corpses of our men, stiff and cold, while numbers of wounded, unable to crawl back to our lines, could be seen moving under any cover or shade they were able to find.'

There are splendid views over the Salt Lake from the edge of the grassy platform.

Continue to a T-junction, with the village of Kucukanafarta a short distance to the left and turn right.

On both sides of the road (but most clearly seen on the left) is an Islamic cemetery, known as the **Boncukkiran Burial Site,** with gravestones consisting of large monolithic blocks of local stone. It is thought to date from the Early Iron Age.

Continue to the guns on the right.

* Krupp Naval Gun Battery/28.1 kilometres/10 minutes/Map S12

The wooden sides of the Turkish naval gun pits have been restored and they are enclosed by barbed wire. One of the guns is more or less intact, the other had its barrel blown off by the British in August 1915. They are on the site of the furthest Allied advance in this area, which was quickly repulsed.

Continue to the T-junction. Turn right and, with due caution, continue to the cemetery on the right. Stop at the side of the road.

* Turkish Military Cemetery, Anafartalar/30.6 kilometres/10 minutes/ Map S13

On the banks of each side of the road are plots in which are the graves of **Lieutenant-Colonel (Yarbay) Halit Bey,** Commander of 20th Regiment, 7th Division, **Lieutenant-Colonel Ziya Bey**, Commander 21st Regiment, 7th Division, killed at Bomba Sirti (Mortar Ridge) and Azmak Dere respectively on 11 August. **2nd Lieutenant (Ustegmen) Halit Efendi,** 4th Regiment and **First Lieutenant Riza Efendi** were killed on the Ariburnu front on 30 May 1915. **First Lieutenant Hasan Tahsin** and the religious leader Muftu Efendi were both killed at Anafartalar on 21 August.

The gravestones on the left bank are neglected and almost indecipherable.

Extra Visit to Camtekke Turkish Cemetery/ (Map P1)
Round trip: 10.6 kilometres. Approximate time: 25 minutes.

Back up or turn round and continue into and through Buyukanafarta along a winding road to a fork. Take the left fork and continue, eventually, to a turning to the left onto a track leading to a group of tall cypress trees, signed Camtekke Cemetery. Drive up it to the cemetery.

Beyond can be seen the large man-made reservoir which looks like a lake. The cemetery, surrounded by the pines and a concrete wall, is a mass grave for 71 soldiers killed in the area in 1915 by an Allied air attack as they were attempting to get water from a well. The marble plaque translates, 'Here we lie, 71 persons in need of your prayers. 1915.' The well, some 30 metres from the cemetery, which is enclosed by a concrete wall and surrounded by cypress trees, still exists.

Return to Buyukanafarta and pick up the main itinerary.

Alternatively, from the cemetery, one can drive to Kocacimentepe along a most scenic, if challenging, road:

Return down the track to the road and turn right. Continue back to the fork and turn left. Continue to a right turn signed to Gaba Tepe. Continue to a right turn signed Kocacimentepe and continue climbing to the crest of the hill along a winding but mostly metalled road.

The drive is approximately 10kms, with breath-taking views to either side.

Extra visit continued

See Kocacimentepe, Itinerary Three above.
Continue to Chunuk Bair and thence to Eceabat.

Camtekke Turkish Cemetery

The Well, Camtekke

Continue in the direction in which you are facing, which leads to the lower route and thence to Eceabat.

* End of Itinerary Four

ITINERARY FIVE

THE ASIAN SIDE

* **Itinerary Five** starts in Canakkale and continues down the Asian coast to Kumkale, examining the Naval Battles. It returns to Canakkale.
Refer throughout to Holts' Map 2 (P)
* **The Route:** Canakkale Walking Tour from the Ferry Terminal - Military/Naval Museum, Cimenlik Fort, the *Nusrat*, Republic Square; British Consular Cemetery; Hamidiye Turkish Cemetery; Hasan-Mevsuf Memorial and Cemetery; Dardanos Battery; Mesudiye Monument and Battery; Turgut Reis Battery Monument and Battery; Erenkoy Turkish Cemetery; Kumkale Plain (Kumtepe Intepe) Cemetery; Kumkale Cakaltepe Battery.
* **Extra Visits** are suggested to Hastane Bayiri Turkish Cemetery; Turgut Reis Battery; Kumkale Fort; the site of Troy.
* **Planned duration,** without stops for refreshment or Extra Visits: 3 hours 55 minutes
* **Total distance: 68.4 kilometres.**

* *Canakkale*

Canakkale is the administrative centre of the region which includes the Peninsula. It was founded in 1452 on the banks of the Saricay (Yellow) River when Sultan Mehmet II built two forts to defend the Straits - Cimenlik on the Anatolian side and Kilitbahir on the Peninsula. A thriving town grew up between the river and the port. Unlike Eceabat, where featureless modern buildings, many of them high-rise, have been allowed to sprawl through the town, many of the interesting (mostly neo-classical style) 19th century stone buildings in Canakkale are in a preservation area. The town therefore retains much of its character and local atmosphere. The modern high-rise apartment blocks are confined to the hillside to the north of the old town. By 1914 it had a population of c16,000, who were evacuated during the 1915 fighting. When Hans Kannengiesser (qv) visited after the 18 March sea battle he found that 'The roads were completely empty – a few badly shelled houses, broken minarets - the latter painted in stripes to make them less observable.'

* *Walking Tour From the Ferry Terminus/0 kilometres/RWC/ Map P*

Stand at the ferry entrance gate and, with your back to the Dardanelles, the **Tourist Information Centre** is to the right, on the corner. This small office normally has a limited range of tourist literature and a photocopied town plan. Details of 25 April ceremonies are posted here. To the left is an assortment of souvenir shops and the 3-star **Anafartalar Hotel**. Beyond it, along the Kayserili Ahmet Paca Caddesi, the pleasant promenade, where soldiers and sailors from the nearby barracks mingle with the local people and the sellers of all manner of refreshments, is the modern 4-star **Akol Hotel** and the traditional 3-star **Truva Hotel**. At the end of the promenade are the Naval Barracks, in which is the **Barbaros Deniz Sehitleri (Naval Martyrs') Memorial (Map P28)**. Unfortunately, as it is in a restricted area, it may not be visited.

Turn right at the corner.

To the left is the **Anzac Hotel** - a favourite stamping ground for young Anzac pilgrims. Ahead is the interesting, five-tiered **19th Century Clock Tower** with its stone dome. To the right is the office of **Dardanel Air,** with details of flights to Istanbul, and shortly after the office of the **Troy-Anzac Travel Agency,** with experienced guides to the battlefields, and the 2-star **Bakir Hotel**. To the left is the **Orka Book Shop,** with a small selection of English-language books/dictionaries. There is an assortment of grocers and *patissiers* along this road and along the first turn to the right is the entrance to the excellent **Liman Yalova Fish Restaurant,** above the fish market. On the parallel promenade to the right is a further **selection of restaurants** and the small **Ferry to Kilitbahir**. This departs more or less when it is full about every half hour (see Kilitbahir entry, Itinerary One). The **Headquarters of the Commonwealth War Graves Commission** (qv) are found by continuing to the crossroads at the end of the road, turning left and then first right onto Cimenlik Sokak. They are on the first floor of the office block on the left marked Bagkur in big red letters. Ahead at the end of the road is the

Military/Naval Museum, Cimenlik Fort/Replica Nusret/Mine Rails/30 minutes/Map P31,32/OP

Park open daily 0900-2100
Museum open 0900-1200 and 1330-1700. **Closed Monday and Thursday.**
Entrance fee: 100,000TL. Fee for camera: 250,000TL. Fee for video camera: 500,000TL

Officially known as the Canakkale Strait Commandery Military Museum, its Exhibition Hall is housed in the beautiful 1870 building that was originally the Strait Fortified Zone Commandery, whose ground floor was a mine depot. On the first floor are displayed arms, uniforms and equipment of the 1915 campaign. On the second floor are pencil and watercolour paintings by Mehmet Ali Laga, who was the official war artist 1914-1918, depicting various battles in the Dardanelles Campaign.

Beside the building are the **mine rails** along which loose floating mines could be dropped into the water. The sinking of the French ship *Bouvet* may well have been the result of a floating mine (the official Naval despatch of 19 March said '*Bouvet* was blown up by a drifting mine...the losses of ships were caused by mines drifting with the current...') although Kannengeiser (qv) later wrote that it was a shell that did the damage.

Walk along the mine rails and stand at the edge of the water facing the Peninsula.
At 12 o' clock is the town of Eceabat and above it the long ridge of the front line.
At 11 o' clock is the Dur Yolcu Memorial. At 10 o' clock is the heart-shaped fort at
Kilitbahir. At 9 o' clock is the **RP** lighthouse on the European shore and the mouth
of the Dardanelles. At 8 o' clock is the tip of the Asian shore. At 1 o' clock, on the
top of the heights is the white obelisk of the New Zealand Memorial and beside it
the dark shape of the Kemal Ataturk statue. Immediately below is the New
Zealand Memorial Wall and Chunuk Bair Cemetery. To its left are the five 'fingers'
of the Chunuk Bair Turkish Memorial and at 2 o' clock is the 18 March 1915
Memorial above Canakkale.

Alongside is the realistic-looking wooden model of the mine-layer *Nusret,*
which was opened in 1992. In it can be seen newspapers and the diary of the period
of Major Nazmi Akpinar. The original *Nusret* was a 60-ton, 40-metre-long and 7.4-
metre-wide mine-layer which laid the 20 mines at Erenkoy Bay on the night of 8
March which wreaked such havoc on the allied fleet. On 16 March, 3 mines were
swept by trawlers but it was assumed that these were isolated floating mines. It
could have been one of her tethered mines that sank the *Bouvet.* What made these
mines so effective was that they had been laid parallel to the shore and not across
the channel as all of the others had, and they were therefore missed during the
sweeping operations.

In the park which adjoins the Cimenlik Fort is a variety of interesting artillery
pieces, including French 5.57cm calibre anti-tank guns.

The Cimenlik Fort (also known as Hamidiye III) is a 150 x 100 metres
rectangular building, with 5.8-metre-thick walls which are strengthened by corner
and intermediary towers. Part of the southern wall was demolished in the 19th
century when bastions and bunkers were added. Inside the outer walls is a four-
storey, 22-metre-high rectangular keep with a 29 x 44-metre base and 7-metre-thick
walls. A small single-minaret mosque adjoins the entrance tower. It was built with
the Fort by Mehmet the Conqueror in 1452 and is known as the Mecidi Mosque.
Beyond the tower is the mosque built in the 19th century by Sultan Abdulaziz
when he installed the long-range artillery guns, the bastions and bunkers. Inside
the Fort are some exhibits about Ataturk's life and from the Canakkale Campaign
and opposite the entrance to the keep is an embedded shell from the *Queen
Elizabeth.* Given appropriate measuring equipment it would be possible to work
out whether the shell had been fired from the other side of the Peninsula, e.g. on 6
March when joined by *Agamemnon* and *Ocean,* the *Queen Elizabeth* shelled the
Canakkale forts from beyond Ari Burnu, or from within the Narrows e.g. on 19
March during the attempt to force the Straits.

*Return to the Ferry Terminal. With your back to the Terminus, walk straight ahead
into the Square.*

Republic Square

An imposing statue of Kemal Ataturk dominates the square, in which there is also
a group of Turkish guns.

Return to your car to start the main Itinerary.

Mine rails, Cimenlik Fort, pointing towards Eceabat and the Sari Bair Ridge

Q: 'Who made that 'ole?' A: 'The Queen Elizabeth' [After "BB"]

The mine-layer, Nusret, with Kilitbahir Fort in the background

British Consular Cemetery, Canakkale

Headstone of
Lieutenant-Commander
Brodie of the E15

Hamidiye Turkish Cemetery and Memorial

Extra Visit to Hastane Bayiri Turkish Cemetery (Map P29)
Round trip: 4.6 kilometres. Approximate time: 30 minutes

Drive directly inland from the ferry terminal through Republic Square, turn left at the traffic lights along Cumhuriyet Bulvari.
On the left is the main **Post Office** (open every day, all day).
Continue over the traffic lights. You will see signs for Hastane Bayiri Sehitligi as you begin to climb uphill.
On the right is part of the University.
Continue uphill on Mehmet Kaptan Cad, between blocks of flats and after the mosque on the right take the first fork right. Some 300 metres later the cemetery is on the right on the junction of Sehitlik Caddesi and a track which leads to the entrance.
The cemetery has imposing gates, within which is the guardian's cottage. The graves are set amongst flowers and in the central avenue is the obelisk memorial. This is a genuine wartime cemetery, with burials made during the campaign. The date on the monument is 1332, the Ottoman date for 1915.
Return to the Ferry Terminus.

* British Consular Cemetery/1.3 kilometres/15 minutes/Map P33

The Cemetery is usually locked. Please check first with the Commonwealth War Graves Commission, tel: 286 2171010.

Drive straight ahead, through Republic Square over two sets of traffic lights (to the right at the first of which are the Turkish Baths) *to a T-junction (1km). Follow the road round to the left and immediately turn left again.*
On the left is the interesting cemetery which contains graves from as early as the 1860s, including those of the family of Frederick William Calvert, Consul in the late 19th Century and a German teacher, Axel Johansson. The British War Graves in Plot I are of 16 soldiers, 6 sailors of the Royal Navy and 2 Marines, 11 New Zealand soldiers and 2 Australian, 1 Macedonian Mule Corps and 9 post-war or non-war graves. These include 2 New Zealand ladies, Rosalind Webb and Jean Walker, who were killed in a car crash near Lapseki on 11 November 1965, en route to the battlefields, and Australian veteran, Basil Wood Bourne, who served as a Corporal in the 3rd Battalion, AIF in 1915. He died near Anzac Cove as he stepped off his coach while on a pilgrimage in April 1965. In Plot II are 3 Russian Nurses, 2 Russian Labourers, 1 Greek Airman and one Greek Labourer. Three Naval burials were made in the cemetery in April 1915. These are of crew members of the Submarine *E15* (qv): **Lieutenant-Commander Theodore Stuart Brodie** RN, age 31, Commander of the *E15*, killed in action 17 April 1915; **A.S. Frederick John Cornish**, age 22, died 18 April 1915 and **E.R.A. 2nd Class Ernest Valletta Hindman**, age 31, died 18 April 1915.

In 1918-1920 33 burials were made here by medical units at Canakkale and later two British graves were brought here from Roosto Catholic Cemetery on the Sea of Marmara.

*Return the way you came and at the first set of traffic lights you meet turn left along the road to Troy, past the market on the left and across the Kopru Bridge over the Sari Cay to the crossroads with the **Archeological Museum** on the left (3.6kms).*
[Canakkale Archeological Museum: Tel: 00 90 286 217 3252. Open daily: 0830-1700.]
Turn right at the traffic lights and continue through the blocks of flats to the first turn to the left. Turn to the cemetery some 50m to the left.

** Hamidiye Turkish Cemetery and Memorial/3.9 kilometres/5 minutes/Map P36,35*

In the white-walled cemetery, with traditional cannon balls at each corner, is the obelisk memorial, with the date 5 mart 1332 (1915 in the Ottoman calendar).
Return 50 metres to the junction.
At the end of this road to the left on the edge of the Straits, but in a restricted area, is
* Fort Hamidiye I/ Map P34
The fort was constructed by Sultan Abdulhamid II c1880 for the defence of the Straits, on the low earthworks built by the French in 1837. It was sometimes referred to by the Allies as Fort No 19. It consists of a shore revette, behind which are parapets and a barbette with ten gun enplacements approached by stone steps and a ramp. In 1915 these were occupied by Krupp guns, four 35cm and six 24cm calibre, all with new range finders and an impressive range (13,000 and 14,000 metres respectively). At the back of the large parade ground are two-storey barracks sunk into the ground and covered with earth and along the eastern side in 1915 were German tented encampments. Then there were also two searchlights, one fixed within the compound and one mobile on the shore beyond. A line of 23 mines stretched across the Straits to Fort Hamidye II (Fort No 16) opposite. On 6 March 1915 it was shelled by the *Queen Elizabeth, Agamemnon* and *Ocean* and returned fire, but the following day, when the French also joined in, the fort was silenced.
Return to the main road and turn right towards Troy. Continue 2kms to a road junction. Do not take the road signed to Izmir (the left fork) but continue straight ahead through an urban area.
To the right is Sari Sighlar Bay where, in December 1914, in one of Britain's first hostile actions of the War against the Turks, and which irrevocably signalled her intentions, the old Turkish battleship *Mesudiye* was sunk by the submarine *B11*. Launched in 1906 as part of Fisher's naval expansion plan, by 1914 *B11* was virtually obsolete. She was commanded by Lieutenant Norman Holbrook with a crew of one other officer and 13 ratings. On 4 December she left her base in Tenedos on her reconnaissance mission and, fully briefed on the Turkish defensive mines, nets and cables, dived outside the entrance to the Dardanelles and made her way up the Narrows. Forced to surface as one of her improvised cable guards came loose, she dived again until she reached the area of the first minefield. There Holbrook spied the *Mesudiye* which was moored as a floating battery to protect Canakkale, only 3kms away. To close on her, Holbrook had to pass five rows of mines and so shallow was the water here that *B11* frequently broke the surface and was soon spotted by her target. A rain of fire was directed on the submarine, from

the *Mesudiye* itself and from all shore batteries in range. Small boats raced towards her, but Holbrook launched two torpedoes just in time and the *Mesudiye* sank, her determined guns still firing at the submarine as it submerged. *B11* then hightailed it back to Tenedos. One of the guns of the *Mesudiye* has been moved to Chunuk Bair - see Itinerary Three. Holbrook was awarded the VC, the first ever won by a submariner, his First Lieutenant won the DSO and every rating the DSM. A town was named after Holbrook in New South Wales, Australia, and in its park is a model of the *B11*, a statue of Norman Holbrook VC, a torpedo commemorating the action of Lieutenant Stoker (qv) and the crew of the *AE2* and a Submariners' Memorial which consists of the whole upperworks of the submarine, HMAS *Otway*.

Cross the Kephes [Kepez] stream (9.8kms) and. as the road rises, turn right at the large board and marker with a shell on top on the roadside to '18 Mart 1915 Hasan Mevsuf Sehitligi'.

*Hasan-Mevsuf Memorial and Cemetery/ Dardanos Battery/11 kilometres/ 20 minutes/Map P39,38,37/ OP

The sign translates, 'Stranger, stop! The place on which you stand is holy ground, a national shrine. March 18 1915 is a memorial day in Turkish history. On that day, enemy forces consisting of 22 warships were arrested in this waterway by a single Turkish artillery battery. Giving the best example to a glorious defence, these few men played the major part in the great Turkish victory, a legend of the Dardanelles. In this ground lie the battery commander Lieutenant Hasan, 2nd Lieutenant Mevsuf and four other unnamed soldiers of the battery. They fought for liberty and they died. Their deep memory will shine in the hearts of brave people. May they rest in peace and God bless them.'

A small road leads to the **cemetery**, approached by stone steps. Behind, white stones set into the slope read, 'Martyrs, rest in peace'.

Continue along the track to the stone monument to Dardanos Hasan and Mevsuf Battery (11.2kms).

Hasan-Mevsuf Turkish Cemetery

View over Kephes Lighthouse from Dardanos Battery

The Dardanos Battery.

It reads, 'The battery was built in 1892 in the reign of Abdulhamit II by Marshal Asaf Paca. On 19 August 1914 three 150mm guns from the battleship *Asar-i Tevfik* were placed near the two existing 150mm guns in Dardanos to increase the total number of guns to five. On this hill, which ran with their blood, the brave soldiers, led by their commanders, Hasan and Mevsuf, became martyrs. The battery withstood the attacks of the enemy from the sea of 19 and 25 February and 18 March and did not let them pass the Straits. Beloved martyrs, the Motherland is grateful to you.'

Continue behind the cemetery to the battery memorial and guns.

The **stone monument** with a red-painted Turkish flag is similar to other battery monuments in the area. The **battery**, which is beyond, was refurbished in the late 1990s. It is enclosed by a wire fence and consists of five Krupp 150mm guns, which in 1915 were in five steel turrets.

From the memorial walk forward to the edge of the plateau.

To the left is the mouth of the Dardanelles and to the left across the Straits is the Turkish Memorial at the tip of the Peninsula. Directly opposite you is the small lighthouse [RP] mentioned in Itinerary One and below to the right front is the Kephes Lighthouse. On 17 April the submarine *E15* en route to the Sea of Marmara was driven ashore below the lighthouse by strong currents. As she surfaced a shot from Turkish field guns hit her conning tower and killed her Captain, T. S. Brodie (qv), and six of her crew. The remainder were taken prisoner. In an extraordinary coincidence the first Allied person to see the stricken vessel was Lieutenant-Commander (later Admiral) C.G. Brodie, the Captain's twin brother who was flying over the area on reconnaissance. To prevent the vessel from being used by the Turks she was torpedoed the following night by picket boats dropping torpedoes over their sides. To the left, over the wooded crest, is the long sweep of Erenkeui Bay. By looking to the left horizon on a line parallel to the adjacent shore, the eye travels across the bay approximately along the line of mines laid by the *Nusret* (qv), and it was on and around that line that the *Irresistible, Inflexible* and *Ocean* were mined and the *Bouvet* sank. From the nothern end of the battery is a splendid view towards Kilitbahir on the left, the Narrows and Canakkale.

Return to the road, turn right and continue, taking the right fork downhill and then up again until you rejoin the main Izmir-Troy road (14.4kms) .

You are passing through the area inhabited by the Dardanians (later known as Trojans), the descendants of Dardanos, the son of Zeus and the Pleiad Electra, who, having slain his brother Iasius, fled across the sea from Arcadia to Samothrace and thence to Asia Minor to found the kingdom of Dardania and the royal house of Troy. The name 'Dardanelles' is an amalgamation of 'Dardanos' and 'Helles'. The legendary Helle, after whom the Hellespont ('Helle's Sea') was named, fell off the back of the winged ram with the golden fleece who was carrying her and her brother Phrixus (who were about to be sacrificed by their father, King Athamas of Thessaly) to safety, and drowned in the mouth of the Straits near the present Cape Helles.

The band of 50 heroes, led by Jason, who sailed on the ship Argos to fetch the golden fleece of the ram, then dried and guarded by dragons in Colchis on the Black Sea, were known as The Argonauts. They sailed up the Hellespont and endured many adventures before they finally carried off the fleece.

The classically educated young officers of 1915, notably those of the Hood Battalion, RND, saw themselves as modern-day Argonauts and for them the excitement of going into battle was heightened because they almost felt themselves the reincarnation of the mythological heroes upon whose exploits they had been brought up.

There is a tumulus, signed 'Dardanos Tumulusi', site of archaeological excavations, 1km from the Hasan-Mevsuf battery.

Continue along the main road to a brick monument with the painted red Turkish flag on the right hand side of the road.

* Mesudiye Battery Monument /15.8 kilometres/10 minutes/Map P40

The inscription reads, 'The guns found in the battery, made in 1901 for the battleship *Mesudiye*, were two fixed recoilless guns, 7 metres in length and 15.5cms in diameter. The Armed Forces General Staff built the battery in 1938 by taking the guns from the Mesudiye to a hill overlooking the Straits. In the hands of new soldiers the Mesudiye Battery has not been silent. In a hawk-like fashion, the battery is still guarding and watching the impassable Canakkale. Beloved martyrs, the Motherland is grateful to you.'

Take the first track to the right and continue to the T-junction with the tarmac road, turn right and stop at a gap in the fence opposite house no 142 (16kms).
On the right is a **Drinking Fountain dedicated to the Canakkale Martyrs** erected in 1964 by the Turkish Highway Society.
Walk into the pine woods to the gun emplacements.

* Fort Mesudiye/Battery/16 kilometres/10 minutes/Map P41,40

The well-preserved emplacements, containing two 155mm guns, are connected by an underground tunnel.
Return to the main road to Troy, turn right and continue to the brick memorial on the left with the red-painted Turkish flag.

* Turgut Reis Monument /17.5 kilometres/5 minutes/Map P42

The inscription on the monument reads, 'In 1891 a pair of cruisers, the 10,060 ton *Barbaros Hayrettin* and *Turgut Reis*, were built. In the 1915 Canakkale Battle they succeeded in the task of preventing the enemy landing at Ariburnu by providing distracting fire between Karaburnu and Gelibolu. Later, prior to the Second World War, the turrets from the *Turgut Reis* were moved here to a new duty in defence of the Straits. The guns in the turrets are long-range, 28cm in diameter and 10.30 metres long.'

Extra Visit to the Turgut Reis Battery (Map P43)
Round trip: 3 kilometres. Approximate time: 20 minutes

Turn left uphill up a steep and circuitous but gravelled road. Follow the road round to a car park by a gun battery.
The guns are extremely impressive, housed in Maginot-line style (post-WW1) cupolas, and well worth a diversion. Some 100 metres above on the hillside is another battery.
Return to the main road and pick up the main itinerary.

Continue to a left turn signed Intepe (21.5kms). Turn left up the road to the cemetery on the right through a new housing development.

* Erenkoy Turkish Cemetery/Memorials/21.8 kilometres/10 minutes/Map P44,45/OP

The cemetery is enclosed by a low wall with pillars surmounted by the traditional cannon ball. In it is a **memorial to Captain Bedri Uckun** of the Turkish Airforce, dated 22 X 9 34 and a **bust to Lieutenant Ali Riza**, also of the Turkish Airforce, 30 November 1915.
The battery at what was known as Erenkeui was commanded by the German Lieutenant-Colonel Wehrle. He hid his batteries in gullies leading down to the Straits, changing the positions at night so that Allied air reconnaissance was always

Mesudiye Battery with Editor Tom Hartman

out of date. He also built many dummy positions. Just before 18 March he moved the batteries closer together, making Allied maps obsolete. The result was that, in spite of the Allies' intense bombardment, Wehrle only lost three dead and eleven wounded. His batteries had scored 139 direct hits on the Allied fleet out of the 1,600 rounds fired, wreaking particular damage on the *Ocean* and the *Irresistible*. Morale amongst his Turkish troops was high. 'Let me just see one more ship go down,' a wounded man is reputed to have shouted as he was being borne from one battery.

Turgut Reis Battery

 Stand to the right of the cemetery facing the Dardanelles.

Ahead is a superb view over the tip of the Peninsula. From left to right can be seen the lighthouse at Cape Helles, the British Memorial, the Turkish Memorial, and, directly opposite, the summit of Achi Baba with its white water station.

Erenkoy Turkish Cemetery and Memorials

Return to the main road and turn left. Continue to a right-hand turn signed Kumkale Sehitligi at the exit sign of Yenimahalle village (26.7kms).

Extra Visit to the Purported Site of Troy (Map P50) RWC
Round trip: 18.2 kilometres. Approximate time: 1 hour 15 minutes

Continue straight on for some 3.5 kilometres and turn right following signs to Troy (Truva).
The story of the Trojan Wars, recounted by the Izmir-born poet Homer in his epics *The Odyssey* (the story of the return home of Odysseus [Ulysses]) and *The Iliad*, is probably the most famous legend in the world. 'Iliad' means 'about Ilium', the area which stretches from the range of Mount Ida to the Straits, and later known as the Troad, whose principal town was Troy. After its early sacking by Hercules [Herakles], Troy was rebuilt as a prosperous city by King Priam. The fateful war was triggered by Priam's handsome second son, Paris. He was taken to Mount Ida and asked to decide who was the most beautiful, Hera, Zeus's wife, Athena the goddess of wisdom, or Aphrodite, goddess of love. Paris awarded the prize of a golden apple to Aphrodite when she promised him the love of the fairest woman in the world. Paris was then sent on a diplomatic mission to Sparta and fell in love with Helen, the beautiful wife of its king, Menelaus. When Menelaus left for Crete, Paris carried her home to Troy. On his return Menelaus asked his brother Agamemnon of Mycenae to lead an army to Troy to revenge him and bring back Helen. Eventually other kings of Greece, including Achilles, Odysseus and Ajax, joined the expeditionary force. In the tenth year of the struggle, the Trojan hero, Hector, was killed by Achilles in an heroic battle and his body dragged three times around the city by his victor's chariot. In turn Achilles was killed by Paris by shooting an arrow into his vulnerable heel. Ajax then committed suicide and Paris was killed. But still Priam refused to give up Helen. In desperation the weary Greeks concocted the cunning idea of appearing to abandon their camp but of infiltrating the Trojan city with warriors, including Odysseus and Menelaus, hidden in the belly of a great wooden horse. The Trojans celebrated the apparent withdrawal of the Greeks and, as they fell into drunken sleep, the Greeks burst forth from the horse, slaughtering the male citizens, sacking the city and taking the women back as slaves to Greece. Rupert Brooke's 1909 poem, *Menelaus and Helen*, opens with a vision of that attack
   Hot through Troy's ruin Menelaus broke
   To Priam's palace, sword in hand...
The comparisons of the *River Clyde* (qv) to the Trojan horse are so numerous as to make it a cliche. For example: 'This afternoon, 2,400 Munsters and Dublins and the Hampshires come on board and conceal themselves in the holds of the Wooden Horse ...in the ship's sides great ports are cut. As soon as the crash comes and we grind ashore, these dragon's teeth spring armed from the ports...', wrote Lieutenant-Commander Josiah Wedgwood to Winston

Extra Visit continued

Churchill. Wedgwood, of the famous pottery company, commanded a unit of the RNAS Armoured Car Squadron who manned the guns on the *Clyde*. Whether there was any historical basis to Homer's powerful tale there is now no telling, but many illustrious historians, like Herodotus and Thucydides, firmly believed there was. The story continued to exert a powerful influence on future generations, enjoying an enormous resurgence in medieval and again in Tudor and Victorian times. It featured strongly in the classical public school curriculum of the Edwardian and Georgian period, thus inspiring the well-read, romantic young men of '14-'18 to emulate the feats of Hector and Achilles as they landed so near the setting of the familiar saga. For instance, the poetic, sensitive Sir Ian Hamilton, passing the mouth of the Dardanelles on his first visit on 18 March 1915, was awed by its historical significance. 'We got a wonderful view of the stage whereon the Great Showman has caused so many of his amusing puppets to strut their tiny hour. For the purpose it stands matchless. No other panorama can touch it...Against this enchanted background to deeds done by immortals and mortals as they struggled for ten long years five thousand years ago - stands forth formidably the Peninsula.' Addressing his troops on the eve of the landings he exhorted them, 'The difference between the spear of Achilles and our steel bullets will not be discernible in the sphere of the Gods.' In *The Secret Battle* A. P. Herbert's central character, Harry Penrose, was 'ridiculously excited' at his first glimpse of the mouth of the Straits, 'where the Greek fleet lay'. He 'talked of Achilles and Hector and Diomed and Patroclus and the far-sounding bolts of Jove.' Patrick Shaw-Stewart re-read the Iliad en route to Gallipoli. It inspired him to write,

> ...Achilles came to Troyland
> And I to Chersonese:
> He turned from wrath to battle,
> And I from three days' peace.
> ...I will go back this morning
> From Imbros over the sea;
> Stand in the trench, Achilles,
> Flame-capped, and fight for me.

His friend Rupert Brooke, before his tragically premature death, was also anticipating an heroic encounter in the steps of his classical heroes, and wrote many fragments of poetry on the voyage of the *Grantully Castle*, including,

> They say Achilles in the darkness stirred ...
> And Priam and his fifty sons
> Wake all amazed, and hear the guns,
> And shake for Troy again.

Nowell Oxland, buried in Green Hill Cemetery, wrote,

> Outward Bound
> ...Though the high Gods smite and slay us,
> Though we come not whence we go,

Extra Visit continued

As the host of Menelaus
Came there many years ago;
Yet the self-same wind shall bear us
From the same departing place
Out across the Gulf of Saros
And the peaks of Samothrace...

Compton Mackenzie compared the Australians to the ancient Greeks: 'Much has been written about the splendid appearance of those Australian troops... Their beauty, for it really was heroic, should have been celebrated in hexameters not headlines. As a child I used to pore for hours over those illustrations of Flaxman for Homer and Virgil which simulated the effect of ancient pottery. There was not one of those glorious young men I saw that day who might not himself have been Ajax or Diomed, Hector or Achilles.'

Though not involved in the Gallipoli campaign, Maurice Baring wrote from the Western Front, where he was ADC to General Trenchard of the RFC,

Such fighting as blind Homer never sung,
No Hector nor Achilles never knew;
High in the empty blue.

The presence of an Allied battleship named *Agamemnon* (qv), added to the classical comparisons.

German officers were similarly inspired. Major-General Hans Kannengiesser described how, his copy of Baedeker in his hand, he 'rode via Hisarlik to the Ilion of the Ancients...and finally at dawn on the outer wall of ruined Troy. A magnificent view of that battlefield of Homer, the Skamander, which divided Greek and Trojan... I recognised the burial mounds of Achilles and Patroclus and saw in imagination the ships of the Achaeans lying both sides of the mouth of the Skamander.'

As for the ruins of the city of Troy, the traditional Greek belief was that they lay beneath a colony that was set up on the hill of Hisarlik, standing proud above the flat surrounding land, so like Homer's flat Trojan plain. In 700BC it was named Ilion (later Ilium). Xerxes, the Persian King, visited it in 480BC and Alexander the Great made a pilgrimage to it, laying a wreath on Achilles' tomb in 330BC. The next famous pilgrim was Julius Caesar, in 48BC. In the 4th century AD Constantine the Great contemplated building the capital of the Roman Empire here before deciding on Constantinople. Many 18th, 19th and 20th century writers, artists, scholars and historians visited, painted, mapped or wrote about the site. The tombs of Ajax and Achilles were supposedly identified.

The six destructive and controversial excavations of Heinrich Schliemann, from 1870 to 1890, including the discovery of 'Priam's Treasure', those of Wilhelm Dorpfeld in 1893-4 and of Carl Blegen from 1932-1938, are well-documented and to an extent marked on the walls of the existing ruins. The

Extra Visit continued

nine successive cultural layers of the colony and city, from 3,200BC to AD400 are indicated. Excavations were restarted in 1988 by Manfred Korfmann and are still continuing.

At the approaches to the site there is a group of cafés, restaurants, souvenir shops and 'Schliemann Houses' and at the entrance, where **a fee is payable**, there is parking, a reconstructed wooden horse, a book stall and a **museum in the Excavation House** used by Blegen. Many of the findings from the site are housed in the **Canakkale Archeological Museum** (qv). A qualified English-speaking guide, Mustafa Askim, can be contacted at the Hisarlik Hotel, Troy. Tel: 0090 286 283 0026.

Open: Summer 0800-1900. Winter 0800-1700.
Entrance fee: 500,000TL per person. 1,000,000 per car.
Tel: 090 286 283 0536.

Replica of the Wooden Horse, Troy

Return to the turning to Kumkale.

Turn right, following the sign to Kumkale. After 6 kilometres the local cemetery is passed on the right and the village is entered.
Shortly after there is a symbolic **memorial** on the right comprising shells, anchors and a sarcophagus.
Drive to the centre of the village to a small right turn called Sehitler Caddesi (33.6kms).

Extra Visit to Kumkale Fort (Map P49) Round trip: 10 kilometres. Approximate time: 30 minutes

Although the Fort is within the restricted area of Old Kumkale, it is possible to drive close enough to it to get a good view of the remains - and to take a reasonable photograph - from just before the Restricted Area sign which prohibits photography!
Continue through the village and drive towards the coast on a well-paved road, crossing several waterways of the Menenderes (Skamandros) River Delta.
After approximately 3 kilometres there is a sign on the right, **Sehitler Armani Zhektar** (Heroes' Wood), by a plantation of pine trees, lined with cedar, planted in 1993, Map P48.
Continue as far as the Restricted Area sign. Stop!
The Fort was built by the order of Koprulu Mehmet Pasha, grand Vizier of Sultan Mehmet IV. In 1915 it was equipped with 9 artillery pieces ranging from

Extra Visit continued

Krupp 28cm to Krupp 15cm calibre. It was shelled on 19 February by Allied warships but despite some damage was still firing when night fell. On 25 April it was shelled again prior to the attempt to force the Narrows and the diversionary attack here was very successful. A Russian contingent from the cruiser *Askold* led by Naval Lieutenant Kornilov landed on the wrong beach and suffered badly from Turkish Maxim fire, but the French Senegalese (who had delayed the landing by refusing to leave their transports for fear of the sea and had to be harangued by General d'Amade) landed at around 0930 hours and with fixed bayonets made a howling bayonet charge off the beach clearing the fort and the village within 90 minutes. The Turkish 3rd Divison moved up from the south and contained the French within 700 metres of

Restricted Area sign, Kumkale Fort

the village and a stubborn Turkish force at the cemetery held out until the French withdrew on the night of 27 April, but 800 Turkish prisoners were taken.

Return to the village of new Kumkale and pick up the main itinerary.

Turn along Sehitler Caddesi.
Driving along this narrow and bumpy road there are magnificent views to the left over the mouth of the Dardanelles, the Helles Memorial, Seddulbahir, Morto Bay

Kumtepe Intepe Cemetery and site of gun battery

Kumkale Cakaltepe Battery

and the Turkish memorial at Cape Helles.
Continue to the cemetery on the left.

Kumkale Plain (Kumtepe Intepe) Turkish Cemetery/Battery/35.3 kilometres/10 minutes/Map P46/OP

The cemetery is enclosed by a white stone wall, decorated with shells and cannon balls. To the right of the coloured wrought iron entrance gate, with splendid star and crescent decoration, is a glass-enclosed sign containing a faded inscription which reads,

'Kumkale Plain Intepe Battery Martyrs' Cemetery. In World War One, on 25 April 1915, French forces landed in the cove between Kumkale and Yenisehir in the Dardanelles. Stationed there on that date was the 15th Army Corps, consisting of the 3rd and 11th Divisions. The headquarters of 15th Army Corps was at Kalvert Farm, of 3rd Division in Saricaeli and of 11th Division in Pinarbasi. On 25/26/27 April 1915 forces of the 3rd Division confronted the French Forces at Kumkale. The French left Kumkale to the victorious 3rd Division on 26/27 April. They left the area while under fire from the Intepe Artillery Battery which consisted of 120mm guns and the evacuation was completed on 27 April at 0200 hours. The casualties of the 3rd Division in the Battle of Kumkale were 17 officers and 450 soldiers killed, 23 officers and 740 soldiers wounded and 5 officers and 500 soldiers missing. Construction of the Kumkale Martyrs' Cemetery, under the chairmanship of the Kumkale Village Chief, was begun by the villagers in April and completed in October. It was unveiled by the Canakkale Garrison Commander, Rear-Admiral Atilla Erkan, on 18 March 1984.'

There is also a faded photograph of a veteran of the action, Hafiz Izzet Misirlis, born 1298 in the Ottoman calendar in Uzunkopru, died 15 August 1959.

Inside the gates is a monument by the tomb with the inscription, 'Here lie 14 heroic martyrs of the 120mm artillery battery who were killed by enemy fire from the sea on 28-30 April 1915 in World War One. Let their soul rejoice.' The inscription continues on the tomb,

'They lie under the blue vault in blood,
O Traveller, soldiers who died for these lands,
These saints did not merely enter this tomb,
In God's mercy, they await your prayers.
Overflow you will, even when buried in history
Horizons too small,
Holy War too little to contain thee.'

Continue along the track, through cotton fields (in October), bearing left to the harbour.

Kumkale Cakaltepe Bataryasi/36.5 kilometres/10 minutes/Map P47

To the right and left of the track are massive gun emplacements, complete with gun. There is a tiny fishing harbour and huts - an ideal spot for a picnic - and stunning views.
Return to Canakkale

* End of Itinerary Five

ALLIED AND TURKISH WARGRAVES & COMMEMORATIVE & CONSERVATION ASSOCIATIONS

COMMONWEALTH WAR GRAVES COMMISSION

[The history of the Imperial War Graves Commission is given in full in Major & Mrs Holt's Battlefield Guides to the Somme and the Ypres Salient.]

Following a report of 1889, the British Office of Works, had 'responsibility for the maintenance and upkeep of soldiers' graves in the Crimea'. This included those in Haidar Pasha Cemetery in Constantinople, where, before the War, the Office had a clerk of works. When Fabian Ware was fighting for what he then called 'an Imperial Commission for the Care of Soldiers' Graves' to be set up at the beginning of 1917, the Commissioner of Works, Sir Alfred Mond, felt that this work could be undertaken by his Department. Fortunately Ware prevailed and the work fell to the Imperial War Graves Commission which received its Charter on 21 May 1917.

Concern had already been expressed about the numerous Gallipoli war cemeteries, 50 in the Anzac area alone, the first of which had been started at the foot of the Ari Burnu Knoll and at Queensland Point on the evening of 25 April. This had to be abandoned with the Evacuation, but it was carefully recorded on maps at the request of Birdwood. Much of the recording had been undertaken by Chaplain W. E. Dexter, a former sea captain. The Pope was persuaded to send Envoys to the area in 1916 to examine the graves, who returned satisfied with their state.

By Article 129 of the 1923 Treaty of Lausanne the Turkish Government granted land to the British Empire which included 'in particular... the area in the region known as Anzac (Ari Burnu)' for the purpose of establishing war cemeteries and erecting memorials. No dwellings may be erected (other than for the purpose of maintaining the cemeteries) nor any jetties or wharfs in this area. 'Persons who desire to visit the area must not be armed [and] The Turkish Government must be informed at least a week in advance of the arrival of any party of visitors exceeding 150 persons.' Thus the tranquillity of the area would be preserved for ever for the men who lay there. The Treaty also covered the land on which all the British cemeteries and memorials in the Cape Helles area would be made. It also made available Turkish records of Commonwealth troops who had died as prisoners of war.

Despite the Treaty, the construction of graves and memorials in Turkey, still officially an enemy country which was 'uncivilised', with inaccessible and difficult terrain, was fraught with problems. After the Armistice, men of the GRU from Egypt under an Australian, Lieutenant Cyril Emerson Hughes (who had served with the Light Horse on the Peninsula, was awarded the MC, became a Lieutenant-Colonel, chief administrator of the IWGC, Middle East, and then Australian Government Commissioner in Egypt), had landed on the Peninsula on 10 November 1918, and camped in old Turkish barracks near Kilitbahir and in dugouts on the Sari Bair Ridge throughout the bitter winter. They found a different situation from that described by the Pope's Envoys: many graves had been desecrated, especially in the Helles area. When Bean's Historical Mission arrived in February 1919, Hughes was able to help Bean compile a Report for the High Commissioner and the Australian Government and GHQ, Constantinople. It confirmed the desecration of the graves, the rifling of bodies for the gold coins that were often carried by the ANZACs as part of their pay, the removal of all wooden markers and the fact that the Turks had attempted to remedy this by creating indiscriminate mounds to represent graves, often in completely spurious positions in their attempt to prove that they had cared for them in order to impress the Pope's Envoys. It was in this area in the winter of 1918/1919 that the GRU had its headquarters section under the New Zealander Captain C.V. Bigg-Wither.

Bean reported that 'Of the 8,000 Australians killed during the Campaign, about 2,000 were buried at Egypt, Malta and Lemnos, 6,500 are definitely recorded as having been killed at Gallipoli. Of these about 3,500... will be identified with certainty... The remainder number about 2,500.' In March he submitted a further Report, which confirmed that Hughes had located about 4,700 graves and that others were still being found. Many of the original burials had been marked with crosses made from biscuit boxes with names painted on them or punched into small plaques of tinplate which were then nailed to the cross, or with pinewood crosses. Bean recommended that the cemeteries remain on their present sites. He concluded that the number of workers available was inadequate (by about one quarter) to complete the task of decently covering the bones that lay on the surface of the land and which would distress visiting relatives - who should not be permitted to come until the work was completed. The true cemeteries were discovered by probing the ground with steel rifle rods. Graves of particular Anzac heroes, like Captain Brian Onslow (qv), Birdwood's A.D.C., Major C.H. Villiers-Stuart (qv), his chief of intelligence, Colonel Henry McLaurin (qv), the Commander of 1st Brigade, and Lieutenant-Colonel A. J. Onslow-Thompson (qv) were refound.

The following spring the eminent architect Sir John Burnet (1857-1938), with his assistants Captains D. Raeburn and G.S. Keesing (an Australian), was sent out to assess the problem and was appalled by what he found: the coastal ground was sandy and badly drained, the cliffs and hills above prone to landslides. He pronounced it 'unreliable and insecure ground unsuitable as foundations for permanent monuments of any size or weight'. His answer was to build fewer cemeteries than planned, concentrated on secure land, protected by stone-lined ditches and girdles of trees to stabilise the ground with their roots. Fearing that the impoverished local inhabitants would be tempted to purloin any materials that appeared valuable (such as bronze) he recommended cemetery walls at least eight feet high, with 'headstone blocks' with sloping faces rather than the upstanding headstones being erected on the Western Front. These Burnet, an opponent of the concept of marking graves by crosses, which he felt appeared 'to interlace with one another...giving the appearance of fences [which was] destructive of all quiet', found aesthetically more pleasing, as well as being practical when graves lay very close together. This deviation from the standard, upright headstone was permitted when local conditions made it appropriate.

In its difficult work the Commission was supported by the Australians and the New Zealanders, whose emotional attachment to the land where so many of their countrymen had lost their lives in their countries' first blooding was deep. They volunteered to send out troops still based in Egypt to help carry out the strenuous work. This offer, after some consideration and initial hesitation by Winston Churchill and the Prince of Wales, then the Commission's President, was gratefully accepted by the Commission, and the Australians continued under the efficient and energetic Hughes. It would have been costly to transport help from the UK and it was felt inappropriate to employ local labour: Russian refugees from Bolshevism and Greek contractors were employed instead. As Philip Longworth says in The Unending Vigil, 'Hatred for the enemy was strong among the general public, though not among the soldiers themselves, and strongest of all among the relatives of the dead.' Just as Winston Churchill wanted to leave the ruins of Ypres as one vast memorial and as a reminder of the horrors of war, so the ANZACs wished the whole Gallipoli area to be left as 'consecrated ground'. It was, however, considered that the variety and size of the cemeteries required made this idea impossible to achieve. Two-thirds of the burials were unidentified, making the memorials to the missing of particular significance.

The work, which continued until 1924, was dauntingly difficult. First the workers had to build their own quarters in Kilye Bay. Then roads had to be built to reach the proposed sites; a quarry had to be blasted; an aerial ropeway, two and a half miles long, had to be constructed to carry materials up to the Lone Pine Ridge. Bullock carts and Thorneycroft lorries laboriously pulled wagons laden with stone to the new cemeteries. When the lorries could not negotiate the primitive roads, Hughes built a pier at North Beach and transported materials by sea. In 1922 work was halted for three months as Mustafa Kemal made his advance and the Commission workers helped the troops who had once been their enemies. The Greek stonemasons then abandoned their work and Italian craftsmen had to be brought in to replace them. Another setback came in spring 1924 when most of the stone quarried the previous year cracked in the hard frost. By the end of that year, however, 31 cemeteries containing nearly 9,000 grave markers were almost complete and by 1926 the major memorials were all complete, bar the engraving of some of the names of the missing. It was, literally, a monumental task.

Burnet also planned the landscaping of his cemeteries with care, taking into consideration local climatic conditions (which varied from dry, blistering heat in the

The Gallipoli War Graves Commission Ropeway Courtesy the Commonwealth War Graves Commission

summer to freezing blizzards in the winter) and complementing the architecture. A horticulturist from Kew established a nursery and advised on the most suitable plants for the area. A dark screen of evergreens was planted behind the white wall that incorporated the Cross of Sacrifice and that and the edging walls had to be high enough to prevent the cross from being too conspicuous and offending Muslim sensibilities. Ornamental trees and shrubs softened these walls and the ground was turfed. Eventually pines and pyramid cypresses thrived, beneath which flowered in abundance the anemones, crocus and scilla. Eucalyptus trees and wattle were planted in tribute to the Australians and rosemary (for remembrance) was a favourite. For many years, even during the difficult period of the Second World War, an Australian veteran, Major Tasman Millington of the 26th Battalion, AIF, who had returned to the area with Hughes in 1919, lived in Canakkale to make sure that his countrymen's graves were well cared for.

After the Second World War professional horticulturists reviewed the cemeteries in the more distant regions. In Gallipoli much of the top soil had been lost by water erosion and by the constant sweeping away of pine needles. A supply of water was desperately needed and the gardeners were set to digging wells and installing water pumping equipment. Soon the cemeteries blossomed with junipers, Judas trees and daffodils. Major maintenance work is constantly being undertaken and in 1998 the walls of the beachside cemeteries at Anzac Cove had to be substantially repaired as a result of sea erosion. The dedication of the gardeners, now local Turks supervised by an experienced representative from Europe, is outstanding. The work is hard and sometimes, because of the unfriendly climate, frustrating. Imagine transporting gardening equipment down the tortuous and rocky paths that lead to such isolated cemeteries as Plugge's Plateau, 4th Battalion Parade Ground and The Farm - and back up again. Occasionally a local donkey (always, inevitably, nick-named 'Murphy') has to be hired to carry new stones to these inaccessible sites. In springtime, over the period of the April landings anniversary, the cemeteries are a riot of colour, places of supreme beauty and peace, a credit to the hard-working staff and a joy to visit.

Each year the Commission holds a formal meeting away from Head Office and in June 1999 the venue was Gallipoli. As a result of their inspection, conducted by local supervisor John Price, recently awarded the MBE, 3,700 pedestal markers were identified for re-engraving. John also conducted HRH the Duke of York around the cemeteries.

In November 1998 the Commission's **Debt of Honour Register** database was launched on the Internet at Canada House in London. It is accessed on www.cwgc.org and finds the site of graves of WW1 and WW2 war dead by family name. The site is extraordinarily popular, with thousands of 'hits' per day.

Head Office: 2 Marlow Road, Maidenhead, Berks, SL6 7DX   Tel: 01628 634221. Fax: 01628 771208. e-mail: general.enq@cwgc.org

Australian Office: PO Box 21, Woden, ACT 2606, Australia. Tel: (06) 289 6477. Fax: (06) 289 4861

New Zealand Office: Heritage Property Unit, Department of Internal Affairs, PO Box 805, Wellington, New Zealand. Tel: (04) 495 7200. Fax: (04) 495 9458.

Canakkale Office: Cimenlik Sokak, Bagkur Ishani No 9, Buro No. 10, Canakkale. Tel: 00 90 286 217 1010. Fax: 00 90 286 212 6705. e-mail: cwgctur@turnet.net.tr

THE GALLIPOLI ASSOCIATION

The Association was founded by Major Edgar Banner, who enlisted (under-age at 17) into the RAMC at Rhyl in October 1914. He sailed for Mudros on the *City of Edinburgh* in March 1915 and served on the Hospital Ship *Aragon* off V and W Beaches during the landings. Contracting fever, he was sent to Alexandria but returned to the Peninsula and was attached to 11 Casualty Clearing Station at W Beach before moving to Lemnos during the Suvla operations. He later served in Salonika and after WW2 he founded the Salonika Reunion Association. In 1957 Edgar and a small group of Gallipoli and Salonika veterans made a pilgrimage to Gallipoli, then still occupied by the Turkish Army, who hosted the veterans. In 1960, when the Salonika Association folded, he was moved to found the Gallipoli Association In 1965, the 50th Anniversary, Edgar organised a great Pilgrimage, mainly for 29th Division Association veterans. The first official meeting of the Gallipoli Association took place on 25 April 1969. By the time of Edgar's death in 1984, age 86, 900 veterans had joined. Sadly, by 1998, only two veteran members remained. There are some 800 Associated Members - relatives of Gallipoli Veterans being particularly welcome.

The excellent magazine, *The Gallipolian*, is produced three times a year and continues to publish fascinating articles about the campaign. An Annual General Meeting is held in October followed by the Autumn Lunch and Gallipoli Day, 25 April, is commemorated by the laying of a wreath at the Cenotaph, followed by a Service in Westminster Abbey and a lunch in Central London. Gallipoli Day is also remembered at several sites around the country, notably at dawn at the RAAF Remembrance Stone in Battersea Park, next to which Clive James unveiled a Ross Bastiaan bronze plaque in 1998. There is then a Service in St Paul's Cathedral, where the Duke of Edinburgh unveiled a Gallipoli Plaque in 1995. Wreath-laying ceremonies/services are also held at Edinburgh Castle, at King's Lynn, at the New Zealand Memorial in Brockenhurst, at the British War Cemetery at Cannock Chase and at other sites with Gallipoli/Australian/New Zealand connections. An important ceremony is held at St Mary's Church, Harefield at 1100 hours as Harefield House was used as an ANZAC hospital during the war and many ANZACs are buried in the cemetery. (Contact Mary Fox on 0171 498 8669.) In Hawick (qv) an annual ceremony is held on 12 July at 1900 hours when a laurel wreath is placed on the war memorial in the High Street and then in Wilton Park. A piper plays *The Flowers of the Forest* and *The Last Post* is sounded. A Gallipoli Memorial Lecture is held each year around Anzac Day organised by the Gallipoli Memorial Trust, normally in Eltham, where the founder of the Lectures, His Hon Judge Paul Batterbury, was educated. A Gallipoli Grove will be planted at the National Memorial Arboretum at Tisbury, Wiltshire. HRH the Duke of Edinburgh is the Association's patron. **Contact: The Secretary, J.C. Watson-Smith, Earleydene Orchard, Earleydene, Ascot, Berks SL5 9JY. Tel: 01344 626523.**

OFFICE OF AUSTRALIAN WAR GRAVES

Department of Veteran's Affairs

The Office has a dual role: to maintain and care for the war cemeteries within Australia and the region as agents for the Commonwealth War Graves Commission; and to commemorate eligible veterans who have died post-war and whose deaths are accepted as being caused by

war service. It has established Gardens of Remembrance in all State capital cities, where standard bronze memorial plaques to veterans are erected. Plaques are also provided for veterans buried in local cemeteries. Since it was established in 1922, the Office has commemorated over 102,000 war dead from all wars including, of course, Gallipoli. Funeral benefits are also provided to eligible veterans.
Contact: Director of War Graves
Office of Australian War Graves, Woden ACT 2606 Australia. Tel: (06) 289 1111.

THE AUSTRALIAN WAR MEMORIAL, CANBERRA

The Memorial is the physical expression of Australia's desire that her war dead should be remembered. It is a combination of Memorial, Museum and Research Centre. In the Hall of Memory the Roll of Honour lists all the war dead on bronze panels around the Pool of Reflection, without rank or decoration. There are 61,720 names listed for WW1. The Roll is supplemented by the Commemorative Book, which lists 2,850 Australians who served with Allied forces or as members of the Merchant Navy or organisations such as the Red Cross. In 1993 a computer database was installed so that visitors can search for names. Around the Pool is the Garden Court, planted with the Roman Cypress for immortality, rosemary for remembrance, aquilegia from Pozières, poppies and anemones from Flanders and the Australian wattle. From the parapet can be seen Anzac Parade, with Memorials to Kemal Ataturk, the Royal Australian Navy, the Royal Australian Air Force and Tobruk on the eastern side and the Hellenci, Australian Army, Vietnam and Desert Mounted Corps Memorials on the western side. In the Memorial sculpture garden is a duplicate of the Ross Bastiaan Chunuk Bair plaque (qv).

In March 1997 the New Zealand Prime Minister, Jim Bolger, announced a competition for a New Zealand Memorial to be erected here. The winning design, by Wellington sculptor Kingsley Baird, was unveiled on 14 June 1999. It is of two 11.5-metre bronze arches, based on the handles of a flax basket ('kete'), representing Australia and New Zealand, one on each side of Anzac Parade.

At the main entrance to the Memorial are the Menin Gate Lions, chipped and shattered by shellfire, presented by the Burgomaster of Ypres. The Hall of Memory houses symbolic works of art by Napier Waller, who served with the AIF and lost his right arm at Bullecourt in 1917. He then taught himself to draw with his left arm. The Hall contains stained glass windows and magnificent mosaic walls comprising 6 million tesserae, fixed by WW2 widows, completed in 1959. The seven-segmented dome represents Australia's seven-pointed star, with the sun at its apex. The space in the Hall is for contemplation and remembrance.

On 11 November 1993, the tomb of the Unknown Australian Soldier was unveiled in the Hall. In it is the body of a soldier removed from Plot III, Row M, Grave 13 from Adelaide Cemetery, Villers Bretonneux on the Somme. His remains now lie under a slab of red Australian marble, with the inscription, 'He symbolises all Australians who have died in war.' Behind the tomb is a high niche containing four pillars sculpted by Janet Lawrence which represent the four elements of earth, air, fire and water. In front of the Memorial is a Stone of Remembrance.

Also in the complex is the Research Centre, which contains a vast archive containing official records of Australian forces, photographs, letters and diaries and 'relics' of war, from uniforms to weapons and personal keepsakes. Many of the items in the original collection were brought back by C. E. W. Bean and his Historical Mission (qv) in 1919. They include a 4.7″ gun from Kojadere, an old ship's boat from Anzac Beach and part of the battered corrugated iron head-cover from Quinn's Post. There are also sketches and pictures by the Mission's artist, Captain G. W. Lambert. Bean was the true inspirer and instigator of the Memorial. He persuaded General Birdwood to authorise an expedition to the old battlefields to examine the ground whilst it was still untouched in order to answer some unresolved questions about Turkish dispositions, ANZAC ground gained and the state of the original burials. A secondary objective was to bring back war relics for a museum. Thirdly, a photographic and artistic record of the ground was to be made. The expedition, led by Bean (who described himself as 'then thirty-nine years of age, lean active, and with an accurate memory'), started from London on 18 January 1919. It comprised Lieutenant John Balfour and Staff-Sergeant Arthur Bazley (Bean's former clerk) to assist him with the records, Lieutenant H. S. Buchanan, an engineer, and Sergeant G. Hunter Rogers to make or check the maps, Lieutenant Hedley Vicars Howe, one of the first to land at Anzac (as a Private), Captain George Hubert Wilkins, an experienced war photographer and George Washington Lambert, a portrait painter who had been brought up in Australia and who had worked as a war artist. They were a motley, dedicated, talented, energetic and somewhat eccentric crew and their extraordinary exploits are fully described by Bean in the poignant record, *Gallipoli Mission*, first published in 1948. Of the relics brought back by the Mission which are displayed in show cases in the War Memorial Bean wrote, 'I still wonder, as I did when we first came on them on those ridges - of what high morning hopes, what grim midday obstacles, and what final tragedy do those cartridge cases or that torn fragment of uniform tell?'

Major Ceremonies of Remembrance are held here on Anzac Day - with a Dawn Service attended by thousands wearing sprigs of rosemary and carrying candles - and on 11 November.

There is a Memorial shop and the publications AWM Journal and Wartime Magazine. **Contact: Australian War Memorial, GPO Box 345, Canberra ACT 2601, Australia. Tel: + 61 (0)2 6243 4392/3. Fax: + 61 (0)2 6243 4325. Website: http://www.awm.gov.au**

ANZAC MEMORIAL, HYDE PARK SOUTH, SYDNEY

This imposing Memorial was dedicated on 24 November 1934 by the Duke of Gloucester. The central motif of the Memorial is the dramatic sculpture, 'Sacrifice' by Raynor Hoff. On 11 November 1995, an Eternal Flame was lit for the first time. Flanking the entrance are two Aleppo Pines.

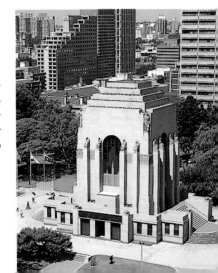

The Australian War Memorial, Sydney

THE AUSTRALIAN RETURNED SERVICES LEAGUE

This looks after Veterans' affairs. **Contact:**
13b Moore Street, Canberra City 2600. GPO Box 708, Canberra ACT 2601, Australia. Tel: +(0)2 6257 2633. Fax: +(0)2 6257 4475. web-site: www.rsl.org.au.

ANZAC OFFICERS DIED AT GALLIPOLI WEB SITE

This data base established by B.W. Dolan can be accessed on **http://www.surfline.ne.jp/3dolans/Anzac.** In Spring 1999 it recorded the names of 486 officers of the Australian and New Zealand Army Corps known or believed to have died as the result of their service on the Gallipoli Peninsula in 1915. This 13-year labour of love supplements the CWGC listing by giving some biographical details and, in many cases, photographs or quotations from the personal messages on the graves of the officers listed.

In process is the listing of the 2,543 men of the 5th Light Horse Regiment, AIF.

The compiler, B.W. Dolan, unlike some of his occasionally over-zealously patriotic countrymen, generously reminds readers that, although his listing is of ANZAC officers only, it is 'in no way meant to diminish the part played by the soldiers of England, Wales, Scotland, Ireland, France, Senegal, India, Nepal, Newfoundland or Ceylon, nor of the soldiers of the Ottoman Empire; all of whom fought and suffered together - and died together- at Gallipoli'. He also quotes an untypical Australian newspaper report of November 1915 which reminded Australians who 'in their legitimate pride at the way their troops have fought during the past seven months' tended to forget that 'they do not form one-third of the Allied force there, and have not incurred one-third of the Allied losses' and that 'the Dardanelles campaign is by no means an Australasian "show" only, as many people imagine.'

In the site are details of the **Gallipoli Medallion**, issued in 1967 to ANZAC survivors of the Gallipoli Campaign or their families by the Australian Government. Claims by those eligible are still being accepted by the Soldier Career Management Agency, Historical Research Section, GPO Box 393D, Melbourne, Victoria 3001, Australia. The handsome bronze medallion is surmounted by a crown and shows Simpson (qv) and his donkey and the date '1915'. On the reverse is a map of Australia and New Zealand with the stars from their national flags. A lapel badge is also available.

NEW ZEALAND NATIONAL WAR MEMORIAL AND HALL OF MEMORIES/RETURNED SERVICES ASSOCIATION

Anzac Day was first celebrated in New Zealand in 1916. Now it starts with a Dawn Service, followed by a Parade and Church Service. There are two National Memorials in New Zealand: the Cenotaph in Lambton Quay (the focus of national 25 April commemorations), and the National Hall of Memories (where visiting Heads of State place their wreaths), Buckle Street, Wellington. Anzac Day Commemorations are, of course, also held at war memorials around the country. The country's main military history museum is halfway between Auckland and Wellington on State Highway 1, postal address **Queen Elizabeth II Army Memorial Museum, Army Training Group WAIOURU, New Zealand.**

The New Zealand Returned Services Association looks after Veterans' affairs. Address P.O. Box 27248, Wellington, New Zealand. The last New Zealand Gallipoli veteran, Alfred Douglas Dibley, died on 18 December 1997 at the age of 101. The last survivor of the landings, Ted Mathews, died earlier that month, also aged 101.

SERVICE DES SÉPULTURES DE GUERRE

(See also the entry on the French National Cemetery, Itinerary One). The French cemetery in Gallipoli is maintained by this organisation which comes under the Ministry of *Anciens Combattants et Victimes de Guerre*, started on 25 January 1918, which maintains French war graves and cemeteries around the world. It is funded by the French Government and looks after 884 cemeteries in 69 countries outside France. Their representative in Turkey is the French Consul in Istanbul. Work on the locating and re-interring of the then estimated 10,000 French dead began in January 1919. A working party of 500 Senegalese troops with 5 French officers camped in huts on Hill 141 and brought in the remains from the wartime cemeteries. They also identified and marked the old French trenches.
Contact: 37 rue de Bellechasse, 757007 Paris, France. Tel: [00 33] 1 48 76 1135.

ASSOCIATION NATIONALE POUR LE SOUVENIR DES DARDANELLES ET FRONTS D'ORIENT

The President of the French Dardanelles and Eastern Front Association, Madame Stocanne, is the daughter of one of the last surviving Gallipoli veterans (age 105 in 1999) and its Treasurer is the husband of one of the grand-daughters of the commanding officer of the the French 1st Division of the Gallipoli French Expeditionary Corps who was mortally wounded near Morto Bay on 12 July 1915.

Each year around 25 April the Association rekindles the flame under the Arc de Triomphe in Paris and around 18 March holds a Conference followed by a Memorial Service in the Val de Grace Church, Paris. They make pilgrimages to Gallipoli and other Eastern Front battlefields. Current membership is approx. 200.
Contact: Madame Madeleine Stocanne. 137 Bvd St Michel, 75995 Paris, France.
Tel: [00 33] 143 548670. Fax: [00 33] 143 290261.

THE GALLIPOLI PENINSULA NATIONAL HISTORICAL PARK (GELIBOLU YARIMADASI TARIHI MILLI PARK) TURKISH MINISTRY OF FORESTRY/1994 FOREST FIRE

The Park was established in 1973 and since then the Park Authority has been responsible for the daily running of the Park, particularly in respect of the upkeep of and access to the Turkish war graves and memorials, landscaping and fire-fighting, but also in respect of all other administrative functions. It encompasses some 30,000 hectares of land, bounded on three sides by the sea - the Gulf of Saros to the north-west, which joins the Aegean Sea to the west and, from the tip of the Peninsula at Cape Helles, to the Dardanelles in the east. Its northern land boundary extends from the Ece [Ejelmer] Bay on the Gulf of Saros [see Holts' Map 3] to Akbas Bay on the Dardanelles coast and some 10,000 people live in the area. The aim of the establishment of the park was the protection and preservation of this historically and ecologically interesting area. However, a programme of afforestation had been started as early as 1964 by the Ministry of Forestry which in many ways destroyed the natural characteristics and flora of the area and drastically changed it from the bare or scrub-covered aspect of the 1915 battlefield. Extensive pine forests were planted which masked many of the existing Allied memorials (such as Lone Pine). Much of the area was accidentally restored to its post-WW1 appearance by the drastic fire of 1994 (see above), which started at 1630 hours on 25 July and lasted nearly 57 hours. It destroyed a total of 4,049 hectares of forest in and around the Chunuk Bair-Ari Burnu areas. Thankfully only one life was lost (see Itinerary Three above) but it sparked off a great debate: whether to let nature take its course and allow the scrub (or maquis) to dominate the scene as it had in 1915 or whether to afforest anew. In fact the Ministry of Forestry started a programme of replanting in some areas only two weeks after the fire, leaving other areas - happily many of them around the WW1 cemeteries and memorials - to recover naturally. Some $1.5 million (U.S.) was voted to the project to plant 5,229,000 young trees and plant 574 kilos of seed. Already by autumn 1998 the rugged beauty of the bare hilltops was being threatened anew, but a moratorium on new planting was negotiated in October of that year, instigated by the new Peace Park Committee.

The Milli Park's headquarters building is in Eceabat (see Itinerary One).
Tel: 00 90 286 814 10 25. Fax: 00 90 286 814 17 30.

THE GALLIPOLI INTERNATIONAL PEACE PARK PROJECT

Within the Milli Park's administrative area there are many diverse interests involved. For example, the Anzac area stipulated by the 1923 Treaty of Lausanne (qv) is administered by the CWGC. Other bodies with authority in the Park area are the Governor of Canakkale, the Mayor of Eceabat, village headmen, the local gendarmery, the National Government and National Security Council and Naval and Military authorities. With all these - sometimes conflicting - interests, a cohesive preservation/presentation policy for the Park was almost impossible.

The problem seems to have found a unity of purpose in the launching in 1998 of an international competition to transform the park into a Memorial for World Peace. The initiative came from the President of Turkey, Suleyman Demirel - who was intensely moved on visiting the Gallipoli Battlefields after the 1994 fire - in order to perpetuate Kemal Ataturk's desire for 'Peace at home, peace abroad'.

Before the competition could be announced to architects around the world, an immense and ambitious project to investigate, chart and record every aspect of the Peninsula had to be undertaken. Professor Doctor Raci Bademli of the Faculty of Achitecture, Department of City and Regional Planning, of the Middle East Technical University at Ankara was appointed in 1996 as technical adviser and co-ordinator. In the Professor the project found a man of integrity and vigour with strong views on the preservation of this beautiful and mainly unspoiled land and who was conscious of its historical, emotional, ecological and strategic importance. With a small budget he assembled a team of part-time enthusiasts - mainly students - who over the next few years undertook the monumental task of mapping the area, hitherto only recorded on highly classified military maps and in an extraordinarily detailed map that was prepared in 1916 by Sevki Pasa, which was rediscovered almost by accident by the team. This done, in a series of 1:25,000 scale maps, the team recorded features such as archeological remains, war remains, cemeteries, memorials and museums, settlements and buildings, the natural environment, flora and fauna. A sophisticated computer data-base was then set up and the results of this impressive research and survey were a 'Book' and a 'Catalogue' containing as detailed and in-depth study of an area as can ever have been undertaken anywhere in the world. The Competition was then announced and competitors were sent the Book and Catalogue, which contained the terms and conditions of the Competition. They formed the new 'Master Plan' for the park, whose objects are:

1. preserving and rehabilitating natural assets
2. conserving and better displaying archeological heritage sites
3. conserving, re-evaluating and better displaying historical sites and battlefields
4. integrating inhabitants with the Park and reorganizing activities and scenarios
5. improving the Park and its management
6. re-evaluating the identity of the Park and creating a new identity.

Three focus areas were identified: 'The Main Gateway' - the area round Eceabat and Kilitbahir; 'The Battlefields' - the Anzac area, and 'The Forum' - the Helles Battlefield area. For some unknown reason, the Suvla area was not included in these focus points.

The winner of the competition would become 'consultant designer or engineer' of the agreed plan, which includes the design of consistent signing to places of interest, the development of the Information Centre at Gaba Tepe and a museum at Alcitepe, the restriction of tourist development to the areas around Eceabat and Kumkale and the probable demolition of unauthorised holiday homes, especially in the Suvla area. The erection of further memorials will be forbidden, as will the development of any industry that is not compatible with indigenous resources. The long-discussed and controversial proposal to build a bridge over the Narrows from Eceabat to Canakkale is not favoured. Should a bridge (rather than a tunnel) be constructed, its Asian end would not be within the Park boundary.

Over 120 entries were received from prestigious architects around the world which were judged in Ankara in July 1998. The Jury consisted of representatives of the offices of the President of Turkey, the Ministry of Forestry, and several international architects. John Price, the CWGC Superintendent in Gallipoli, also served on the committee. The total prize money was $765,000, the first prize being $120,000. The winner was allocated a budget of $60 million. The winning entry was submitted by a team of young Norwegian architects, the B & K Architecture Studio of Oslo - Lasse Brogger and Anne-Stine Reine. In 1998 the authors walked the length of the Kirectepe Ridge with John Price (qv) and the two architects and asked them why they thought they had won in the face of such strong opposition. They replied that it was because they hardly wanted to change a thing - comforting news for all lovers of this hauntingly beautiful land, redolent of so many stories of valour and desperate effort on both sides in the struggles of 1915.

Inevitably the tragic earthquake of August 1999, with its appalling loss of life and habitation, will strain Turkey's resources for years to come and plans for the implementation of the Peace Park may well be delayed. Changes of Government since the original concept was agreed have also resulted in delays. Professor Bademli is confident, however, that the special fund allocated for this worthwhile project will not be affected and it will eventually go ahead.

GALLIPOLI COMMEMORATIVE STAMPS/BANK NOTES

In 1998 the New Zealand Post issued a first day cover and stamps 'to reflect the friendship that exists between Turkey and New Zealand'. Similar stamps were issued in Turkey. The New Zealand 40c and the Turkish 125,000TL stamps depict the Turkish statue which features on the cover of this book. The New Zealand $1.80 and the Turkish 125,000TL stamps feature Lyndon Smith's 1964 statue of 'Mother With Children' in the Hall of Memories at the National War Memorial in Wellington.

In 1965 the Australian Government issued three stamps to commemorate the 50th Anniversary of the Gallipoli Landings featuring The Man with the Donkey, John Simpson Kirkpatrick. The New Zealand Government featured Anzac Cove on two stamps issued on 14 April.

In 1955 the Turkish Post issued a 15 kurus stamp with a bas relief map of the Peninsula and Canakkale and a 20 kurus stamp featuring the Man with the Shell, Seyit Onbasi. In 1990 the 1,000TL stamp featured the Canakkale Memorial at Helles. It also features on the 500,000TL bank note.

On 18 March 1935 the Australian Post Office issued two stamps commemorating the 20th Anniversary of the Campaign, featuring the Cenotaph at Whitehall. On the 21st Anniversary the New Zealand Post issued two stamps on 27 April depicting a Kiwi soldier at Anzac Cove.

Group on the Kirectepe Ridge: on left Eileen Price; third from left Anne-Stine Reine; second from right John Price (CCWGC Area Superintendent); fourth from right Lasse Brogger.

TOURIST INFORMATION

Also read carefully the section 'Prior to Your Visit...' above
It is wise to contact your local Turkish Tourist Information Office before you leave to enquire about current regulations about visas, currency restrictions etc..

Australia: Suite 101, 280 George Street, Sydney, NSW 2000
Tel: +61 (0)2 9223 3055. Fax: +61 (0)2 9223 3204

France: 102, Avenue des Champs Elysées, 75008 Paris
Tel: +33 1 4562 7668 Fax: +33 1 4563 8105

Great Britain: 1st Floor, 170-173 Piccadilly, London W1V 9DD
Tel: +44 (0)171 629 7771. Fax: +44 (0)171 491 0773

Turkey: Ministry of Tourism, Ankara.
Ismet Inonu Bulv. 5 06100. Bahcelievler
Tel: +90 (312) 212 8300. Fax: +90 (312) 213 6887

In 1998 a visa was not required for citizens of Australia or France for a stay of up to 3 months. UK citizens could purchase a 3-month visa on entry at the airport or border post.

There is no limit on the amount of foreign currency that may be brought into the country, but a limit of $5,000 worth of Turkish currency may be brought in or taken out. Keep your money exchange slips. They may be required if you change money back or when taking souvenirs out of the country. Keep all your receipts for major purchases (you may get a tax refund) and note that exporting antiques from Turkey is forbidden.

In Canakkale/On the Peninsula

Canakkale Police: From ferry terminal drive directly inland through Republic Square to traffic lights and turn left. The Police Station is on the corner. Tel: 286 217 11181

Canakkale Main Post Office: The Post Office is just past the Police Station on the same road on the left.

Canakkale Hospital: The hospital is on the same road as the Post Office, further up on the right-hand side. Tel: 286 217 1044

Canakkale Tourist Information Office: Iskele Meydani, 67 (near the Ferry Terminal) Tel: + (90) 286 217 11187

Dardanel Air: This small airline,with smart Beechcraft 1900D aircraft, flies from Canakkale to Edremit (about 20 minutes) and thence to Istanbul (about 40 minutes) on Mondays and Fridays. The modern airport building is to the east of the town at Havaalani [see Map 2], about a 10-minute taxi drive from the centre. Schedules change according to the season, but at the end of 1999 only a limited service was available.
Contact: Istanbul: Valikonagi Cad. YKB Vakif Binasi No: 173 Kat 8/1 Nisantasi Istanbul. Tel: +(90) 212 234 3738. Fax: +(90) 212 234 2628. Canakkale: Saat Meydani No: 17 Canakkale. Tel: +(90) 286 217 0887. Fax: +(90) 286 212 8653.

TroyAnzac Travel Agency: Tours of Gallipoli and Troy for individuals or groups. Near Clock Tower, Canakkale. Tel: + (90) 286 217 5849. Fax: + (90) 286 217 0196
Car/Motorbike/Bicycle Hire: **Gezgin Rent a Car**, Cumhuriyet Meydani Tekki Sk.

Carpet Men

Sock Lady

Pretzel Boy

Scarf Man

CWGC Worker, Ali

Praying Mantis, Anzac

Cotton, Kumka

Wild Marigolds

Goats, Suvla

No. 2/A. Tel: +(90) 286 212 8392.
Note that you will need your driving licence, that traffic drives on the right and that the Turkish Highway Code is similar to most European ones and seat belts are required to be worn.
Eceabat Gendarmerie Emergency Tel. No: Freephone 156
Eceabat Down Under Travel Agency: Run by Ilhami Gezici ('T.J.') a knowledgeable Turk married to an equally knowledgeable Australian. Can provide individual tours, large and small buses. Kemalpasa Mh. Cumhuriyet, Cad. No.5A, Eceabat.
Information on CWGC Graves location is also available from these offices.
Tel: +90 286 814 2431. Fax: +90 286 814 2430. e-mail: d.under @ excite.com
Taxis can be hired from the ranks at the ferry terminals in Canakkale and in Eceabat.

Some Hotel Suggestions

Canakkale
**** Hotel Akol. Canakkale's smartest hotel. Tel: +90 286 217 9456
*** Hotel Anafartala. Just next to the Ferry Terminal. Good restaurant. Tel: +90 286 217 4454
*** Hotel Truva. Well-established, experienced at handling groups and battlefield pilgrims. Tel: +90 286 217 1024
* Anzac House. Favourite Aussie and Kiwi Meeting Place. Clean basic rooms and battlefield information. Tel: +90 286 217 0156. Fax: +90 286 217 2906
Near Canakkale
Ozan Motel. At Guzelyali (10 km south on the Izmir road). Tel: +90 286 232 1084
Tusan Hotel. Off the Izmir road. Tel: +90 286 232 8746/7. Fax: +90 286 232 8226.
Eceabat
Eceabat Down Under Travel Agency - see above
Kumkale
Kum Motel and Kum Camping. On the coast near Gaba Tepe. The area that will be developed when the Peace Park is established. Tel: +90 286 814 1455.
Seddulbahir
Pansiyon Helles Panorama. Run by retired CWGC worker Erol Baycan and his wife. Superb situation and views. Immaculately clean. Good home cooking. Tel/Fax: +90 286 862 0035/286 212 9497

Canakkale Scuba Club

Over 200 wrecks, including those of WW1 have been identified in the waters round the Peninsula and can be visited through the club.
UK agent: http://www.crusadertravel.com

Thanks to our Turkish Military and Police friends

Remember, it can be wet and muddy on the Peninsula

ACKNOWLEDGEMENTS & SOURCES

We are deeply indebted to Professor Dr Raci Bademli, Co-ordinator of the Gallipoli Peninsula Peace Park International Competition, Ankara, for generously making available to us the results of his remarkably comprehensive survey of the Gallipoli Peninsula in all its aspects and for giving us permission to quote from the resultant 'Book' and 'Catalogue' and to use his extraordinarily detailed maps; to Lasse Brogger and Anne-Stine Reine, winners of the Competition for explaining their concept for the Park; to the Turkish Army for their ever-courteous support and practical assistance on the ground in the Peninsula. Our thanks go in London to the Military Attaché, Colonel Dundas, and in Gelibolu to Colonel Tahsin Daggez, Chief of Staff of 2nd Corps, Colonel Bilgin Yavuz, General Secretary of 2nd Corps, Lieutenant Mehmet Gunes, Lieutenant Simen Gidem, Sergeant Alper Tunga Dost and Private Ayhan Bakar and Sergeant Faruk Ergun of the Eceabat Jandarma. As always, we have received tremendous support and assistance from the Commonwealth War Graves Commission - both at Headquarters in Maidenhead (especially from Liam Hannah, Nigel Haines and Peter Francis) and from Superintendent John Price, his knowledgeable wife Eileen and the ever-helpful Volcan Susluoglu in the Canakkale Office. We are deeply indebted to them, especially for their work in checking our itineraries and distances and for the photographs on pages 92, 194. Our thanks also to the CWGC for permission to reproduce the photograph on page 251. As the inimitable Rose Coombs blazed the trail for battlefield guides of the Western Front, so Phil Taylor and Pam Cupper (now Mrs Taylor) produced the 'Bible' of Gallipoli Guides in 1989 and we acknowledge their research and dedication. Our thanks go to Brigadier I. J. Duthie, Head of the New Zealand Defence Staff, London; to Major Easey of the Armed Forces Chaplaincy Centre for information on the Rev W. Finn; to Gavin Richardson for information about the Hawick Plaques; to Arthur Coxon for information about his father; to Grace Wallis for permission to quote from the Dardanelles Diary of Private Robert Edward Atkinson: to Ross Bastiaan for information about his marvellous Australian plaques and the photograph on page 130; to the Imperial War Museum's Nigel Steel, Chief Historian and author of several works on Gallipoli, Brad King, expert on the RNAS, and Bridget Kinally of the Photographic Collection for permission to reproduce the pictures on pages 104, 105, 134, 138, 219; to Pam Flynn of HMSO for permission to reproduce the plan of Suvla Bay on page 213; to Jillian Brankin of the Australian War Memorial for permission to reproduce the photograph of Suvla Point on page 214; to Major Huw Rodge and his wife Jill, of Dragon Tours, who made our 1998 tour of the Peninsula so painless and whose guest on that tour, Wayne Ryder, the Bugler of the 1st Battalion the Royal Welch Fusiliers, appears on the back cover of this book; to J.P. Thierry of the Historical, Péronne and to the BBC for permission to use the picture of David Jason on page 222.

Finally, our eternal thanks to our source-of-all-knowledge editor, Tom Hartman, and to Elaine Parker and David Geewater for keeping us 'on the road'.